KIDS IN THE MIDDLE

❧

The Rutgers Series in Childhood Studies

The Rutgers Series in Childhood Studies is dedicated to increasing our understanding of children and childhoods, past and present, throughout the world. Children's voices and experiences are central. Authors come from a variety of fields, including anthropology, criminal justice, history, literature, psychology, religion, and sociology. The books in this series are intended for students, scholars, practitioners, and those who formulate policies that affect children's everyday lives and futures.

Edited by Myra Bluebond-Langner, Board of Governors Professor of Anthropology, Rutgers University, and True Colours Chair in Palliative Care for Children and Young People, University College London, Institute of Child Health.

Advisory Board

Perri Klass, New York University
Jill Korbin, Case Western Reserve University
Bambi Schieffelin, New York University
Enid Schildkraut, American Museum of Natural History and Museum for
    African Art

KIDS IN THE MIDDLE

❧

*How Children of Immigrants
Negotiate Community Interactions
for Their Families*

Vikki S. Katz

Rutgers University Press
New Brunswick, New Jersey, and London

Library of Congress Cataloging-in-Publication Data
Katz, Vikki S.

Kids in the middle : how children of immigrants negotiate community interactions for their families / Vikki S. Katz.

pages cm. — (The Rutgers series in childhood studies)
Includes bibliographical references and index.
ISBN 978–0–8135–6219–3 (hardcover : alk. paper) — ISBN 978–0–8135–6218–6 (pbk. : alk. paper) — ISBN 978–0–8135–6220–9 (e-book)

Children of immigrants—United States. 2. Immigrants—United States. 3. Communities—United States. 4. Family—United States. I. Title.
HV741.K365 2014
305.9'069120973—dc23   2013029879

A British Cataloging-in-Publication record for this book is available from the British Library.

Visit our website: http://rutgerspress.rutgers.edu

Manufactured in the United States of America

אל תקרא בניך אלא בוניך

"Call us not thy children, but thy builders."

Kriyat Habonim

CONTENTS

TABLES

ACKNOWLEDGMENTS

This book and the project that prompted it have spanned a number of years. As such, I am grateful to a great many people for supporting me through its development and publication.

Peter Mickulas was my intrepid editor at Rutgers University Press and a champion for this project from the very beginning. I thank him for his insights, humor, and professional dedication to helping me produce the book I had hoped for. The production team at the press made bringing this project to fruition a pleasure. I thank Myra Bluebond-Langner for agreeing to publish this book as part of the Childhood Studies series. I also thank the two anonymous reviewers who greatly improved this manuscript with their challenges and insights.

Earlier versions of chapters 4 and 5 have been published by *Journal of Children and Media* and *Social Problems*, respectively. Invited talks at Ben Gurion University, DePaul University, Drexel University, the London School of Economics, the University of California–Los Angeles, the University of Pennsylvania, and the University of Southern California, as well as conference presentations to the American Sociological Association, the International Association of Media and Communication Researchers, the International Communication Association, the Migration and Childhood Workshop, and the National Communication Association, all provided opportunities for useful feedback that helped me refine my ideas and arguments.

The University of California–Los Angeles was my first intellectual home and where I was introduced to the processes of academic inquiry. From the very beginning, Roger Waldinger treated me as a valued member of his research team. His generosity as a teacher and role model—from my undergraduate days, through graduate school, and now—has taught me a great deal about asking good questions and being self-critical. He showed me what real mentorship looks like. He was also convinced that this was a book even when the research was in its formative stages; I thank him for all the ways his support has helped me realize this goal.

My undergraduate years provided me other professors who inspired me to follow their footsteps into academia. G. Jennifer Wilson, UCLA's assistant vice provost for College Honors, lit me up with her love of scholarly inquiry. She continues to be a dear friend and role model for me in more ways than she realizes. I still feel the presence of my friend and mentor Jim Bruno, who was a professor of education at UCLA and whose advice I wish he was still here to give me. Jim taught me so much about fully living the academic life and integrating it into a life well lived. I hope he would have liked this book.

My graduate years at the Annenberg School for Communication and Journalism at the University of Southern California (USC) gave me every opportunity and encouragement to grow. Sandra Ball-Rokeach was my advisor and continues to be both my teacher and my friend. I thank her for the many ways she demonstrates to me the best of academic work, professionalism, and mentorship. I also thank her for allowing me to include analyses of survey data collected under the auspices of her Metamorphosis Project. I am grateful to Michael Cody, Peggy McLaughlin, and Robert Rueda for their contributions to shaping and developing this project.

Larry Gross was and continues to be the most involved and supportive "unofficial" advisor anyone could ever hope for. I thank him for conversations and encouragement that continue to be a major part of my professional support system.

The Annenberg Family and Annenberg Foundation gave me the gift of a fellowship that supported my five years of graduate work and a subsequent two-year postdoctoral fellowship. I thank Wallis Annenberg and her family for their unparalleled generosity. I also thank the Urban Initiative at USC and First 5 Los Angeles for providing financial support for different aspects of data collection.

In 2009, I joined Rutgers University's Department of Communication in the School of Communication and Information. I am very grateful to my colleagues for their support and encouragement, which, along with a well-timed sabbatical leave, ensured that I had the resources I needed to complete this manuscript.

My dear friend and colleague Matthew Matsaganis has been my sounding board, travel companion, and generous reader of many iterations of this manuscript. Lucy Montgomery has also been my editor and my cheerleader, always seeming close even when we were separated by many time zones. David FitzGerald has also probably read more versions of certain chapters of this book than he cares to remember and has done so generously. Judy Manouchehri deserves special thanks for her many patient, careful readings; I am lucky to have a friend outside the academy who makes my projects hers and contributes so heartily to them.

I am grateful to many colleagues for conversations, counsel, and feedback on this project, including Lourdes Baezconde-Garbanati, Sarah Banet-Weiser,

Joanna Dreby, Nelly Elias, Howie Giles, Carmen Gonzalez, Ellen Helsper, Amy Jordan, Catherine Lee, Dafna Lemish, Meghan Moran, Marjorie Faulstich Orellana, Jack Linchuan Qiu, Renee Reichl Luthra, and Holley Wilkin. Their thoughtful questions and ideas improved my thinking and writing, but any mistakes or omissions herein are mine alone.

Beni Gonzalez and Michelle Hawks were my extraordinary research assistants for the project on which this book is based. As USC undergraduates who had been (and continue to be) child brokers in their own immigrant families, their understandings of what we were seeing were far more "insider" than mine and added a layer of richness to what I learned about these children and their families. Michelle's support for this project may be never-ending; a 3:00 a.m. email asking her to come to Los Angeles with me in 2011 to reinterview these families was met with complete enthusiasm. I consider myself privileged to have worked with them both. A special thanks also to Carmen Gonzalez, who made time in her overloaded schedule to visit families with me on a few occasions when Beni and Michelle could not.

I am very grateful to the teachers, administrators, physicians, nurses, support staff, social workers, and service providers who generously shared their stories and perspectives with me in the schools, clinics, medical practices, and social service offices of Greater Crenshaw. And I am not sure there are words to adequately express, in either language, my appreciation for the parents and children who humbled me with their trust, opening their hearts, homes, and histories to me, Beni, and Michelle. I can only hope that they feel I did justice to their stories in the pages that follow.

Other scholars have noted that a first major research project is often autobiographical; this book is no exception. My parents emigrated from South Africa with my brother and me, leaving behind elderly parents, siblings, friends, and their way of life. My parents reinvented themselves in the United States so that they would not, as my mother once put it, be "left behind." I was thirteen when my family landed in the San Francisco Bay Area, old enough to understand the everyday strains that acclimating to a new place places on a family in transition. But the experience made a team out of the four of us, forging a closer family unit in ways that may not have been necessary or possible had we not immigrated.

I started graduate school knowing that I wanted to study how immigration changes families that, unlike mine, do not arrive in the United States with the built-in advantages of being native English speakers and holding advanced degrees that are both recognized and valued. While our transition was not always easy, we were so fortunately situated in comparison to many families, including those who are the focus of this book.

The families who participated in this study embodied the optimism so often associated with immigrants. During our interview with Paula, who lived in a one-bedroom apartment with her husband and four children, she contrasted living in the United States with her native El Salvador. She told us that every morning when she wakes up, she bends down to kiss the concrete floor next to her bed, grateful to have the opportunity to live in the United States. The courage and tenacity that immigrant parents and their children so often demonstrate in the face of serious challenges deserves acknowledgment. I hope this book will be a small contribution toward deepening our understanding of the everyday lives of these twenty families and of the many others like them. These families' inclusion in the social fabric of American life must be a central concern for all of us, because they *are* us.

I dedicate this book to my family:

To my father, Ian, who has read every word in this book more than once, often editing late at night and early in the morning, all the while insisting that it was "his pleasure" to do it;

To my mother, Cheryl, who has contributed her perspectives on this book's contents for years and who supported me by always reminding me why writing it mattered;

To my brother, Jeff, who lived with me while I wrote this book and whose patient readings and excellent analytical questions sharpened many of my ideas into actual points; and

To my husband, Dan, whose keen legal mind also challenged me to think about what I was writing from nonacademic perspectives and who lived through the late night and early morning mania that appear mandatory for completing a book project.

Thank you to all of you, for everything.

KIDS IN THE MIDDLE

❖

❧

CHILDREN, FAMILY, AND COMMUNITY

Luis is eleven years old.[1] He is soft spoken, with warm brown eyes partially hidden by long, thick hair he shyly retreats behind from time to time. Luis is the eldest of Ana and Felipe's three US-born sons; both parents are undocumented immigrants from Mexico. Felipe works in a clothing factory for an hourly wage as the family's sole breadwinner; Ana hasn't worked since her youngest son was born two years ago. Both parents have had limited employment options in part because of their unauthorized residency status, but also because they, like many of their contemporaries, cannot speak, read, or write proficiently in English.

The focus of this family is not the toddler tugging at Luis's pant leg, angling for his big brother's attention. Luis's seven-year-old brother, Julio, is severely epileptic. His condition was initially misdiagnosed when he was an infant, resulting in two untreated, grand mal seizures that left him so brain damaged that he will never be able to speak.

So Luis speaks for Julio—and for their parents—when they go to the many doctor appointments that Julio needs. Luis, a straight-A student, routinely misses school or forgoes completing his homework to help his parents communicate with English-speaking staff at the emergency room, at scheduled doctor visits, and at Julio's rehabilitation services, for which Luis helped his parents complete the required paperwork.

As the primary English speaker in his immigrant household, Luis uses his language proficiency, familiarity with US cultural norms, and ability to connect with content via various media formats to help his family access available community resources. Luis regularly makes phone calls and searches for local news and information in community newspapers and online, sometimes at his parents' request and sometimes on his own initiative. He presents his findings to his parents so that together they can make decisions about locating and securing goods and services they need.

By performing these tasks, Luis is a crucial link between his Spanish-speaking parents and their English-speaking environments. He is hardly unique. While no representative data specifically document how many children assist their parents as he does, 61 percent of children of immigrants in the United States have at least one parent who has difficulty speaking English. Among children with a parent from Central America, that proportion rises to 68 percent, and for children with a Mexican-born parent, to 82 percent (Urban Institute 2009). Furthermore, the odds of children of immigrants having at least one parent with limited English proficiency have risen steadily, from 49 percent in 1990, to 55 percent in 2000 (Johnson et al. 2005), and to 61 percent today (Urban Institute 2009). These trends suggest that for children of immigrants—and particularly for those of Mexican or Central American origin—having parents who need help navigating community interactions may be the norm, rather than the exception.

Bringing Children's Contributions into Focus

While this book focuses on children of Latino immigrants, children like Luis are not unique to a single immigrant group, to a particular receiving community or country, or to contemporary migration flows. Half a century ago, Ephraim Kishon (1967) observed that immigrant mothers in Israel learn their "mother tongue" (i.e., Hebrew) from their children.[2] Biographical accounts by US-raised children of Italian and Jewish immigrants describe these forms of family assistance as a normal aspect of their childhoods in the early twentieth century.[3] Children of Holocaust survivors interpreted Yiddish and English for their parents on the streets of New York and Toronto (Epstein 1979; Fass 2007). And now, in the post-1965 immigration era, children of immigrants from Central and South America, Africa, the Middle East, Asia, and Southeast Asia help their families navigate interactions in their adopted communities.[4]

Children's assistance is often an important feature of immigrant family life, but their contributions have generally been relegated to footnotes or passing comments—at least, until recently. There is burgeoning interest in children of immigrants' roles and responsibilities among researchers in North America, the United Kingdom, and Europe.[5] To date, most have explored how children facilitate their parents' interactions in schools and, secondarily, how they contribute to family-owned businesses (Buriel and De Ment 1998; Chao 2006; Orellana 2009; Orellana, Dorner, and Pulido 2003; Park 2001; Song 1999; Tse 1996; Abel Valenzuela 1999). Scholars have also begun documenting how children of immigrants influence family learning processes, notably those related to political socialization (Bloemraad and Trost 2008; Félix, Gonzalez, and Ramírez 2008; Wong and Tseng 2008).

Studies in locations like schools and family businesses are important because the characteristics of physical sites influence how immigrant families are received by people they encounter there. However, parents and children do not experience their communities as a set of discrete locations. What children do to help their parents in one location affects what they do in other places; a strategy that works in a school setting may, for example, be deployed again when the family has to communicate with a doctor. The same is true for the communication processes underlying political socialization, since these forms of family learning can influence other social outcomes as well. Furthermore, family responsibilities can redirect children from personal pursuits, like participating in after-school activities; these time and energy displacements will not be revealed in studies focused on one site or family learning process.

The goal of this book is to move beyond location- and process-specific studies, to examine how children develop and hone both individual and collective strategies for assisting their families across multiple physical locations. Drawing on four years of ethnographic data, I document how children, as the primary English speakers in their households, influence family interactions at home and in schools, healthcare facilities, and social services in one settlement community. Addressing everyday challenges—such as how to apply for food assistance or find a local doctor—provides natural opportunities for individual and collective learning within families. By considering different kinds of tasks and experiences across home and community locations, I was able to identify how parents and children developed strategies to understand their community, to locate local opportunities, and to take advantage of them.

While I focus on children's contributions to family functioning, their efforts are not considered in a vacuum. What children do is first contextualized within their family systems of parents and siblings because these domestic dynamics are crucial to understanding why children's activities varied across demographically similar families. Second, children's contributions are considered in context of constraints and opportunities in their families' homes and local institutional sites. These data reveal how much local spaces matter. Community-level features and rapid demographic change affected how families communicated with other residents and with local service providers. When families entered local schools, healthcare facilities, and social services, the institutional dynamics in those particular sites and the particular service providers they encountered there deeply influenced how effective families' strategies were for achieving the goals they had for those interactions.

Accounting for children's contributions reveals, in part, why some immigrant families manage to leverage institutional resources and opportunities more fully than others. Such knowledge can inform efforts to address persistent social disparities affecting immigrant families. Given that over 20 percent of children growing up in the United States today has at least one immigrant parent—and that a full third of them have a parent who is Mexican-born—fully understanding these families' needs is both important and urgent (Child Trends 2010). This examination of families' experiences in one community, which shares many commonalities with settlement communities across the nation, is intended as a contribution in that direction.

Understanding immigrant family wellbeing is important; how children's family responsibilities affect the choices they make about their own needs and opportunities is equally so. I explore whether the strategies that facilitate familial goals can simultaneously constrain children's own choices. Thus far, these relationships have been much debated. Lisa Dorner, Marjorie Orellana, and Christine Li-Grining (2007) have argued that children's responsibilities to their immigrant families positively influence their academic performance; Guadalupe Valdés (2003) has framed these skills as a form of giftedness. On the other hand, an extensive literature on children as carers suggests that family responsibilities can detract from children's connections to school and other resources that foster intellectual and social development.[6] Moving beyond the home-school lens permits examination of how children's broader family responsibilities may influence their academic engagement.

IMMIGRATION AND FAMILY CHANGE

Children's family responsibilities evolve out of a larger set of changes to family life resulting from migration and settlement. These changes affect all family members but vary by gender and generation. Over the past few decades, feminist scholars have documented how gender affects migration and settlement experiences and how related changes influence family relationships.[7] Barrie Thorne and her colleagues (2003) have argued that age and generation are equally important dimensions of immigrant family life since children and parents experience migration-related family changes differently.[8]

Whether adults migrate with their children or become parents after arrival, parenting practices are affected by moving to and living in a new place. The demands of low-wage work have particularly far-ranging impacts on changing family dynamics.[9] Employment options in the United States for immigrants from Mexico and Central America are generally constrained by truncated formal education, limited English proficiency, undocumented immigration status, or a combination of these factors. Roger Waldinger and Claudia Der-Martirosian (2001) argued that immigrants' social networks can further limit exceptional individuals' options by restricting them to work niches occupied by longer-settled friends and family. Given these constraints, immigrant parents tend to find work in low-skilled employment sectors like child or elder care, housecleaning, or construction, which pay low wages and almost never provide formal benefits like health insurance or retirement plans. In some families involved in this study, parents' employment did not even offer much financial stability from week to week.

I had not intended for employment to be a focal topic in interviews, but parents and children spontaneously discussed parents' work worries so frequently that these stresses were clearly chronic features of family life. Their most common complaints were employers who paid below minimum wage, withheld pay or overtime, or changed employment conditions or payment without notice. For example, Graciela (age thirteen) often talked about phone calls she made to people whose houses her mother cleaned in different parts of Los Angeles. Sometimes, even longtime clients would leave her less money than usual or expect her to clean up after long-term houseguests without paying more for the extra work. Graciela would have to call these English-speaking employers and explain her mother's objections—carefully, so as to make her mother's points clear without jeopardizing her livelihood.

Graciela's phone calls reflected how intimately involved these children were in the everyday maintenance of their families. Evelyn (age fifteen) told me that because she wrote checks to pay the household bills for grandmother and herself each month, she was acutely aware of their financial conditions. Her grandmother never had to tell her which months they had no money for nonessential items; Evelyn already knew.

In any family where parents must work long hours at one or multiple jobs to make ends meet, children's domestic responsibilities generally increase to compensate for their parents' extended workdays. Children often shoulder primary responsibility for cooking, cleaning, and household shopping. Elder siblings may take younger children to school, help them with homework, and put them to bed at night.[10] These patterns are common among low-income families, regardless of whether they are headed by native-born or immigrant parents.

Graciela's and Evelyn's experiences, however, reflect that children of immigrants make contributions to household functioning that go beyond the responsibilities children assume in working poor families more generally. Parents who have difficulty with interactions and tasks requiring English proficiency or US cultural knowledge (such as making phone calls to employers or writing checks) must depend on others to help them. They tend to depend on their children, either by choice or because their homogeneous social networks and limited institutional links preclude regular access to adults who could be their intermediaries. Thus, in under-served communities where immigrant families encounter few linguistic and cultural accommodations, children emerge as essential contributors to family survival strategies.

CHILDREN AS BROKERS

I focus on how children act as "brokers" by facilitating their immigrant parents' connections to and understandings of their local environments.[11] Brokering activities most often involve negotiating language, as children do when they enable a conversation between their parents and an English-speaking neighbor or service provider, for example. Cultural brokering is often also intertwined into these interactions, since child brokers engage at least two sets of cultural norms with regard to appropriate behavior and talk. They may also have to negotiate the norms of an institutional culture, depending on where these interactions take place.[12] Finally, brokering activities often involve engaging media devices or content as well when, for example, children make a phone call for a doctor's appointment, complete a sibling's intake form to attend school, or go online to check if the family qualifies for a food assistance program. Depending on the situation, child brokers may invoke their linguistic, cultural, and media-related skillsets separately or simultaneously to connect their families to local information, news, and resources.

Children of immigrants' abilities to shoulder these responsibilities relate to their developmental stages and attending US schools. Developmentally, children are more adept at learning language than adults. They also develop unaccented English more easily than their immigrant parents because native tongue phonology is more likely in early language learners (Lippi-Green 1997, 46). School attendance also provides daily opportunities to practice and have their mistakes corrected by native speakers, be they teachers or peers.

Children also become familiar with US cultural norms in school. Roberto Gonzales (2011) argues, "For generations, the public school system has been the principal institution that educates and integrates children of immigrants in to the fabric of American society. . . . This assimilating experience is profoundly different from what most adult immigrants encounter."[13] Whereas immigrant parents enter workplaces where they often interact primarily with other Spanish-speaking immigrants, children interact with schoolmates and teachers from whom they acquire some measure of US cultural knowledge (Suárez-Orozco, Suárez-Orozco, and Todorova 2008). What children learn with regard to cultural norms affects family communication (McDevitt and Chaffee 2002); for example, Janelle Wong and Vivian Tseng (2008) found that the civics content children learn in schools can, through family talk, influence the political socialization of their immigrant parents.

Children's greater cultural knowledge (relative to their parents) can also inform how they broker media content for their families. US-produced media can be cultural teachers for immigrant parents and their children by familiarizing them with local news and norms.[14] Media brokering has been almost entirely overlooked in prior research, despite how frequently media are implicated in children's brokering responsibilities. Children broker parents' connections to content as well as to new communication technologies, like the Internet. Even in working poor communities where broadband penetration rates remain relatively low, children are more likely to develop new media proficiencies than their parents (de Block and Buckingham 2008; Federal Communications Commission

2010; Pew Research Center 2011). They develop these skills at school by teaching themselves or by learning from their friends (Ito et al. 2009).

Media brokering is not unique to children of immigrants. Even in middle-class, native-born families, children can broker media for their families by, for example, teaching their parents how to send a text message or how to navigate a particular website (Clark 2013; Strasburger, Wilson, and Jordan 2009). However, children like Luis, Graciela, and Evelyn broker their parents' connections to communication technologies more often and for a wider range of tasks than the native born because their media brokering is more likely to also invoke their knowledge of English and US culture.

Child brokers' responsibilities are also distinctive from those of professional and informal interpreters. Most obviously, they are not professionals, nor are they adults. Children broker in social spaces generally reserved for adults in Western society, such as discussions of a parent's medical condition. As such, they risk being viewed as violating cultural expectations of appropriate childhood, which has consequences for how they and their families are perceived by service providers and other professionals who are gatekeepers to local resources (Cohen, Moran-Ellis, and Smaje 1999; García-Sánchez 2014; Reynolds and Orellana 2009).

Children also broker interactions commonly marked by social distinctions based on class, race, immigration status, income, and education. Children's awareness of these social differences, coupled with their efforts not to appear transgressive of either adult's expectations of child-appropriate behaviors, can make them reluctant to ask questions or openly advocate on their families' behalf (Dorner, Orellana, and Li-Grining 2007). They may also struggle with complex information that at least two adults are depending on them to communicate accurately.

Perhaps most importantly, child brokers differ from professional intermediaries because they live with and are cared for by the adults for whom they broker. While professionals aim to be "invisible" and impartial in interactions they facilitate (Willen 2011), child brokers are not and cannot be seen as disinterested parties. They navigate complicated and sometimes contentious interactions to try and achieve desirable outcomes for their families. In tense situations, children sometimes softened their parents' words or chose to explain their dissatisfaction in great detail, trying to secure cooperation from service providers.[15] For all these reasons, children's brokering activities need to be understood in context of the family systems in which they take place.

FAMILY INFLUENCES ON CHILDREN'S BROKERING

A family systems approach moves beyond considering families as the sum of individual members' experiences. Instead, the family is seen as an interactive, dynamic context in which individual members experience each other and the world around them (Galvin, Dickson, and Marrow 2005; Olsen 2000; Yerby 1995). Alyshia Gálvez describes this kind of family-centered approach to understanding immigrant families as one "in which individuals play roles that are complimentary to and not reducible to the roles other members play"; she goes on to note that "look[ing] at families as a relevant unit of social analysis, a site for decision-making, resource allocation, emotional and economic support, and more, does not mean that inequalities within the family can be overlooked" (2011, 46–47).

I use this perspective to uncover how children's brokering activities factor into the strategies families develop to engage with local resources. I contextualize children's activities within their own family's dynamics. In doing so, I detail how children affect family functioning, while also considering how parental authority, for example, influences these efforts and can highlight asymmetries in the positions that family members hold in relation to each other.

Three basic tenets of the family systems approach guide my analyses. The first is that as a self-organizing unit, individual family members manage tensions between their needs for closeness as a cohesive unit and their needs for differentiation as individuals. The second is that as systems, families balance opposing forces of stability and change. While these systems are dynamic, communication patterns and routines also become embedded parts of family functioning over time.[16] Finally, families systems are "open" systems, meaning that families are studied in context of their interactions with other systems in their environments. These include other families as well as the systems that families encounter in local sites, such as staff members working in a local clinic.

These three tenets correspond to three levels of analysis—namely, the individual, family, and intersystem levels—all of which helped shape and influence children's brokering efforts. To varying degrees, children engaged in their independent strategies when they brokered by using school-learned methods to extract meaning from unfamiliar words and concepts, negotiating cultural knowledge and norms, and engaging media as resources to supplement their skills. The utility of these efforts—and indeed, the likelihood that children would engage in them at all—depended heavily on whether parents modeled independent communication strategies that children could use as a guide when handling difficult brokering tasks.

At the family level, children's brokering efforts were supported by collective sense-making activities they engaged in with their parents, and sometimes with their siblings as well. Pooling their respective skill sets and what they had learned through their independent efforts often enabled children's and parents' abilities to collaboratively address family needs. These collective activities provided natural opportunities for language learning, increased cultural and technological familiarity, and other forms of skill-building for all involved members. The usefulness of pooling parents' and children's abilities was also clear in cases when parents had to depend on each other because their children were not available or when children had to address an issue when their parents were not present. These events, which I called family triage, were much less effective than when parents and children worked together.

Children's efforts were also influenced by relationships with other systems. Older cousins and family friends could support them by helping with challenging brokering tasks. On the other hand, some children were spread thin by responsibilities beyond their own family systems when they were expected to help extended family and parents' friends who did not have children old enough to broker for them.

LOCATING CHILDREN'S BROKERING

Children's brokering activities were also directly affected by where those interactions took place. The community itself matters, since its features influence how people communicate in local spaces.[17] For example, Greater Crenshaw had been a predominantly African American community before large numbers of Latino immigrant and second-generation families settled there. The rapid demographic shift had contributed to residents' perceptions that institutional resources were scarce. In local social services offices and healthcare settings, when an interaction reinforced feelings that members of the other group were being favored for resources, voluble protest was often immediate. As a result, Latino and African American residents seldom talked or shared information with each other in local waiting rooms.

Characteristics of the specific sites where children and families interacted with each other, other residents, service providers, and professionals deeply influenced the nature and outcomes of those interactions. Features of the family home affected what strategies children and parents developed there to independently and collaboratively manage everyday challenges. In chapter 4, I describe how differences in the organization of family homes, particularly in terms of their media environments, influenced children's skill-building and abilities to help address family needs.

Outside their homes, the institutions families entered affected the strategies children and parents could deploy there, and to what effect, to achieve their goals. Schools, healthcare facilities, and social services were not the only local institutions that featured prominently in families' lives, but prior research suggested that immigrant families connect with these early and often.[18] These institutions also provide services and goods that sustain basic needs (i.e., food assistance programs, pre- and post-natal care) and that can facilitate social leverage (i.e., education for children, English-as-second-language classes for parents). Considering institutional encounters in context of each other made it possible to compare how families' individual and collective strategies were deployed in different settings and to evaluate the reasons for variance in the success of these strategies.

Brokering has also been used by other scholars to describe institutional interactions; two of these applications are particularly relevant to these families' experiences. Mario Small (2006) describes how well-connected local entities (childcare centers, in his work) can be "resource brokers" when inter-organizational relationships enable residents to access goods, resources, and services across different institutions. Small emphasized that low-income families did not consciously connect with institutions because they were resource brokers. Rather, he found that families who entered such places enjoyed "unanticipated gains" over residents who did not, because one meaningful connection to a local institution could spawn additional connections with little or no additional effort on their part (Small 2006, 274).

Institutions can be resource brokers when their links to other organizations are formalized through mandates for staff members to connect residents to certain resources, as is the case when a social services agency provides a mandatory referral to appropriate doctors, for example. Individuals working in local institutions can also be resource brokers when they take personal initiative to alert families to relevant resources, going beyond their formal responsibilities in the process. Chapter 2 describes the kinds of resource brokering that occurred in places that child brokers visited with their families. Limited funding meant that resource brokering often fell to individual providers, with little institutional support for their efforts. Children's brokering affected how much providers and educators knew about these families' needs and, therefore, influenced whether their families were alerted to a broader range of local resources.

The dispositions of local service providers deeply influenced the receptions they provided for child brokers and their parents. Douglas Massey and Magaly Sánchez have argued, "As [immigrants] encounter actors and institutions in the receiving society and learn about the categorical boundaries maintained by natives, they *broker* those boundaries and try to influence the meaning and content of the social categories defined by those boundaries" (2010, 16 [italics in original]). Massey and Sánchez view immigrants' efforts to broker social boundaries as how they ultimately negotiate entry into mainstream American life. The success of immigrants' brokering efforts depends on (a) the characteristics and motivations of immigrants themselves, (b) the reception the native-born provide for immigrants, which is contingent on their perceptions of their own social standing, and (c) the interactions that occur between them in local settings like schools, workplaces, businesses, and public spaces (Massey and Sánchez 2010, 16).

Like Massey and Sánchez, I consider immigrant settlement as a local process that unfolds over time in places like the schools, healthcare facilities, and social services I observed in this community. However, whereas Massey and Sánchez viewed boundary-brokering interactions as an individual-level phenomenon, I argue that these are often family efforts that involve children as well as parents.[19]

Children contribute to how their families prepare for boundary-brokering inter-actions by gathering information to inform family decisions. They are also often the facilitators of interactions their families have in these local spaces. How those interactions unfold depends a great deal on the motivations and perceptions of providers that families encounter there. Families who depended on their chil-dren's brokering efforts often revealed limitations in local institutions and their staff members' abilities to accommodate local population diversity. The resulting discomfort many providers felt when they interacted with these families affected the nature and outcome of these boundary-brokering interactions.

BROKERING AND IMMIGRANT SETTLEMENT

Children's brokering is integral to how their immigrant families construct and shape shared understandings of their adopted communities. These understandings enhance families' familiarity and comfort with local people and places and, over time, build a sense of belonging and connection to their adopted community.

Children can help make and maintain important local connections that parents would find difficult to initiate independently. For example, facilitating relationships with African American neighbors who have lived in the area all their lives can alert immigrant families to services and opportunities. When children broker these kinds of relationships, they do more than build their families' local support system. They potentially provide access to opportuni-ties for social leverage, invoking Ronald Burt's general definition of a broker as someone "in a position to bring together otherwise disconnected contacts" (Burt 2001, 36; Small 2006).

Likewise, enduring relationships with service providers can offer access to institutional resources that help families survive and thrive. By speaking for their family members to secure services, filling out paperwork that determines eligibil-ity for resources, and so on, children's brokering can initiate and maintain their families' connections to such resources. Sustained connections to local services and institutions are markers of successful boundary brokering that can facilitate families' community integration.

Child brokers took justifiable pride in what they did to help their families. For many, their sense of self was deeply rooted in their identity as the family helper. Consequently, when they had to choose between self-interest and a family need, the latter was often their instinctive choice. They seldom made these choices because their parents asked them to put their family's needs first. Because parents were not fully familiar with school requirements and opportunities, they were often unaware when their children were not completing schoolwork or attending after-school enrichment programs to be available to help their parents.

The possibility that children's efforts to help their families broker boundaries at the expense of pursuing their own opportunities raises concerns about potential conflicts between individual and family needs. Vivian Louie (2012) explored the "immigrant bargain" between parents and children, whereby parents' migration-related sacrifices are redeemed by the (usually academic) successes of their children.[20] I develop this concept further in chapter 6 by considering that children's brokering reveals potentially conflicting definitions of success in immigrant families. Helping families address immediate and urgent needs was often how child brokers honored the immigrant bargain and their parents' many sacrifices, in the short term. However, these efforts could circumscribe brokers' abilities to redeem the immigrant bargain with long-term academic successes. I did not find evidence for the link between brokering and higher educational attainment that others have reported.[21] More than half the children I interviewed were struggling in school, often failing at least one class. Many child brokers exhibited limited language capacities in English, Spanish, or both. These children's low rates of school achievement and limited bilingual capacities raise important questions about the quality of brokering they performed for their parents, even with the best of intentions.

Being home to help their parents was also no cure-all for the realities of living in an under-served community.[22] I interviewed young people who brokered diligently for their parents but were also routinely suspended from school for fighting. I interviewed Maria, pregnant at nineteen, whose heavy familial responsibilities had fueled her desire to have something "just for herself," as she phrased it. Hernando (age twelve) isolated himself from neighborhood boys because he feared the draw of the streets and breaking his mother's heart by falling into gangs and drug dealing, as his older brother had. There is no doubt that I saw family responsibility shielding children from the attractions of street life and enhancing parental control over children's behavior. However, this shield was far from impermeable.

My findings suggest relationships between children's brokering and social disparities they and their families experienced in trying to make meaningful local connections. Some children and families had more success in achieving goals for which they engaged their brokering skills than others in similar circumstances. Their relative successes were largely explained by communication norms in these families; the same was true for children who struggled with brokering and whose families had more trouble making and maintaining local connections.

In the chapters that follow, I take a measured approach to assessing children's brokering activities and their effects. I try to balance competing tendencies by not over-celebrating children's brokering successes, as this would risk glossing over the serious structural difficulties these families face in securing local resources. However, focusing only on structural barriers would fail to recognize the innovative strategies that children and parents develop to address everyday challenges and the very real gains they often make in this regard.

GUIDE TO THIS BOOK

This first chapter situates this project within prior research on children's brokering, immigrant family change, and families' community interactions and institutional experiences. The chapters that follow highlight the considerable contributions that children make to their immigrant families, in context of how their efforts are influenced by family dynamics and how they are received in local healthcare facilities, social services, and schools. Rather than doing a location-specific study, I explore how child brokers develop and hone individual and collective strategies to influence their families' experiences across home and community locations. Brokering also affects children's development, as evident when familial needs conflict with their own needs.

Chapters 2 and 3 provide background on the community and the families. Chapter 2 describes Greater Crenshaw and the social changes that have shaped the area where families lived. The institutional landscape that child brokers and their families encountered and the forms of resource brokering that took place in these sites are detailed, as well as the research design for the project that informed this book.

Chapter 3 introduces the child brokers and families who are at the center of this inquiry. I describe who these child brokers are, how their responsibilities evolve as they age, and how differences among families affected children's responsibilities. Drawing on interviews with parents and children, as well as a randomized telephone survey of six hundred adult residents in Greater Crenshaw, I compare interviewed families with their African American, English-speaking Latino, and Spanish-speaking Latino neighbors on a range of community integration indicators to situate their experiences in broader local context. Convergence between interviews and survey data provides detail on parents' social networks and links to community organizations to identify the gaps children were most likely to broker for their families.

Having set the scene, chapter 4 analyzes families' interactions around children's brokering activities at home, such as making and returning phone calls in English, answering mail, and going online to retrieve local news and information. While children took front-stage roles in information gathering at home, making sense of what they found required collaborating with parents. Together, families developed shared understandings about how to engage with the community to address their needs. Family interaction at home is therefore closely tied to immigrant families' community interactions, which in turn influence future information seeking and decision making at home. Chapter 4 examines the family system as a strategic unit, to identify how and why some family communication arrangements are more likely to enable children's brokering than others.

Chapters 5 and 6 explore how children's brokering influences family interactions with community institutions. Chapter 5 jointly examines children's brokering in healthcare and social services facilities, since healthcare facilities are often mandated to refer families to social services they need, and vice versa. Brokering in healthcare settings was particularly difficult for these children due to providers' communication styles, the demands these interactions made on their bilingual abilities, and the heightened emotion associated with the reasons their families were seeking healthcare in the first place. Risks of miscommunication in these encounters were compounded by the fact that many of these institutions' most valued resources required completing complicated paperwork. The penalties for errors in these documents could be dire. Child brokers' difficulties with the formal English required for these documents hinted at limitations in their educational experiences.

Chapter 6 turns to children's experiences with schools, beginning with how their brokering responsibilities affected their relationships with teachers and administrators, who were seldom aware of children's family obligations. Mismatches between schools' and families' expectations with regard to "involvement" by parents, students, and their siblings influenced how children brokered parent-teacher meetings and school-related materials at home. Children's academic achievement is also commonly viewed as validating immigrant parents' sacrifices by honoring the immigrant bargain (V. Louie 2012; Smith 2002). Children's brokering allowed them to honor their parents' sacrifices in the short term by providing them assistance as needed. However, these efforts could constrain their capabilities to honor the immigrant bargain in the long term by precluding their full access to school resources. Chapter 6 raises important questions about the relationship between children's individual needs and the collective needs of their families.

Finally, chapter 7 summarizes key findings from the empirical chapters with regard to how children's brokering activities influence, and are influenced by, interactions with their parents and local service providers and professionals. I draw from these findings to suggest changes to institutional policy that can enhance local institutions' responsiveness to increasing community diversity and improve families' access to resources and services they need. Family change and children's development are explored through the experiences of three families who were re-interviewed four years after their initial interviews. While these findings cannot be considered representative, they foreground how short-term and long-term strategies affect what kinds of gains families make as collectives and as individuals—and why a holistic approach to researching children's brokering enhances what we understanding about immigrant family settlement and second-generation development.

❦

CHAPTER 2

SETTLING IN GREATER CRENSHAW

This chapter provides background on Greater Crenshaw, an urban community located in South Los Angeles, a few miles from downtown.[1] The community and the institutions within it had been profoundly shaped by social and demographic shifts that had taken place in the preceding decades.[2]

GREATER CRENSHAW, PAST AND PRESENT

From the 1920s to the 1950s, South Los Angeles grew and flourished as a set of predominantly blue-collar neighborhoods populated by families connected to the local steel, automotive, and food-processing plants. These communities were also fiercely segregated; Josh Sides (2004b, 585) describes the "incredibly successful" efforts of segregationists to maintain these all-white neighborhoods. Supreme Court rulings on *Shelley v. Kraemer* (1948) and *Barrows v. Jackson* (1953) heralded a shift in these policies, effectively ushering in a new era of residential integration. These changes did not come easily; local mobs used violent tactics to discourage African American settlement, including fire bombings and cross burnings on front lawns.[3]

Over time, it became clear, even to the staunchest opponents, that residential integration was inevitable. This recognition sparked the beginnings of white flight from the area, an exodus that continued apace through the early 1960s. Middle-class African Americans and whites alike struggled to maintain the market value of their homes and the stability of their neighborhoods as increasing numbers of whites decamped to outlying suburbs.

Times were changing. Unemployment increased, particularly among African American men, as the manufacturing jobs that first lured residents to the community moved to regions where tax burdens were lower and land was cheaper (Leidner 1965). By the end of the 1960s, the area's South Central and Centennial High Schools became the respective birthplaces of the Crips and the Bloods, two of the largest and most notorious street gangs in the United States. This local development was, according to Sides (2004b, 593), "undoubtedly fueled by the decline in legitimate employment opportunities" for young men in the area. Through the 1970s and 1980s, gang activity expanded and became increasingly violent, with different cliques vying for control of crack cocaine sales.[4]

The area also bore the deep imprint of the Watts Rebellion that rocked Los Angeles in the summer of 1965, setting off a new round of disinvestment from South Los Angeles communities.[5] The 1992 uprisings following the Rodney King verdict again decimated large swaths of the area.[6] These events further tied images of lawlessness and violence to South Central Los Angeles, as the area was known until 2003, when the city council changed it to South Los Angeles in an attempt to dismantle these negative stereotypes and encourage new commercial investment.[7]

South Los Angeles once again found itself in demographic transition in the 1990s and 2000s as large numbers of immigrant and second-generation Latinos primarily from Mexico, but also from El Salvador, Guatemala, Nicaragua, and Belize, began to settle in the area (Medina 2012). In 1990, 80 percent of Greater Crenshaw's residents were African American; by 2000, this proportion had decreased to 47 percent, with Latinos comprising 37 percent of the population (US Bureau of the Census 2000). By 2005, the randomized telephone survey conducted as part of this study revealed that approximately half (46 percent) of adult Latinos living in the area were foreign born.

These demographic shifts have not been uniform across the community. Some parts of Greater Crenshaw have become homogeneously Latino, others more mixed, and the more middle-class edges of the area have remained primarily African American. Immigrant residents' access to Greater Crenshaw's schools, healthcare, social services, and commercial outlets has varied accordingly. I found that immigrant parents living in predominantly African American parts of the community depended more heavily on their children's brokering than those living even a few blocks away.

Greater Crenshaw as Receiving Community

While I was developing this study, I was often asked why I had chosen to focus on Spanish-speaking immigrants in Los Angeles. Some suggested I select a "real" language minority group so that I would encounter families who actually needed their children to broker for them. No doubt, the challenges of smaller immigrant groups are important. However, my fieldwork contradicted popular perceptions of Los Angeles as a uniformly bilingual city. Despite being the first major US metropolis to have a second language (i.e., Spanish) spoken in as many homes as English,[8] Spanish-speaking parents in Greater Crenshaw had difficulty interacting with and understanding service providers, completing applications, and making meaningful connections to local institutions without assistance from their children or other English speakers.

Unlike many parts of Los Angeles where Latinos have been settled for a generation or more, Greater Crenshaw was an ideal place to explore how Latino immigrants navigated a community where they were a relatively new presence and, specifically, how their children's brokering contributed to their settlement activities. Los Angeles and its surrounding region have had a large Spanish-speaking population since the days when California was Mexican territory.[9] As a result, many parts of the city have longstanding Latino communities that routinely have their language stores refreshed by newly arrived immigrants. Greater Crenshaw is an excellent reminder that while the characteristics of entire cities certainly influence settlement, local communities are immigrants' primary contexts of reception, and their social integration is a locally based phenomenon.

Greater Crenshaw may be somewhat exceptional within Los Angeles, but as a low-income urban community now almost equally populated by African Americans and Latinos, the area resembles immigrant-receiving communities in many parts of the United States. Migration patterns have changed; immigrants from Mexico and Central America are moving to a wider variety of urban centers and smaller cities. They are also less likely to settle in ethnically homogeneous neighborhoods than in previous eras.[10] When Latinos do migrate to large cities, they tend to settle in urban neighborhoods with large African American populations. Together, Latinos and African Americans now comprise the majority population in seven of the ten largest urban areas in the United States (Telles, Sawyer, and Rivera-Salgado 2011). Greater Crenshaw therefore shares demographic similarities with immigrant-receiving communities across the country. It also faces many of the same challenges, including limited and under-resourced local services, high crime and high school dropout rates, and other stressors common to low-income US urban centers.

Research Design

This book is based on an ethnographic study of Greater Crenshaw that I conducted over four years, between 2006 and 2009. My goal was to explore the strategies that child brokers and their families develop and deploy in different community locations and how these efforts are influenced by the people and institutional characteristics of these sites. I focused on healthcare facilities, social services, and schools because prior research suggests these as among the most important local connections immigrant families make (Brittain 2003; Domínguez 2011; Gálvez 2011; Valdés 1996). Family wellbeing requires connecting with these institutions soon after arrival and maintaining linkages to them over time. Moreover, these resources can help families address basic needs and facilitate their social mobility.

To develop a well-rounded understanding of these families' experiences, my investigation included in-depth interviews with parents, children, and the professionals who interacted with them in local schools, healthcare facilities, and social services. These interviews were supplemented by extensive field observations in a subset of these institutional sites over an eighteen-month period and a randomized telephone survey of local residents.

A Random Digit Dial survey of six hundred Latino and African American adult residents of Greater Crenshaw in late 2005 enabled me to draw a more representative interview sample than would have been possible through snowball or convenience sampling. Survey data also facilitated comparisons between families with child brokers and other residents on a range of demographic and community indicators (see chapter 3).

To be eligible for interviews, Spanish-speaking respondents had to have one or more children between eleven and nineteen years old who helped them with English-language media, telephone calls, mail, and school materials, either "often" or "very often."[11] The sixty Spanish-speaking parents with children in this age range often required such assistance (see table 2.1).

I selected this age frame because it appeared to correspond with the most intensive period of children's brokering. Children's transition from elementary into middle school at approximately age eleven was a transition point, in that many parents saw their children as capable of assuming more family responsibilities, including more and increasingly complex brokering tasks. By age nineteen, child brokers had completed or left high school and tended to be less involved

TABLE 2.1

PARENTS' NEEDS FOR BROKERING ASSISTANCE

	Very often/ often (%)	Sometimes (%)	Rarely/never (%)
Parents who needed help with			
English-language radio and TV	54	33	13
English-language newspapers	53	22	25
Mail to the house	62	22	16
Making or receiving phone calls in English	58	25	17
School materials children bring home	49	26	25

SOURCE: Analyzed and prepared by the author from a survey of Greater Crenshaw conducted by the Metamorphosis Project at the University of Southern California, 2006.

in their parents' everyday routines because they had moved out of the house, entered college or the workforce, or had children of their own.

My two bilingual undergraduate research assistants contacted eligible parents by phone. Twenty parents and the twenty-two children they identified as their primary brokers participated in interviews; two parents had two children whom they felt shared these responsibilities equally. Each home was visited at least twice, for a total of sixty-five interviews ranging between 45 and 120 minutes in length. Parents and children were interviewed separately, at home, in their preferred language. I conducted all parent interviews in Spanish with one of my two research assistants, who ensured the fidelity of my non-native understandings in these interactions. Conducting interviews as a team also allowed me to observe and record activities naturally occurring among other family members during the interview, including children brokering for their other parent, grandparents, or neighbors. I interviewed children on my own, and all but one chose to be interviewed in English. Interviews with parents and children were semi-structured and included complimentary questions related to family communication dynamics, children's brokering activities, family migration history, and experiences with local institutions, resources, and residents.

To better understand children's brokering experiences, we secured agreement from three interviewed families to have my research assistants and me shadow their visits to local healthcare facilities, social services, and schools in the months subsequent to their interviews. Families were selected in part because we had already established rapport with them. These families also had more frequent contact with local institutions (healthcare facilities in particular) than other interviewed families, which provided more observation opportunities. These visits made it possible to compare children's and parents' recollections of past brokering with current brokering events. Young people sometimes glossed over difficult brokering experiences during interviews, but their challenges were clear during visits to local institutions.

I also interviewed twenty-nine English-speaking professionals who worked in Greater Crenshaw schools, healthcare, and social services offices that families frequented, including places that my research assistants and I had visited with families. Semi-structured interviews with teachers, administrators, service providers, social workers, medical professionals, and support staff each lasted approximately one hour. Questions focused on their work history, impressions of changing community demographics, and perspectives on children's brokering and its impact on their work experiences.

Finally, I conducted extensive observations in two middle schools, one clinic, and one social services office over an eighteen-month period following these interviews. Hours spent in waiting and consultation rooms, school hallways, and classrooms, helped me develop a textured understanding of the interpersonal and organizational dynamics child brokers and their families encountered in

these local institutions. I also frequently witnessed children's brokering serendipitously during these field observations.

Interviews and field observations generated thousands of pages of verbatim
interview transcriptions and field notes, which I compiled with my research
assistants following each interaction with families and on my own after each
site observation. I analyzed these data using Steven Taylor and Robert Bogdan's
(1998, 137) constant comparative method, which requires coding and analyzing data as it is collected. In keeping with this approach, I coded specific words,
phrases, and recurring activities, meanings, and feelings in order to explain data
patterns and specify relationships between emerging concepts. In doing so, I paid
particular attention to instances when parents', children's, and providers' perspectives on children's brokering experiences either converged with or contradicted each other (Barry 2002).

Accounting for the perspectives of all participants in brokered interactions
was crucial to understanding how and why these experiences took the courses
they did. The places where these interactions occurred were equally important.
The remainder of this chapter details the institutional environments child brokers and families encountered in Greater Crenshaw, including the four sites
where I conducted extensive field observations.

Healthcare and Social Services in Greater Crenshaw

Like residents in many low-income communities, child brokers and their families encountered limited options for healthcare and social services. King/Drew,
the area's only full-service hospital, had faltered for years and was shut down
entirely in 2007. It was dubbed "Killer King," and reviews and audits showed
that administrative negligence had led to a number of preventable deaths and
accidents.[12] Without King/Drew, residents could choose local clinics or private
providers or venture farther afield to places like Children's Hospital Los Angeles,
which, for many, required a long bus ride with a number of line changes. Most
of these families went to local clinics and providers, if they accessed healthcare
services at all. Social services ranged in size from the locally grown to branches
of state- and federally funded operations.

Healthcare facilities and social services generally depended on grants or other
time-limited funding that made for tight budgets and, often, rather precari-
ous future outlooks. They were also generally understaffed. As a result, families
reported extensive wait times for what were usually hurried interactions with providers who had overwhelming caseloads. Most of these families under-utilized
services because they were undocumented or had no insurance coverage. Many
reported using emergency rooms for acute care as needed. Parents were more likely
to seek out resources for their children than for themselves, such as "well child" visits to pediatricians that were subsidized by state initiatives for uninsured children.

Because immigrant Latino families had not lived in Greater Crenshaw in large numbers for very long, local institutions had adjusted to the area's demographic shift at varying paces. As a result, parents encountered limited accommodations for Spanish speakers; most professionals spoke minimal or no Spanish and most institutions lacked the resources to employ adequate numbers of dedicated translators. I conducted formal interviews at four local healthcare facilities, including a private pediatric practice, a local pediatric practice with four partners, a regional hospital located near the community, and Union Clinic. I also conducted interviews at three social services organizations, including an affiliate of a statewide program enrolling children in no- and low-cost health insurance programs, a locally-based organization providing diverse support services to young people and their families, and a local Women, Infants, and Children (WIC) office. I conducted extensive field observations at Union Clinic and WIC.

Healthcare Provision at Union Clinic

Union Clinic was founded in Greater Crenshaw in the early 1970s and had moved to another part of South Los Angeles for a period of time. In the mid-2000s, it had moved back to Greater Crenshaw. Ms. Barnes, an African American registered nurse (RN), said, "Slowly but surely, I see patients coming back from the neighborhood . . . ladies [who] may be in their fifties now, saying that they remember coming here and bringing all their kids when they were growing up. . . . [I]t shows that [this clinic] was really needed here." Union Clinic was located on major bus lines and drew large numbers of residents. Their client base was largely African American and Latino and, to a lesser degree, Asian- and Belizean-origin immigrants. Ms. Barnes commented that Belizeans "come quietly into the neighborhood"; these immigrants' phenotypical similarities to African Americans made them less visible newcomers to the area. Staff reported frequent challenges communicating across languages, as well as with specific dialects. Clinic materials announced translation capacities not only in Spanish, but in Tagalog, Japanese, Vietnamese, Thai, and West and Central African languages, among others. However, the translation unit was frequently inundated with requests. Providers often depended on children's help or on ad hoc assistance by bilingual staff members, such as receptionists, who had not been hired as dedicated translators.

The clinic drew doctors and practitioners from across Los Angeles who resonated with the institution's holistic, community-based ethos to provide a wide range of services to residents. Administrative staff and some of the nurses lived in or near the community, but most doctors lived in other parts of the city. As a result, they tended to be less familiar with the community and with local services beyond Union that could be useful for their patients. Many providers at Union had worked there for over ten years. Others, as Ms. Levande, an African American woman who ran the support groups for chronic disease management there, said, "come in and stay a few months and go." The clinic survived largely on grants, so there was also a good deal of staff turnover at the end of funding periods.

Union Clinic provided general and specialized pediatric and adult healthcare, as well as treatment and management of chronic conditions including diabetes, hypertension, and HIV/AIDS. Union provided services within their facility and through mobile clinics that partnered with local schools and other organizations to make vaccinations and other routine care readily available to the community. The clinic also accepted a range of health insurance coverage and offered sliding-scale payment options.

Serving Families at Women, Infants, and Children (WIC)

WIC is a federally funded program that provides nutritional education, supplemental food, healthcare access, and breastfeeding support to low-income pregnant women and mothers with children up to age five. California has more WIC enrollees than any other US state; over 60 percent of California infants are enrolled in the program (California WIC Program 2011). Eligibility requires a household income below 185 percent of the US Poverty Income Guidelines. In 2006–2007 dollars, this threshold was $43,290 for a family of five (US Department of Agriculture 2013), the median household size for interviewed families.[13]

WIC tends to be mentioned by name in research involving low-income immigrant mothers, reflecting both the widespread usage of this program and its importance to women who, very often, are connected to few other resources. Ms. Fenstein, a white nutritionist at this WIC site, addressed recipients' unusual relationships with the program: "Once they're in the door, they pretty much stay because they know that this program is unique in that we won't share [their] information . . . so they feel more comfortable, especially if they were referred to us by another family member they trust." All interviewed families had been or were still WIC recipients, making it a natural choice as an observation site. As Ms. Fenstein indicated, WIC was unusual partly because families connected through recommendations from family members or friends. Because they came to WIC through trusted channels, mothers were more comfortable with this institution than with many others. WIC was also the only institutional site I encountered that had enough Spanish speakers for parents to confidently manage their interactions independently, though they were often accompanied by their older children anyway.

Staff members at this WIC site were also overwhelmingly female, which augmented the ease many mothers felt there. Like at other WIC sites, staff consisted of supervisors, nutritionists, and "peer professional" staff. Supervisors and nutritionists were generally not community residents and were largely native English speakers, though some were proficient in professional Spanish. Peer professional staff members were required to have a high school diploma. They generally lived in the community they served and, according to Ms. Dorsey, a regional supervisor, were usually WIC-eligible themselves. She noted that these similarities helped them relate to recipients and provided added motivation to become knowledgeable about other local resources: "It benefits them [staff members]— you know, [they] learn things about their own community, they become experts of what's in their own community for themselves and their families, and then they share that." Therefore, although WIC is federally funded, its community-based model made it function more like a local organization. Its peer-professional staff, in particular, had personal motivations that could help them link families to resources well beyond WIC's doors.

RESOURCE BROKERING IN GREATER CRENSHAW

Connections to local institutions were important for families in their own right, but also for the broader local linkages that personnel like WIC's peer professional staff could facilitate. Institutions that families frequented in Greater Crenshaw varied in terms of their capabilities to act as resource brokers, which Mario Small (2006, 274) defined as "organizations possessing ties to businesses, nonprofits, and government agencies rich in resources, which then provide the neighborhood institution's patrons with access to these resources." Interinstitutional connections could be great enablers for children too, because brokering a connection to one institution could manifest multiple helpful linkages for their families, with little or no extra effort on their part.

Resource brokering was especially valuable when it alerted families to resources they would not have even known to ask for. Ms. Fenstein said, "Being brand new to the country, I think a lot of people aren't aware of what is actually offered to help, and even speaking with friends and family, they don't necessarily learn about everything until they come to a program that can give them a few extra numbers and more information about what's available." Ms. Fenstein highlights how institutional connections could substitute for connections and information missing from families' homogenous social networks (Domínguez and Watkins 2003; Wilson 1987, 1996). Small argues, "The truly disadvantaged may be not merely those living in poor neighborhoods, but those *not participating in well-connected neighborhood institutions*" (2006, 275 [italics in original]).

Because Greater Crenshaw institutions faced constraints broadly related to inadequate funds and staff, resource brokering at the institutional level was usually limited unless it was formally mandated. Later chapters indicate that child brokers and their families generally depended on individual providers as their gateway to resources in and beyond local schools, healthcare facilities, and social services. Because families tended to depend on a trusted individual—when they could locate one—rather than an institution more generally, their local connections were often tenuous. Their chances of accessing resources across organizations also depended heavily on individual providers' local knowledge, time, and energy.

From an institutional perspective, providers' personal knowledge stores were a resilient asset in that they did not depend on time-limited funding streams or formal initiatives. However, they were challenged by large client rosters and institutional subdivisions that provided few opportunities for staff to pool their local knowledge. This decentralization meant families depended on providers taking considerable initiative to champion them, particularly when they had non-routine needs. When providers did so, children and families could be connected to resources they may not have located on their own or known to ask for.

Effective resource brokering requires stability, both over time and in terms of resilience to financial or political shifts. It also requires building meaningful relationships that engender trust between families and the providers who can be gatekeepers to resources (Small 2006).

Stability over time means that transfers of resources to families remain consistent. In this sense, families being connected to particular providers, rather than having generalized ties to institutions, made these relationships vulnerable. If trusted providers left or retired, families' access often left with them. Hilda was among the parents whose healthcare connections had dissolved when her family's doctor left the area. Making new connections was difficult; her family had not had a consistent healthcare provider since that time, over five years prior.

Resilience to political or economic shifts could challenge even the most dedicated staff members. When I interviewed service providers at Secure Pathways, an organization providing a range of support services to young people and their families, they were preoccupied with just-announced changes to the mayor's agenda for "at risk" youth that placed their funding in immediate jeopardy. Ms. Ramos, a third-generation Latina caseworker there, told me,

> I just found out last night [about the proposed cuts] and parents are really upset because they feel that this program and the field trips and the other things that . . . [we] provide at this agency—maybe, you know, that's why the violence [in the area] has gone down. Now if they're gonna take it away, what are these kids gonna do now? What's gonna happen to the options that they have? Not all of them took advantage of it, but the ones who did—now what's gonna happen [to them]?

While Secure Pathways ultimately maintained much of its autonomy, even the possibility of such overnight shifts emphasized how vulnerable many years of work and relationship-building could be to forces beyond providers' control.

Finally, effective resource brokering depends on being able to connect families with services and resources related to sensitive issues. Doing so requires deep levels of trust. As Silvia Domínguez and Celeste Watkins (2003, 123) found among low-income women in Boston, "mothers must trust these agencies before they can include them in their social support networks." For these families, trust had to be developed not only with mothers (and fathers), but with the children who brokered these interactions. Greater Crenshaw providers who had frequent contact with child brokers and their families were more likely to be knowledgeable about the specific challenges they faced. Child brokers and their parents were also more likely to directly request help or resources from a provider with whom they had an established relationship, reflecting Barry Wellman and Milena Gulia's (1999) finding that relationships fortified by frequent contact are most likely to be sources of support.

Clearly, enduring relationships could improve families' communication with providers, enhance providers' understandings of family needs to more effectively recommend appropriate services, and perhaps make families more comfortable making direct requests for assistance. The rarity of these kinds of relationships complicated interactions between families and service providers. Providers' impressions of these families and perceptions about children's brokering also directly influenced how they interacted with them.

Some providers worked in places that provided more support for their individual efforts than others. In Greater Crenshaw, formal mandates from funders or other powerful entities often directed staff members to required forms of resource brokering. For example, WIC is formally mandated to connect recipients with three local doctors who can provide them appropriate care. For many mothers, WIC linking them automatically with providers of prenatal care spared them or their older children from having to initiate those connections independently. Institutional mission statements were also formal mandates because they guided staff members' behaviors and influenced institutional decisions to prioritize particular expenditures or resource brokering.

Formalized resource brokering could also be more passive, requiring little direct input from people who worked in these places. Bulletin boards and tables with flyers and brochures from other organizations were common forms of passive resource brokering that alerted families to resources beyond that organization. Parents and children often explored these materials during protracted waits for appointments. They sometimes used that time to develop shared understandings of these materials. Having these flyers in hand made some children more confident asking doctors and service providers to clarify their content during appointments.

Passive resource brokering can also be informal. For example, institutional sites can facilitate what Small (2010, 20) called "normal accidents" by providing opportunities for residents to talk with each other and share information (Perrow 1984). Mothers of child brokers often exchanged niceties with other immigrant mothers in Spanish while they waited to be seen, though I rarely heard exchanges of local news or information. Likewise, African American women tended to pick waiting-room seats closer to other African American women. Therefore, while waiting rooms could have facilitated normal accidents, I never witnessed these accidents crossing racial or linguistic lines.

Instead, these were places where intergroup tensions often simmered close to the surface. Ms. Brinkley, an African American WIC site manager, said, "In the center I do notice a little tension. . . . Parents are very guarded . . . to the point that if a Hispanic child may accidentally hit [an African American] child, then there's an uproar in the center where we have to stop working and literally go over there." Doctor Victor, an African American pediatrician, reported a similar experience in her practice. "We've had outbursts in our waiting room [between Latino and African American parents]. What they don't realize is that there are four physicians; and if I'm moving fast, you know, you might have gotten here first, but I'm going to see the next patient on my list. They take insult at the slightest hint of preference." Perceptions of resource scarcity diminished residents' opportunities to broker resources among themselves not only in local healthcare and social services sites, but also in the schools.

EDUCATION IN GREATER CRENSHAW: BELLUM AND TYLER MIDDLE SCHOOLS

I interviewed teachers and administrators at Tyler and Bellum Middle Schools, both located within Greater Crenshaw. Most interviewed families had at least one child (often the child broker I had interviewed) who was currently or had previously been a student at one of these schools. By contrast, children went to high schools all over the county, particularly if they managed to matriculate into one of the district's competitive magnet high schools. Over eighteen months, my time on campus included observations of a sixth-grade classroom in each school and interviews with seventeen additional parents who had children in these classes. These parents were African Americans as well as both immigrant and second-generation Latinos from Mexico, Belize, El Salvador, Guatemala, and Nicaragua. Their interviews provide additional context for understanding child brokers' families' experiences in these locations.

Tyler and Bellum Middle Schools were natural foils for each other in terms of the racial and ethnic makeup of their student bodies. Table 2.2 shows that Bellum Middle School served a predominantly African American/black student body and Tyler Middle School served a predominantly Latino population. Latino students almost entirely made up the remainder of Bellum's students, and the converse was true for Tyler. In this respect, Bellum and Tyler looked like urban schools across the United States in that their student bodies were almost entirely Latino and black.[14]

Intergroup tensions were everyday features of these educational environments. Gang activity and fighting were common in both schools (though more so at Bellum). Aside from the racial and ethnic profiles of their student bodies, both schools also faced challenges typical of inner-city education environments, including high levels of food insecurity that state and federal funding attempted to offset with free or reduced-cost school lunches. A considerable proportion of Tyler's student body was classified as English Language Learners. Many teachers had emergency rather than full teaching credentials, a high proportion were first-year teachers, and, overall, these teachers had many fewer years of experience than the California state averages (see table 2.2).

Both schools had been designated Title 1 schools under the No Child Left Behind Act, meaning that the campuses qualified for additional federal, state, and local funding due to the high percentage of students from low-income families.[15] Both schools were also in the bottom 10 percent of California schools on the Academic Performance Index, which is calculated primarily by students' scores on standardized proficiency tests. Table 2.3 shows percentages of students at Bellum and Tyler Middle Schools that tested at grade-level proficiency in English and math for the total student population and by racial/ethnic group. The number of students at Bellum and Tyler Middle Schools who tested at or above grade-level proficiency was particularly low when one considers that California was ranked forty-ninth among the fifty states in student proficiency when these data were collected (National Assessment of Educational Progress 2005).

TABLE 2.2

PROFILES OF STUDENTS AND TEACHERS AT
BELLUM AND TYLER MIDDLE SCHOOLS

	Bellum Middle School	Tyler Middle School	State of California
STUDENT POPULATION (%)			
African American/black	68	23	8
Latino	31	75	48
Eligible for free or reduced cost lunch program	78	83	52
English language learners (ELL)	14	36	25
TEACHERS (%)			
With emergency credential[a]	37	45	5
With full credential[a]	87	71	95
First-year teachers	11	13	6
Mean years teaching	10	6	13

SOURCE: California Department of Education, 2007, "Data and Statistics," http://dq.cde.ca.gov/dataquest/.

[a]Percentages do not add up to 100 percent because these numbers also reflect teachers transitioning from emergency to full credentials.

TABLE 2.3

PROFILE OF CALIFORNIA STATE TESTING RESULTS

	Bellum Middle School			Tyler Middle School			California Average		
Grade	6th	7th	8th	6th	7th	8th	6th	7th	8th
STUDENTS TESTING AT OR ABOVE PROFICIENCY (%)									
All students									
English	18	21	17	16	17	13	42	46	41
Math	16	10	5	15	15	15	42	39	38
African American students									
English	13	19	15	15	15	9	29	32	27
Math	9	5	5	6	4	2	24	22	13
Latino students									
English	26	26	21	15	18	14	28	32	26
Math	29	20	7	17	19	17	29	27	16

SOURCE: See table 2.2

On-campus Environments

Bellum Middle School was frequently referred to by teachers and administrators as the "last African American–majority school" in the Los Angeles Unified School District. This moniker reflects the symbolic importance of this school in local politics and to African American residents, many of whom saw Bellum as the last vestige of the Greater Crenshaw that had been "their" community. The designation was a misnomer. Although 68 percent of Bellum students were classified as black/African American at the time of this study, a considerable number of Belizean-origin and (to a lesser degree) African-origin students were included under this umbrella designation. The fact that parents and personnel alike persisted in referring to Bellum as an African American–majority campus reflected the increasing diversity of the area, the local invisibility of phenotypically black immigrants, and how highly salient race was to the experiences that child brokers and their families had on this campus.

Tyler Middle School was one of ten schools in California receiving preferential funding in a pilot effort to accelerate student performance in high-poverty schools. Evidence of these additional funds could be seen everywhere around campus: new computer labs, the Parent Center with two full-time staff members, and the general upkeep of the campus, which was markedly better than at Bellum. Tyler faced many of the same community challenges as Bellum, but additional resources went a long way toward improving the on-campus experience. For example, the Parent Center had one African American and one Spanish-speaking Latina staff member who worked together to create parent support programs. These included parenting skills programs to improve homework management and disciplinary effectiveness. An active parent volunteer program monitored major routes to and from school each morning and afternoon to ensure that students could get to and from school without fear of being harassed by gang members. Tyler also offered a wider range of after-school programs and home-work help options than Bellum.

The communication environments of these two schools were also very differ-ent. Immigrant parents who braved Bellum's campus did not find any Spanish-speaking staff; even the English as Second Language (ESL) coordinator there did not speak Spanish. By contrast, Tyler had consciously invested its addi-tional resources to foster an institutional culture responsive to the demographic changes in their student body. This included having a large number of visible, bilingual staff members, ranging from office managers to the white principal, who spoke fluent Spanish. Even with all these overtures, Tyler struggled to draw immigrant parents through the front door; many were reluctant to make regular contact with the school.

While most of the children knew little about the schools beyond their immediate area, they were often aware that their own campuses were devalued spaces. They knew that the threats of violence that permeated their campus and community were not present everywhere. In interviews, teachers often referred to students who had gained entry to schools in other parts of the dis-trict as having "won"—necessarily implying that students who stayed in local schools had lost.

There were other reinforcements of devaluation on campus. Ms. Rhines, the ESL coordinator at Tyler, told me that a local mother had secured permission from the administration for her daughter (who was zoned to go there) to spend that day on campus. "The mom told me this herself; she said, 'My daughter is here so that she can learn how it is to value the education that she has—she's [bused to] some school in the Valley and she's not doing so well. She's changed, so I am sending her here today to observe so that she can value the education that she's got.'" Unusual parenting tactics notwithstanding, that this mother used Tyler as a cautionary tale—and the administration allowed her to do so—could only send negative messages to current Tyler students.

I was witness to a similarly frank devaluation by a teacher at Bellum as I signed in with the security attendant at the school gate, as I had to do on every visit. While recording my details from my driver's license, the security attendant asked me, "You here to pick up your kid?" An African American teacher, pass-ing by with her sixth-grade class well within earshot, responded before I could, saying, "Boy, you blind? You think that nice lady would send her kid here?" The message to her students was clear; by virtue of my race and (presumed) class, I had choices as to where my kids would be schooled, and no one would choose to send a "nice" kid to Bellum.

Teacher-Student Relationships

Teachers on both campuses identified the same structural challenges to connecting meaningfully with students. Teachers were often new and staff turnover on both campuses was high.[16] Ms. Rosenfelt, a Jewish math teacher at Tyler who had taught at local schools for thirty-seven years, said, "When new teachers come in, they [administrators] hand you your keys . . . and that's it. There is not enough help and support. . . . [There are] so many new teachers. Most of them are gone or going. The ones who made it, that were here when I got here, they seemed to know what to do to survive here." New teachers had to devote considerable time to preparing classes and learning their way around campus. Few lived nearby, and their limited knowledge of the local area and its resources meant they were seldom effective resource brokers for families.

Safety concerns on both campuses further limited student-teacher communication, as teachers found themselves in perennially disciplinarian roles.[17] Gang-related and other on-campus fighting was symptomatic of widespread disciplinary problems at Bellum in particular, where the (unofficial) school motto was this: "Our first job is to keep the kids safe; the second is to educate them." I heard some version of this motto in every teacher and administrator interview on that campus. Ms. Hernandez, the ESL coordinator there, was "horrified" when a Latino student recently came into class dripping blood from his side, gashed with a knife when he tried to break up a fight between two other students. He did not tell her what had happened; she only saw he was bleeding when she noticed him becoming increasingly pale over the first ten minutes of class. She said, "Here, it's not just coming to school and doing your work. You have to go outside. Hang out with your friends. Deal with boys and girls. Worry about not getting pushed around or jumped, you know."

Teachers were forced to devote substantial energy to enforcing rules and meting out punishments, giving them little time to focus on students who were not making trouble. Mr. South, a white social studies teacher at Bellum, said when the parents of "good kids" come to parent-teacher night, "What I really want to tell them is the truth. That [your kid] is great, does all her work, never makes problems. And because of that, I've ignored her the entire year because I'm too busy dealing with hooligans." Children of immigrants were often considered good kids, partly because they tended to be quiet. However, these silences meant that teachers often knew little about their students' family lives. Veteran teachers like Ms. Rosenfelt were exceptional, and her clear understanding of how brokering responsibilities influenced her students' school experiences was hard-won over her many years in the area. Other, newer teachers were more likely to attribute students' frequent absences, incomplete homework, and visible fatigue to lack of interest. Students and parents were unlikely to share their challenges with teachers unless they already trusted them. I explore these disconnects between teachers', students', and families' understandings and expectations in chapter 6. These mismatches had consequences for children's school experiences and for interactions they brokered on campus.

In Greater Crenshaw, immigrant parents and their child brokers encountered a community that gave them a mixed reception. Though providers, teachers, and other professionals generally had good intentions, limited time, funding, and support, combined with anxieties about having to communicate via children, meant that they often did not fully understand the needs of child brokers and their families. Within these constraints, child brokers and their families, to varying degrees, worked together to identify and secure resources and build relationships with providers and professionals in these institutions.

CHAPTER 3

CHILD BROKERS AND THEIR FAMILIES

The chapters that follow draw on the experiences of twenty families in which children brokered at home and at local schools, healthcare facilities, and social services. This chapter introduces these children and their families, explains why certain children are more likely to shoulder these responsibilities than their siblings, and describes what kinds of gaps they are enlisted to bridge in their parents' social networks and local connections.

Introducing the Children

Parents generally relied on their eldest child to broker for them. These children had spent their early years in language environments where they were primarily, if not entirely, surrounded by their parents' language. Many did not encounter English on a consistent basis until they started school. Their younger siblings' environments were different; Spanish became intermingled with the English their elder siblings spoke with them and among themselves. This pattern was consistent with prior research finding that eldest children are more likely to be proficient in their parents' language than their siblings, across immigrant groups (Stevens and Ishizawa 2007). Karen Pyke (2005) even documented cases where eldest siblings had to broker for their younger siblings because they spoke so little Chinese or Korean that they could not communicate fully with their own parents or grandparents.

Sometimes, gender trumped birth order, as girls were far more likely to broker than their brothers. Daughters were primary brokers in seventeen of these twenty families; in the two families where parents had two children who brokered equally, sons were identified along with a daughter. This pattern is partially explained by brokering activities being embedded in the kinds of care work that traditionally fall to women, such as assisting with household management, helping younger siblings with homework, and securing resources that ensure family wellbeing, like healthcare or food assistance.[1] Daughters were also more likely to be home to help because they were kept under stricter parental surveillance than their brothers in many of these families.[2] Research on family communication patterns has also found that mother-daughter communication tends to be more intensive than among other family members (Guilamo-Ramos et al. 2006; Miller-Day and Fisher 2006); Virginia compared her daughter Regina (age fourteen) to her son, saying, "She and I converse a lot, so she speaks Spanish much more." This gendered dimension of family communication may also help explain why daughters were more likely to broker for their mothers than were sons.

Whether child brokers were the eldest, the eldest daughter, or the eldest sibling still living at home, they tended to spend most of their free time with their parents. Sometimes, family rules determined which children were most likely to be home and therefore available to help, as was the case with parents who kept a closer watch on their daughters. Other times, children stayed close to home because of long-established patterns of being needed; eldest children had often helped parents for as long as they could remember and were therefore used to being on hand to help at home and accompany parents to errands and appointments.

In either case, primary child brokers were likely to be more bilingually proficient than their siblings. These skills were developed and supported by frequent use; younger siblings had less experience communicating in two languages, making phone calls for parents, deciphering household bills and mail, and so forth. Regular practice gave children opportunities to build on past experiences and engage their parents in mutual learning activities that fostered their language development. The importance of practice was clear in families where an eldest sibling moved out and everyday brokering tasks were bequeathed to a younger sibling (Park 2001; Song 1999). These younger children often struggled at first, but over time, their brokering capabilities increased with use.

Helping parents also engendered closeness between child brokers and their parents; many felt that they had more rewarding relationships with their parents than their siblings because they brokered.[3] Collaboratively working toward shared goals increased children's attachment to their parents, and children realized how brokering positioned them within their families. Although some child brokers made a point of noting that they helped their parents much more than their siblings did, they seldom resisted these obligations. Rather, they took considerable pride in being able to broker; Juana (age thirteen) said, "I'm just glad that when my mom needs help, I can do it. I can make things easier for her." Having their parents' trust conferred a sense of authority and status within the family, and in relation to their siblings, that child brokers prized highly. The embedded rewards of being the family helper and the "good" child were powerful motivators for these young people. These rewards help explain why brokering responsibilities often persisted into early adulthood and sometimes past the time when parents needed such intensive assistance. These rewards also explain why many child brokers reflexively put their families' needs ahead of their own, prioritizing helping their parents over finishing their homework, for example.

Brokering activities provided psychic rewards for children but were also a way for children to reward their parents. Child brokers often framed their assistance as a way to pay back the many sacrifices their parents had made for them by migrating. Children knew that their parents come to the United States motivated, at least in part, by a desire to provide their children with more opportunities. The costs to their parents were separation from their own families of origin and feeling humbled by their foreignness, limited language capabilities, and low-paid, low-status jobs, from which they often returned exhausted and still worried about paying their bills. Being able to "make things easier" for parents, as Juana phrased it, was part of how children gave back. Their parents' gratitude motivated them to continue to enact these roles over time.

There were, then, overtones of morality and family loyalty associated with being the family's primary broker. These were sometimes made even more explicit by parents. In two families where a younger child was the primary broker even though an older child still lived at home, parents explained this apparent aberration by saying their eldest was either "shy" or "lazy." The former explanation implies some parental assessment as to which child was best suited to brokering responsibilities. The latter carried the kind of moral judgment that Miri Song (1999) documented among Chinese immigrant parents in the United Kingdom, who pointedly compared children who exhibited individualistic tendencies to their "good" siblings, or to good children in other families, in order to draw them back into the family fold.

This and other manifestations of parental authority highlighted that while brokers often enjoyed special status in the family as their parents' primary helpers, they were still children. In interviews, they referred to themselves as "children" or "kids," even if they were in their late teens. They also distinguished between tasks they could do and "grown-up stuff," a term they frequently used to describe brokering tasks that exceeded their capabilities. These young people were cognizant of their social positioning; while their brokering responsibilities could elevate their status over their siblings, they were well aware that they were not equals to their parents and other adults.

Twelve of these twenty-two children were in middle school (grades six to eight) at the time of our first interview, and seven were in high school (grades nine to twelve). Maria and Vida (aged nineteen and eighteen, respectively) had dropped out of high school when they were pregnant, and Maya (age nineteen) had just begun her first year at a local university (see table 3.1). With few exceptions, schools had always been English-only environments for these children. In 1998, California had passed Proposition 227, a ballot proposition that had effectively ended bilingual education in the state. Even child brokers who had entered schools as new immigrants themselves were limited to a maximum of one year of bilingual instruction before being transferred into English-only classrooms. Many child brokers, even if they were US-born, struggled with subjects that were heavily dependent on language comprehension, like history. Math, on the other hand, was less language dependent and often a subject where child brokers performed strongly (see chapter 6).

The majority of child brokers were US-born; four were immigrants themselves. Rolando (age seventeen) had crossed the border alone, without papers, when he was fifteen. Vida (age eighteen) had migrated with her family when she was nine years old and still struggled to read and write in English; Yanira (age fourteen) was in similar straits, having moved to the United States six months prior to our interview. Children who were immigrants themselves faced significant struggles as they simultaneously tried to learn English and broker for their families. Rolando's, Vida's, and Yanira's undocumented status further complicated their brokering experiences. They had to be visible for their families while managing their own anxieties about needing to remain largely invisible (Gonzales 2011). On these fronts, US-born brokers had less to worry about, since they were all citizens and had been learning English since they started their formal schooling. These advantages were relative, since many still struggled with limited linguistic and cultural proficiencies, as compared to peers with native-born parents.

TABLE 3.1

CHARACTERISTICS OF CHILD BROKERS AT TIME OF FIRST INTERVIEW

	Proportion of sample (N = 22)	*Percentage of sample*
AGE (median)	14	–
SEX		
Female	17	77
Male	5	23
Pregnant or parents themselves	2	9
IMMIGRATION STATUS		
Immigrant, unauthorized status	3	14
Immigrant, authorized status	1	4
US-born citizen	18	82
EDUCATION		
Attending middle school	12	55
Attending high school	7	32
Left high school without graduating	2	9
Attending college	1	4

While there were commonalities among families in terms of which children brokered most frequently, what they brokered varied according to age, abilities, and families' needs. Older children were more likely to have developed greater bilingual capacities, cultural sophistication, understanding of meta-language, and the ability to reflect on their brokering behaviors (Buriel and de Ment 1998; Dorner, Orellana, and Li-Grining 2007; Orellana, Dorner, and Pulido 2003). Family configurations and needs, however, were the primary determinants of what responsibilities children were given, whether they were eleven, fourteen, or seventeen years old. The three families my research assistants and I observed in months subsequent to their first interviews demonstrate how diverse these twenty families' characteristics and circumstances were, and how their children's brokering experiences varied as a result.[4]

Luis's Family

Luis and his family were introduced in the opening chapter of this book. He was eleven at the time of our first interview and a sixth grader at Bellum Middle School, earning mostly As and Bs. The eldest of three sons, Luis did not participate regularly in after-school programs because he was needed at home. Luis's family had particularly acute needs for a wide range of community connections because Julio, his seven-year-old brother, was severely epileptic. Untreated seizures in infancy had caused serious neurological damage, leaving Julio unable to speak or do many things independently. In frustration, he lashed out, sometimes hitting his siblings and his mother. Julio's condition and his attendant medical needs preoccupied his family and strained their limited financial and social resources.

His family's extensive medical and social needs put pressure on their sometimes-shy son to speak for his family often and in an unusually wide range of contexts. His mother, Ana, was thirty-nine years old at our first meeting. She and Luis's father had lived in the United States for fifteen years, in Los Angeles for eight, and, after a short stint in the Midwest, had returned to Greater Crenshaw eight months earlier. Their return to the community after an absence meant reorienting and connecting, in many cases, with new services and resources. Ana had spent less than three years in school in Mexico and she had minimal capabilities communicating in English. She and her husband were both undocumented, and their fears of being discovered caused family tensions during their frequent visits to healthcare and social services institutions for Julio. Luis often missed school and did not complete his homework on "bad days," as he referred to times when they sought emergency care for Julio.

The first day I interviewed him followed a "bad day." Because of a late night trip to the emergency room, Luis had been chastised at school for not finishing his homework and for falling asleep in one of his classes. He enlightened neither teacher as to the reasons for these behaviors. This family's difficult circumstances had, in essence, turned them inward; they had few close ties in the area, making them all the more dependent on Luis's brokering. He helped dutifully to the best of his abilities but showed tacit resentment for how much he was needed, which he directed particularly at his father.

Ana was acutely aware of her dependence on her oldest son but accepted it as a critical component of her family's survival strategy. In that first interview (and in subsequent ones), she would repeatedly say, "God blessed me with my first child." The unspoken comparison to the challenges her second son's condition created for their family always lingered. Financial pressures were also particularly acute for this family, who lived on less than $15,000 per year. Not only did Julio's condition frequently result in unanticipated costs, but caring for him prevented Ana from being able to work steadily. When we first interviewed her, she had started part-time work as a seamstress in the same factory as her husband. Subsequent meetings revealed that her employment was sporadic and contingent on both Julio's health status and their limited abilities to locate child care for their toddler son.

Graciela's Family

Graciela was thirteen when we first met, the second eldest of four siblings (aged sixteen, eleven, and four) who lived with their mother, Ileana. Graciela's parents were separated and in the process of divorcing at the time. Ileana later admitted to us that at first, she had worried we were immigration officials when she met us. She was thirty-eight years old and had emigrated from Guatemala without documentation seventeen years before. She had lived in Greater Crenshaw for the last fourteen years and was awaiting her residency papers, having regularized her status through her husband, who was a naturalized citizen. He had steady work at a golf course and did not require brokering assistance because he had migrated from Mexico at eleven and matriculated into US public schools. He would often come over to visit his children after school. At Graciela's urging (and with her assistance), Ileana had successfully formalized their child support arrangements through the courts, a move that had negatively affected Graciela's relationship with her father.

Ileana worked as a housecleaner in different parts of Los Angeles. She understood a few words of English but depended on Graciela to broker most of her interactions with her employers. Graciela would make phone calls to her mother's employers when clarifications needed to be made or grievances aired. She also would go with her mother to help her clean when she had school vacations. Graciela accompanied her mother to doctors' visits for herself or other family members; Ileana only depended on Spanish-speaking staff in those locations if Graciela could not come to help her. Despite having an older brother, Graciela took on the vast majority of brokering tasks because, she explained, her brother was shy and would get "too emotional" in challenging interactions.

Ileana differentiated herself from many parents by consistently placing her needs second to her daughter's schoolwork. Ileana would forbid Graciela to accompany her to appointments if it precluded Graciela attending a school-related event or adversely affected her schoolwork, even if it made her own interactions more challenging. She also actively encouraged Graciela to seek out educational resources and opportunities. Despite having only a couple of years of formal education herself, Ileana routinely sought out her children's teachers, communicating with them through Graciela's assistance. These interactions had encouraged her to financially prioritize purchasing supplies and materials that piqued her children's interests and enriched their learning. In Graciela's case, this meant visits to the library and the purchase of poetry books. Graciela contrasted this with her father's approach, saying, "My dad will give me the money to go here and do this and that, and tells me to make the right choice. My mom *makes* the right choice."

Her mother's proactive approach and encouragement were reflected in Graciela's own behaviors. She was unusually involved in after-school programs, including one that paired college students with middle schoolers for homework help and mentoring. At the time, Graciela was in eighth grade at Tyler Middle School with a straight-A average and had been admitted to a competitive magnet high school for the next school year. She was also taking multiple enrichment courses in leadership development, math, and political science after school and on Saturdays.

Liliana's Family

Liliana was sixteen, a junior at a nearby charter high school, and on track to go to college when we first interviewed her and her mother's husband, Carlos, who was then thirty-three. Liliana and her mother left El Salvador when she was five years old and were both permanent US residents. Her mother had married Carlos when Liliana was in elementary school. He had left school in Mexico in the ninth grade to help support his family. He had crossed the US border with his father eleven years earlier, moved to Los Angeles six years before, and had been in Greater Crenshaw for the last five years. He and Liliana's mother had a son, Gavin, who was five years old at that time. When we first interviewed them, Carlos was awaiting his green card. He and Liliana had completed his application together, an experience they both described as daunting.

Two things differentiated Carlos and Liliana from many other families we interviewed. The first was Carlos's attitudes and behaviors, which facilitated both his independence and Liliana's efforts to help him. Carlos went out of his way to push himself beyond his co-ethnic networks, actively seeking out people with whom he could practice English (including me). He kept notebooks of English words that he would review and ask Liliana to define for him as needed. His notebooks were also part of his media consumption; he told us, "I felt that

[English as a Second Language] classes were a waste of time, so I started studying at home on the television." His notebooks were also close at hand when he surfed websites in English, often with Liliana nearby.

The second differentiating feature was the nature of his relationship with Liliana. Their easy give-and-take, particularly compared with other fathers who relied on their children's brokering, facilitated her efforts. He said, "I believe it is mutual. . . . I ask her to translate, but not with the intention to have her read everything to me—or to have her read things for me all the time if I understand perfectly. . . . It used to be very difficult for me to read in English, but not any-more. . . . I'm not saying that my daughter hasn't helped me, because thanks to her I learned the language. She always corrected me."

The nature of their connection may have been different because Carlos was not her biological father, which gave them some flexibility in how they negotiated their relationship. They relied on each other like family, referencing each other as "my father" and "my daughter," though he had not formally adopted her. Kath Weston (1997) details how the families we choose have different dynamics from the involuntary nature of relationships within families of origin.[5] While Liliana obviously did not decide to have Carlos become part of her and her mother's life—he and her mother had made that decision—she did make choices, along with Carlos, about the nature of their relationship. The flexibility and mutual appreciation they demonstrated for each other enabled her to broker for him when needed.

Indeed, Liliana found brokering for Carlos far less stressful than brokering for her mother. In comparing the two, Liliana said, "My mom, most of the time, just asks for help. My dad, he figures out everything on his own, mostly every-thing. When he's *really* confused he comes to me." In contrast to her husband, Liliana's mother, Adriana, consumed only Spanish-language media, and her regular clients where she worked as a cosmetologist were mainly Latina. Liliana would go to work with her mother on the weekends to broker between Adriana and her English-speaking clients. Carlos commented, "Sometimes it seems my wife is less interested in learning English . . . [but] the girl only has a few more years of school so [Adriana] has to learn English little by little." Carlos's com-ment reflected his recognition that Liliana finishing high school would prompt changes to the family system that, in turn, would affect his wife's dependence on her brokering assistance.

Introducing the Parents

Like Adriana, the parents who participated in interviews were all Spanish domi-nant and foreign born, though not necessarily newly arrived; they had lived in the United States for an average of sixteen years, in Los Angeles for thirteen years, and in Greater Crenshaw for eight. That many depended on their children's assistance, even after living in the United States for a decade or more, reflects that immigrants' integration is a gradual process, with local familiarity and comfort accruing over long time periods.[6]

Table 3.2 presents the characteristics of interviewed parents alongside those of other Greater Crenshaw residents, differentiated by race/ethnicity. Latino residents are differentiated by whether they responded to the telephone survey in English or Spanish.

Interviewed parents were demographically similar to other Spanish-speaking Latino residents. However, they had larger households, lower annual incomes, and lower levels of education than African American and English-speaking Latino residents. Eighteen of the twenty families lived on less than $35,000 per year, and many on less than $15,000. Though these incomes should have made these families eligible for poverty relief programs, many were ineligible due to parents' unauthorized immigration status.[7] Over half (60 percent) of parents had less than eight years of schooling; two mothers had no formal education at all because civil wars had disrupted the education systems in their native Guatemala and El Salvador, respectively. Three-quarters of parents were married or living with a long-term partner.

Mothers were more likely to agree to participate than fathers; only five fathers were formally interviewed for this study. A few factors contributed to this gender imbalance.[8] Fathers generally spoke more English, in relative terms, than mothers, so this gender skew partly reflected that they needed less assistance from their children. The imbalance was also partially due to gendered differences in parents' family responsibilities. Michael Jones-Correa (1998) found that even when immigrant Latinas worked full time, they retained their primary nurturer roles and were therefore more likely to interact with local schools, healthcare facilities, and other services. As a result, they were more likely to encounter residents and providers across ethnic and linguistic divides than were their partners (Domínguez 2011, 35; Jones-Correa 1998). Mothers also reported more frequent community encounters than fathers did, and they required their children's brokering assistance to manage these interactions.

But using multiple methods revealed another dimension to this gender discrepancy. Males whose survey responses indicated that their children frequently brokered for them generally denied these needs when asked to discuss them further in an in-person interview. Fathers who did agree to be interviewed were often reluctant, in their speech and body language, to admit that they needed help, particularly to younger women.[9] My research assistants and I noted that when men talked about needing their children's help, they tended to look down or away from us, refusing eye contact until we moved onto less emotionally vulnerable topics. A number of children also reported that brokering for Dad generated more tension. Aurora (age sixteen) said, "[My dad] is just more impatient, I guess. Like, my mom, if I tell her I'm busy and I'll help

TABLE 3.2

DEMOGRAPHIC CHARACTERISTICS OF GREATER CRENSHAW RESIDENTS

	African Americans	English-speaking Latinos	Spanish-speaking Latinos	Parents interviewed
N	294	130	170	20
Age (median)	44	28	37	35
Female (%)	64	50	45	75
IMMIGRANT GENERATION (%)				
First	–	20	71	100
Second	–	65	25	–
Household size (median)	2	4	4	5
Household income below $35,000 (%)	56	58	95	90
EDUCATION (%)				
Eighth grade or less	2	5	47	60
Attended/completed high school	31	48	41	35
Attended/completed college	33	17	5	5
MARITAL STATUS (%)				
Single/never married	42	45	20	25
Married/live-in partner	28	45	68	75
Divorced/separated	19	9	9	–
RESIDENTIAL TENURE				
Years in United States	–	29	19	16
Years in Los Angeles	32	23	14	13
Years in Greater Crenshaw	15	13	8	8

SOURCE: Analyzed and prepared by the author from data from a survey of Greater Crenshaw conducted by the Metamorphosis Project at the University of Southern California, 2006.

NOTE: Percentages may not total 100 percent as less common response categories have not been included in this table.

her in a little while, she's okay with it mostly. But my dad will just say, 'No, I need you right now.' He'll get really mad if he has to wait even two minutes when he's trying to pay bills and stuff."

This gendered dynamic revealed how brokering differentially related to parental roles and expectations. For men, depending on their children was more likely to conflict with their scripts for competent fatherhood and threaten their traditional frames for appropriate masculinity. These feelings could be further exacerbated by their child's gender; Aurora's father, Tulio, said he often wished he had a son to broker for him; he thought that would be less embarrassing than depending on a daughter. While women could also experience role conflicts, the interdependence required for successful brokering was usually understood as a form of mutual nurturing, which integrated more easily into mothers' relationships with their children.

LIVING IN GREATER CRENSHAW

Children were called upon to help make connections that their parents found difficult or prohibitive to make alone. The remainder of this chapter provides necessary context about parents' social networks and local connections, to identify the limitations that children's brokering efforts were most often deployed to address.

Parents' Social Networks

Immigrant parents whose children brokered for them had strong social networks in the area, compared with other Greater Crenshaw residents. They had significantly more close friends and family living in Los Angeles, if not in the neighborhood, compared with other Latino and African American residents.[10] They also reported significantly more frequent discussions with neighbors than other Latinos living in Greater Crenshaw.[11] Both of these patterns reflect the chain migration patterns that characterize Mexican and Central American migration, in that people tend to migrate to places where they have existing support systems.[12]

These kinds of support systems serve many important functions for new immigrants. Having people to watch your kids, come to your celebrations, and listen to your heartaches are all critical forms of social support for immigrants' mental and emotional health and day-to-day survival (Domínguez 2011; Domínguez and Watkins 2003; McKenzie, Whitley, and Weich 2002; Menjívar 2000). These relationships were most often strong ties to similar others, and reciprocal exchanges reinforced in-group solidarity. Silvia Domínguez's (2011, 22–24) study of immigrant women living in public housing in Boston found that social support from friends and family could also indirectly facilitate social mobility by, for example, providing child care and other assistance that facilitated one woman's pursuit of higher education.

These kinds of support networks are very important, but they have their limits. Mark Granovetter (1973) explained how heavy investments of social energy into these relationships can be draining and may constrain capabilities to make and maintain the kinds of "weak ties" he famously documented as being crucial to getting ahead (see also Domínguez 2011, 22). Domínguez (2011, 11), like Cecilia Menjívar (2000) in her earlier work on social networks among Salvadoran immigrants, found that despite close ties, her respondents were "socially isolated . . . [and] they live in contexts with homogeneous social networks in which everyone is alike and information gets recycled."

This recycling of information highlighted the limitations of immigrant parents' networks. The friends, extended family, and neighbors in parents' social networks were generally also new immigrants with limited English proficiency and education. As a result, they all faced the same difficulties in accessing news and information that could enable their local connections.[13] That a number of parents reported "lending out" their children to broker for nearby friends and relatives was further evidence that their closest ties faced their same constraints to navigating their community encounters.[14]

Connections to Community Organizations

Community organizations can provide residents from diverse backgrounds with opportunities to interact, share common concerns, and build relationships with each other (de Souza 2009; Small 2006). Survey respondents were asked to specify their affiliations to local religious, cultural, political, recreational, and educational organizations. English-speaking Latino and African American respondents were most likely to name organizations with diverse memberships that could facilitate relationships across racial, ethnic, and class boundaries and open new avenues to local resources. By contrast, immigrant parents with child brokers reported fewer organizational ties than did other residents. Parents who reported organizational connections were most often involved with Evangelical or Catholic churches or with hometown associations. A study of Greater Crenshaw churches found that Evangelical churches had exclusively immigrant Latino congregations and that Catholic churches held separate Spanish-language services, effectively creating sub-congregations that seldom interacted with each other (Chàvez and Ball-Rokeach 2006; Ebaugh and Chafetz 2000). Overall, immigrant parents' organizational connections were extensions of their homogenous social networks, not spaces that facilitated building diverse local ties.

Accessing Local Resources

The consequences of parents' truncated social networks and organizational affiliations were evident in the challenges they faced in accessing local resources. Compared with other Greater Crenshaw residents, parents with child brokers had significantly more difficulty securing healthcare for themselves and for their children, as well as finding trusted advice on raising children.[15]

All Greater Crenshaw residents indicated that finding healthcare for themselves was more difficult than doing so for their children. This pattern reflected state- and county-wide programs that provided no- and low-cost health insurance to under-served children at that time.[16] Such coverage was largely unavailable for their working poor parents. African Americans reported less difficulty accessing healthcare than their Latino neighbors, but these evaluations were relative. Nationally, African Americans and Latinos have lower rates of health insurance coverage than other US groups and, therefore, tend to receive less care, and at later stages of illness.[17] It is against this backdrop of systemic health disparities that children tried to broker their families' connections to healthcare resources.

Parents with child brokers were disproportionately likely to be immigrants, as compared with other Latino and African American residents. They were therefore more likely to be undocumented. Unauthorized status was a major reason that parents reported significantly greater difficulty accessing health resources for both themselves and their children, even relative to other Greater Crenshaw residents. Hirokazu Yoshikawa's (2011) study of undocumented parents in New York City found that they generally do not qualify for services available to other working poor families with US-born children. Furthermore, even when their citizen children are eligible for services, undocumented parents often do not access them for fear of revealing their immigration status (Yoshikawa 2011). For a number of these families, these fears were draining features of their everyday lives; Ana's stories were peppered with references to how she and her husband weighed the benefits of pursuing opportunities for their son Julio against the potential threat of revealing their residency status.

For respondents with child brokers, finding trusted advice on childrearing was even more difficult than securing healthcare for them. As I noted in chapter 1, children's responsibilities were not a panacea for community ills; some got into fights, dropped out of school, or got pregnant, even while they served as their parents' primary link to community life. If parents sought support for problems with their child broker, they did so without that child's aid. Since parents generally depended on their children's brokering to make connections beyond their own social networks, navigating the community for counsel about their children was likely even more difficult than the tasks they could address as a family unit.

CHILDREN'S BROKERING, BRIDGES, AND SOCIAL LEVERAGE

The limitations in parents' social networks, organizational affiliations, and their abilities to access local resources all reflect that they had few "bridges"; that is, individuals who crossed racial, ethnic, or class lines to encourage development of heterogeneous ties (de Souza Briggs 2003). As opposed to social support networks, which help families "get by," bridges offer access to social leverage, or what it takes to "get ahead" (Domínguez and Watkins 2003; Putnam 2000). For immigrant families in under-resourced communities like Greater Crenshaw, bridges can be important enablers of social mobility and local integration.

In insular neighborhoods, bridges can be difficult to come by; Ricardo Stanton-Salazar (2001) noted that young people find few role models in their urban schools who can be bridges, though these individuals can be critical to their academic success. The same is true in other social domains. Whether a bridge is a native-born neighbor, a service provider, a teacher, a coworker, or a fellow churchgoer from a different social background, these people can help families access a more diverse set of resources because they operate in different social networks.

The most basic requirement for building relationships with bridges is finding opportunities for contact with them. Child brokers provided opportunities for such contact in two ways. The first was positional, since having children brought parents into contact with a range of local institutions to address needs related to their schooling, health, and supervision. These positional needs provided families with opportunities to communicate with others outside their immigrant social networks, including service providers and other parents.

Children also actively facilitated opportunities for contact by brokering in-person interactions, searching online for information on local services, making phone calls to secure appointments, and filling out paperwork to determine eligibility for benefits. Through these activities, children directly facilitated contact with potential bridges and were critical to whether their families were able to convert casual contact into meaningful relationships. Enduring relationships across class, ethnic, and linguistic lines can facilitate increased social and human capital, as well as access to needed services and resources (de Souza Briggs 2003; Domínguez 2011). All of these opportunities could be important forms of social leverage for families.

Service providers and professionals working in local institutions were potentially valuable connections for parents not only as individuals with different experiences, skills, and connections to share, but also as representatives of institutions that were repositories for resources and services. Whether prompted by personal initiative or institutional mandate, resource brokering by providers could open great opportunities for resources and support to these families.

Unsurprisingly, survey respondents with child brokers reported significantly more family interaction than other Greater Crenshaw residents.[18] Family interactions were critical supports for children's brokering efforts. Although providers often perceived brokering activities as independent actions by children, these activities were most effective when they involved many (if not all) family members. Before they ventured into the community, family members engaged each other privately to assess their needs and took steps, independently and collectively, to make sense of how to address those challenges. The next chapter explores the family home and how members developed strategies for understanding their community, and for deciding how best to engage with it.

❧

CHAPTER 4

COMMUNITY BEGINS AT HOME

The interactions that children broker in local institutions do not begin in doctors' waiting rooms or school admissions offices; they begin at home. Since children's brokering is most visible in public spaces, prior research has been largely focused on these locations.[1] In this chapter, I argue that children's public brokering is shaped by domestic forms of these activities, making the family home a central component of understanding how child brokers and their families interact with their community.

I engage a family systems perspective to explore what children do for their families and how families differ with regard to how they engage each other and their environments. Understanding the family system requires considering multiple levels of family interaction, beginning with how individuals negotiate their place in that system. To do so, family members manage tensions that emerge from their needs for closeness and connection, on the one hand, and their needs for differentiation as individuals, on the other. This tension is a dynamic negotiation among family members, as the optimal balance of these needs will differ from one circumstance to another.

Over time, developments within the family alter how individual members manage these tensions. At the system level, the family unit balances opposing forces of stability and change. Family members influence each other's growth and learning, which in turn affects how they understand and connect with their community. Families' capabilities for change are also influenced by the stable interaction patterns that become embedded, enduring elements of how that system functions (Gavazzi 2011; Katz 2010; Lievrouw and Livingstone 2005).

Finally, at the intersystem level, the family is an "open" system, meaning that each family is influenced by other systems in their environments. For example, family members often shared information with each other that they had gleaned from interactions with neighbors, service providers, and local organizations when it was relevant to a family challenge. Similarly, identifying a family need often prompted children to seek out and broker information that could help their family address it. These information-gathering and sense-making practices revealed that community connections can encourage family communication, just as family communication can encourage community connections.

Aurora (age sixteen) provided an example of the linkages between domestic and community interactions by recounting how a negative experience with a local doctor prompted her family's decision to find a new provider. To do so, Aurora and her parents talked with their neighbors and friends. When this approach did not yield the assistance they needed, Aurora searched online for local pediatricians and called the insurance company to ensure that the new doctor would accept their coverage, before accompanying her mother to that doctor when her sister was ill. Aurora's experience emphasizes the recursive relationship between what children do at home and do in the community; having brokered a connection to a doctor that the family decided was not worth maintaining, Aurora's brokering was central to her family's renewed efforts to make a better quality, sustainable local connection.

Her story also highlights how important media connections were to children's brokering activities. Children engaged a range of media to locate resources, to check and double-check their comprehension of important documents, and to learn alongside their parents. These children engaged with traditional mass media (i.e., locally available newspapers and newsletters, radio, and television) and new media (i.e., computers, the Internet, and mobile devices), as well as media forms that are often overlooked, such as landline telephones, "freebie" local newsletters, mailed items, and newsletters that came home from school in children's backpacks. The media connections that families made to address their needs influenced how they perceived their community, as well as the strategies they developed to engage its resources.

Given the centrality of media to children's brokering activities, I begin by overviewing the domestic media environments in these families before turning to how individual-, system-, and intersystem levels of family life influenced children's brokering activities at home.

FAMILY MEDIA ENVIRONMENTS

Child brokers reported helping their parents connect with a wide range of media that required some measure of English language proficiency, US cultural familiarity, or technological know-how. Parents' own media connections were primarily related to entertainment. Newspapers, if purchased, were perused primarily for sports scores, television programming was largely limited to *telenovelas* (soap operas) and soccer matches, and radios were most likely to be tuned to Christian music stations. Victoria (age twelve) described her parents' media connections as follows: "As a family, we always watch [TV] in Spanish . . . mostly we watch soccer, football . . . and when my mom listens to the radio she listens to . . . Spanish [music stations]. So, it's pure Spanish. She never listens to, like, rock or pop or any news in English."[2] In many families, child brokers were the ones who initiated media connections for local information.

A review of media devices that families had at home also uncovered what was missing from these media environments (Livingstone 2002; Wilkin et al. 2007). Parents' limited finances meant that these families did not purchase every media device they may have desired. Therefore, the media they chose to buy gave more insight into their priorities, as compared with wealthier families who can afford one (or more) of every conceivable device. Every family in this study had at least one television, radio, and landline telephone, though it was common for telephones to be cut off for days or weeks at a time before being reconnected when a late bill was paid. Many families did not have cellular phones; those who did usually shared them among members. Personal devices like iPods and smartphones were similarly rare at that time.[3]

More than any other medium, television dominated the environments of these family homes, temporally (in terms of time spent watching) as well as spatially. In many apartments, the television's size was more akin to a movie screen, taking up most free space in small living rooms. Every family also had a cable subscription, which usually included premium content like stations carrying Latin American soccer and additional Spanish-language channels.

By contrast, although seventeen of the twenty families had computers, twelve of them did not have Internet access for some or all of the time that we were in contact with them. Echoing the sentiments of many other parents, Aurora's father, Tulio, explained by saying, "The Internet, it is much too expensive for us." Cable subscriptions, however, were more costly than basic Internet connectivity in Greater Crenshaw at the time. Parents' choices therefore reflected both a preference for expanded television content and their limited familiarity with (and, sometimes, fears of) what Internet access might expose their children to (Tripp 2011).

Where media devices were located in the home influenced how they were treated, who used them, and how. Most families had a television in the living room and another in the parents' bedroom. The television's location determined the primary language for programming; parents' bedrooms were universally Spanish-only zones. In the living room, it depended on who held the remote control. Children reported watching Spanish-language programming alongside their parents but preferred English-language content when watching alone or with siblings. Aurora (age sixteen) said, "When I put English stuff on, [my parents] just go to sleep . . . and I kinda get them, because I imagine myself putting on, like, the Korean TV channel and not understanding. I would just go to sleep [too]."

Computers were located in either living rooms or children's bedrooms. Most parents preferred having the computer in a communal area, if space allowed, to better monitor their children's activities. These desires to keep tabs on their kids were not necessarily matched with computer-related capabilities; Juana's (age thirteen) joking comment that "the only time my mother touches the computer is to dust it" reflected the pattern in many families, where parents only connected with online content through their children (Benítez 2006). Nonetheless, children were more conscious of their online behaviors when computers were located in shared spaces.[4] They were also more likely to treat the computer as a shared resource, rather than one that belonged exclusively to them (Livingstone 2002). For example, Alicia (age twelve) showed me the new laptop that had been a recent Christmas gift, saying, "We keep it [on the living room table] so that everyone can use it." While locating computers in communal areas made them more likely to be shared, children were also more likely to see them as intended for games and entertainment, since it was difficult to concentrate on school-related tasks in these high-traffic spaces.

Brokering, Connection, and Differentiation

The negotiations parents and children had over media devices and content were integrated into their more general negotiations over their needs for connection and interdependence, on the one hand, and differentiation or independence, on the other.

Family systems researchers emphasize the inherent push-pull between individual and collective needs of family members. In his work on families with adolescents, Stephen Gavazzi (2011, 36) found that "family members [who] are able to simultaneously experience themselves as both separate yet connected individuals" experience the highest levels of individual and family functioning. However, what constitutes these optimal levels of functioning—and what is perceived as a balance between connection and differentiation—is necessarily defined by what both individuals and families need to function.

For many parents, their children's brokering capabilities were one of the ways, if not their only way, to make connections beyond their immediate social networks. Most parents were connected to immigrant friends and relatives who faced the same difficulties they did in accessing resources. Having truncated, homogenous social networks and living in an under-served community made them very dependent on their children's assistance, as they generally had few (or no) alternative sources of support.

Children's assistance was clearly important to their families, and every child broker talked about being proud and happy to be able to help his or her parents. Being needed, however, also had its challenges. Almost all the children I interviewed also admitted to occasions when they had felt frustrated or wished they didn't have to broker for their parents. Luis (age eleven) was often irritated when his father made him read the same letter or bill repeatedly to ensure he had brokered it correctly. Like other brokers, he usually helped anyway, which demonstrated that parents tended to retain their authority even as they depended on their children's help.[5] I saw evidence of only one child who had flat-out refused to broker; Marta's daughter Alicia (age twelve) had assumed primary brokering responsibilities because her elder sister was "not willing to be helpful," as Marta phrased it. Whether refusals were episodic or chronic, they revealed that not all children placed family needs ahead of their own, or at least not all of the time. However, even occasional refusals to assist parents were the exception, rather than the norm.

Children admitting to occasions when they would have preferred not to broker invoked prior research on "kinscription" patterns among low-income immigrants. Kinscription refers to obligations one has to other family members' needs that effectively redirect time, energy, and resources from an individual's own goals (Domínguez and Watkins 2003; Stack and Burton 1993). For these children, family needs were most likely to redirect their energies from their schoolwork.[6]

While kinscription certainly took place in these families, brokering responsibilities generally evoked feelings of pride and satisfaction in children, to the extent that these activities evoked any emotion at all. Most parents and children simply saw brokering as an unremarkable aspect of their family routines. When I asked Graciela (age thirteen) how she felt about brokering for her mother, she shrugged and said, "If she needs help, I do it—she's our mom. She's always been there for us, and she just needs a little bit in return." This answer was typical, in that she described her assistance as an everyday fact of life. Graciela's answer also clearly invoked what Robert Courtney Smith (2002, 151) has described as the "immigrant bargain," whereby children repay their immigrant parents' sacrifices with their successes. Their successes can be their academic or professional advancement (V. Louie 2012), but the immigrant bargain can also be honored with demonstrations of family loyalty and respect (Reese 2001). In these families, children's brokering was an integral function of the family system, as well as a tangible way for them to signal both their commitment to their families and their gratitude for parental sacrifices.[7]

The immigrant bargain explains why child brokers did not react to kinscription as adults often do. In separate studies with Latino immigrants, Cecilia Menjívar (2000) and Silvia Domínguez (2011) both documented how low-income immigrant adults often actively avoided family reciprocity situations that could drain their limited personal and financial resources. By contrast, children like Graciela viewed their obligations to assist their parents as a given. Children's abilities to reciprocate their parents' many sacrifices were embodied in their brokering activities.

Brokering activities were, by their nature, expressions of connection and interdependence. Even when children performed brokering tasks independent of their parents, these actions were motivated by their family members' needs.

Brokering activities were also expressions of expediency. Children were aware, either implicitly or explicitly, that their parents had nowhere else to turn if they refused, which made them more likely to put their desires for differentiation aside when their parents needed their help.

IDENTIFYING SPECIFIC BROKERING STRATEGIES

Many children described their independent efforts to locate information that could address a particular family challenge. These individual-level activities were generally followed by family interactions to understand what they had found and discuss how to proceed (i.e., system-level interactions). These family-level activities were, in some cases, supported by others in the community, like extended relatives and friends (i.e., intersystem level).

Critics have charged that the family systems approach produces broad descriptions rather than specific, explanatory findings. However, these families' experiences revealed specific processes and strategies that influenced children's brokering activities across these three levels of their family systems. These strategies directly impacted the information families had on hand to make decisions about local resources. They were also transferable, in that strategies that were successful at home were deployed when children brokered in public places, and vice versa.

CHILDREN'S INDEPENDENT BROKERING STRATEGIES

When children brokered independently, they engaged their relatively greater proficiency in English, familiarity with US culture, and media literacy to locate and decode resources that could help their families make informed decisions. Their independent strategies took three main forms: using context to extract meaning, negotiating cultural knowledge, and engaging media to supplement their own skills.

Context for Meaning

Whether children needed to broker verbal, audio, or text-based content, they often relied on context to enhance their comprehension of complex words or concepts. Victoria (age twelve) described how she employed a strategy her homeroom teacher had taught her earlier that year: "Ms. James said to try reading around what I don't understand so I can see what it is about . . . because some of the time, I have to read rough words, and then I tell [my mom], I'm like, 'What is this word?' and she's like, 'Don't tell me. What does your English teacher tell you to do?' She says to look around the sentence and find out what it is."

Victoria's description of her comprehension strategy shows how she consciously applied a method learned in another social context (i.e., school) to a brokering challenge at home. She also made reference to "rough words" that were beyond her level of understanding; this method helped her handle the challenges such words presented. Finally, her mother's retort that she should use what her teacher had taught her, reflects how important parental directives often were for reinforcing children's own brokering strategies.

Consistent formats and social scripts also made it easier for children to extract meaning independently from conversations and documents. For example, school newsletters or report cards that presented information in the same format each time or phone calls to set up doctors' appointments that required the same details made children more comfortable handling these tasks independently. Consistency not only made children more confident to broker routine activities, but, over time, also allowed them to hone their strategies for completing these tasks.

Negotiating Cultural Norms

Consistency was less likely to be a feature of tasks that required children to negotiate cultural norms. Children most frequently brought up phone calls to parents' employers as times when they had to manage culturally complex interactions. These phone calls required children to engage knowledge of both languages, while also managing the cultural expectations governing these interactions from the employers' and their parents' perspectives. These conversations therefore rewarded proactivity, because children had to make quick decisions about how to best present potentially negative information. These exchanges also required engaging reserves of emotional intelligence, to present information in ways that were most likely to produce desirable outcomes for their families. And, they had to accomplish all of these things while carefully managing their own cultural appropriateness and social positioning as children who were invoking their parents' voices and demands.

These cultural negotiations stretched many children's capabilities not only by virtue of the multifaceted demands they created, but also because missteps could have serious consequences. Evelyn (age fifteen) often called her grandmother's employers. Since her grandmother cleaned different houses each weekday, she often needed Evelyn to juggle her schedule. I asked her if people ever got upset about these changes, and she said, "Yeah, that has happened . . . but you know, I don't want to talk back when they're rude, you know, 'cuz she can lose her job for that." She described how she carefully managed employers' dissatisfaction by keeping her voice deferent, but firm. She had also learned how to best prepare for these calls so that they went smoothly; she told me that employers were more amenable to changes when she could immediately offer them a range of alternative days when her grandmother could work.

The cultural negotiations Evelyn described meant she engaged her independent skills after first consulting with her grandmother, as was the norm. Graciela (age thirteen) described an unusual interaction with a parent's employer that had occurred a couple of years before we first met. A woman for whom her mother, Ileana, had worked for many years had announced that she was moving out of Los Angeles. Ileana was anxious about losing a large portion of her income. On her own initiative, Graciela called this client with whom she had spoken many times over the years, explained the difficulty and worry that the move was causing, and asked if she might recommend Ileana's work to others. The client arranged for Ileana to work for one of her friends, who had a bigger house and therefore paid more than the client she had lost. Graciela's face lit up recounting this story, saying, "I was so excited. I couldn't wait to tell her what happened when she came home."

Graciela's story reveals her assessment that her and her mother's relationship with this particular employer would permit her careful transgression of the traditionally passive roles children are expected to take in Western culture—particularly in regard to arenas like family finances, which are generally reserved for adults (Ariès 1962; Orellana 2009; Zelizer 1985). That she did so without first consulting her mother required an additional assessment of risk and benefit, as few children would have dared so independent an interaction with a parent's employer. However, Graciela and her mother had an unusual relationship in that Ileana encouraged and nurtured her daughter's ability to make independent decisions.

Media as Resources

Child brokers also connected with a variety of media to supplement their comprehension skills and cultural familiarities. They often used dictionaries and reference books to negotiate written materials and to prepare for phone calls where they anticipated having to make specific requests for information. Many children not only consulted dictionaries as references in English, but also used them to ensure their translations into Spanish were as accurate as possible.

For those who had access, the Internet was a particularly useful tool to double-check their brokered understandings, to find local resources and information, and to physically locate places by using mapping functions to get driving directions or bus routes. However, many child brokers did not have Internet access at home or only had sporadic connectivity. Some parents had disconnected the Internet, fearing it exposed their children to unseen risks.[8] Other parents disconnected the Internet from time to time, either because funds were especially tight or as a means to punish what they perceived as misbehavior (for example, online time being a distraction from homework). As mentioned previously, parents' decisions related to Internet connectivity were also influenced by their preference to spend limited discretionary income on cable television.

Regardless of the reason, lacking a home-based Internet connection constrained children's access to an unusually useful resource. The Internet facilitates customizable interactions with nonlinear content; so, unlike a TV news broadcast where viewers have no choice but to wait for the weather forecast at the very end, Internet users can zero in on interesting content, in any order they choose. Furthermore, online content is less temporally constrained, meaning that more information is available at any given time (versus a 6:00 p.m. news broadcast). Lacking a home-based Internet connection could therefore constrain children's efforts to locate useful community information.

Consistent with prior studies, children who had at least a relatively consistent Internet connection at home reported going online to address a wider range of family questions and needs. They also reported more success in locating information online, compared with brokers who did not have a home-based connection.[9] Furthermore, child brokers who were not online at home generally did not go online on a regular basis, since they connected at school or local libraries sporadically at best.[10] Constrained connectivity affected what children could access on their families' behalf; their limited new media literacy could also constrain their academic progress, as these skills are increasingly prerequisites for educational and professional success (Dailey et al. 2010; Thoman and Jolls 2004).

Limitations to Broker's Individual Strategies

Children also encountered other constraints in brokering for their families. Sometimes, tasks were simply beyond a child's capabilities. A number of children spontaneously referred to such materials as "grown-up stuff," reflecting that they recognized the limits of their capabilities and saw them as a function of age. Victoria (age twelve) told me that she could understand English and Spanish, "no problem . . . but some of the people are old and they, like, talk ancient and stuff. . . . [H]ow can I understand that?" Victoria highlighted the difference between the informal English she could speak and the formal or "ancient" English spoken by "old" people, or adults. When I asked her to explain who spoke "ancient," she referred to her teachers and to doctors. When I asked her if she thought I spoke ancient, she assessed me quite seriously and said, "Not right now, but you look like you could."

Struggles to understand "grown-up stuff" and "ancient" language revealed that child brokers were often less fluently bilingual than some researchers have presumed them to be.[11] "Getting stuck" was a term that four child brokers used spontaneously in their interviews to describe times when their language capabilities were not commensurate with the task at hand. Maria (age nineteen) said, "When I have to talk from English to Spanish I get confused. . . . I get stuck." Three other brokers referred to these moments as "getting mixed up." These experiences were hard for many children to talk about, particularly boys. Maria's brother Jose (age seventeen), avoiding eye contact with me, said, "When they [my parents] ask me a question, you know, and I don't understand it, so that I—I cannot ask a question for them, that's when I get really nervous, 'cuz I don't know what to say when I'm stuck."

Getting stuck was more common with print materials, which even posed difficulties for children who had no trouble brokering conversations. Hernando (age twelve) said, "I help with the [mail] that comes in, like papers from the bank. But some [of] those are really hard because there's a lot of words I don't really know; like I don't really [understand] that much from those words from the bank and everything." Print materials were more likely to reveal the limits of children's capabilities than conversations, which they could generally manage in informal English, asking for clarification or otherwise gleaning clues through interaction. Beyond consulting dictionaries or using context to try to decipher meaning, paperwork gave children few decoding options. The nuances in such documents and the "ancient" language they employed caused considerable anxiety for children who knew their parents depended on them to understand these materials.

The other reason print media were so challenging was children's acute recognition of how important these materials were and of how costly a mistake could be for their families. These documents often served as gatekeepers to services and goods their families sorely needed; assistance programs, naturalization, health insurance, and other resources all required completing extensive paperwork. Such documents are often challenging even for native-speaking adults; they are considerably more difficult for children of immigrant parents. Liliana (age sixteen) talked about helping her stepfather, Carlos, with his immigration forms when she was thirteen. She recalled that a lot of the experience "was going 'Oooo, I don't know what that means.' . . . I had to look up like every word. . . . I was so scared I'd make a mistake." These anxieties often exacerbated children's brokering limitations, particularly if they had had negative experiences completing paperwork in the past.

In these instances, parents could provide the support their children needed to successfully complete challenging tasks. The strategies that parents developed to understand their environments, both independently and in conjunction with their children, deeply influenced children's brokering activities and their outcomes.

Parents' Independent Strategies

How parents navigated their English-speaking environments on their own may seem tangential to child brokering, but when it came to these efforts, their kids were taking notes. As their children's first and most influential teachers, parents' communication styles and behavioral strategies serve as powerful models for them (Reese 2001; Valdés 1996). In interviews, children and parents were both asked how parents manage in situations requiring English when their children are not around. The convergence between responses made it clear that children were fully aware of how their parents handled challenges in their absence.

Parents' independent strategies clustered into avoidant and proactive strategies. Parents who modeled avoidant strategies tended to put off even small tasks until their children were home. They also showed visible trepidation when interacting with English speakers, even when their children were there to help them. Aurora (age sixteen) said, "[My mom] just waits for me to get home; she doesn't do things [requiring English] herself." Most parents, even if they were not otherwise avoidant, screened phone calls on the answering machine to identify whether callers spoke Spanish. The answering machine had double utility; it allowed parents to identify people they wished to speak to and also provided a full record for their children to know whom to call back and why, if the caller left a message in English.

In families where parents modeled avoidance of particular groups of people or fear of the community itself, child brokers were more likely to see their environment as a threatening place. In an almost-verbatim rendition of the fears his mother had expressed in her interview, Hernando (age twelve) said, "Over here [in this neighborhood] there's a lot of gangsters, . . . a lot of bad influences and with drugs and things like that, . . . so I need to be in the house." He avoided the neighborhood boys, was bused to a school in the suburbs, and rarely went anywhere without his parents. His mother's community fears were clearly internalized in her son's avoidant behaviors, which also made the interactions he brokered for her that much more stressful for him.

Other parents exhibited proactive strategies when they had to manage without their children. These strategies were often other-oriented. Many parents reported seeking out other Latino residents who spoke enough English to be intermediaries for them. Virginia said, "You can always find someone to speak Spanish to if you're on your own, so that helps." On calls to public utilities or other companies, many parents would request Spanish-speaking representatives so that they could resolve issues independently. Children whose parents sought out Spanish-speaking assistance tended to replicate this strategy, seeking out English speakers when they needed to double-check their comprehension. Children mirrored the proactive communication strategies their parents modeled in Spanish when they interacted with English speakers, improving the fidelity of their brokering in the process.

Many parents also used consistent formatting to enable their independent activities, just as their children did. For example, many parents said they could manage most household bills independently once they were accustomed to the formats. Marta said, "I can manage with bills because they all come the same: balance, payment amount, and due date. No complications to deal with. And, of course, numbers are the same in English and Spanish." Similarly, Juana (age thirteen) indicated that her mother dropped off bill payments to neighborhood utility offices on her own because, she said, "It's like, 'Here you go,' and they say, 'Thank you; goodbye.'" Parents could manage these tasks as long as they were consistent. When there were unexpected charges or changes to formatting, children were generally enlisted to resolve discrepancies.

Children's awareness of their parents' strategies was evident in spontaneous comparisons they made between more and less proactive parents. For example, Milagro (age thirteen) said that her mom usually went to the doctor without her, either during her workday or directly afterward. On the other hand, Milagro was constantly at doctors' appointments with her father, Alejandro. Milagro said, "[My mom] is just more independent. I mean, sometimes she needs my help and I help her with pleasure, but she's a little stronger [than my dad] in most things. She's better off than my dad . . . [because] she takes the challenge[s]."

Parents who modeled proactivity not only normalized these behaviors for their children, but sometimes explicitly demanded it of them. Liliana (age sixteen) said, "You know how sometimes you have to fill out papers? Oh my God, [my mom] gets mad when I make mistakes with her forms. 'You know what it says,' she tells me, and she makes me check it [in the dictionary] three times to make sure I got it right." Exacting parental expectations not only made children more conscientious brokers, but also made them more likely to hold themselves to similarly high standards for future interactions. Juana (age thirteen) said,

> I had trouble in English [before I started school], and then when I was in school, I forgot all my Spanish! It was really hard for me [to broker] back then; I didn't know so many words, and my mom would say, 'That's not how you say that,' and I would get so mad at myself 'cuz, like, I had to get it right. So you get used to it; you learn how to speak Spanish. . . . Sometimes I get really mad [at myself]. . . . Sometimes I say something and [my parents] tell me it's wrong and I'm like, 'What's the difference? You can understand what I mean.' But I know that's not good enough . . . [and] I'm really proud when they're proud of me.

Juana's description of what she expected from her own brokering clearly reflected both her parents' high standards and her own motivation to make them proud of her.

Child brokers were acutely aware of the social discourses that marked them as not only children, but the children of low-income, low-status immigrants. Parents who modeled courageous behavior made it easier for children to be similarly brave in challenging interactions. As their children's first teachers, parents laid the foundation for their family's communication styles and behavioral norms. Parents who modeled more proactive communication styles and behaviors encouraged the same in their children, thereby also facilitating their brokering capabilities. Over time, these communication practices tended to become mutually reinforcing; parents and children could encourage and enhance each other's learning and community engagement. By the same token, when parents exhibited fearful, avoidant behaviors, their children were likely to mirror their behaviors and find brokering tasks more stressful and difficult.

FAMILY-LEVEL STRATEGIES

Activities that parents and children engaged in independently became that much more powerful in family-level exchanges where information was shared and understandings were negotiated. The prior discussion hints at the reason; families learned a great deal from the interactions they had with each other. These parents and children engaged in particular forms of "scaffolding" activities to learn from each other, pooling their collective skills and knowledge to enhance family discussions and decision-making.

Scaffolding is a term associated with Lev Vygotsky's situated learning theory, which posits that learning occurs through active engagement with others. Vygotsky (1978) distinguished between what learners can do without help (their actual development levels) and their "zones of proximate development." These zones encompass skills and content that lie just beyond the limits of a learner's actual development levels. Scaffolding occurs when a more competent partner assists a learner with skills and content in those zones until their help becomes unnecessary, like a scaffold against a finished building.

In these families, scaffolding was not a one-way process; parents and children contributed their respective skill sets to these interactions. Children contributed their greater dexterity with English, US cultural norms, and media forms and content. Parents contributed their adult understandings of how the world works and what the family needed, as well as their greater Spanish proficiency. Because parents and children came to these interactions both as learners and as more competent peers, scaffolding provided opportunities for all family members to simultaneously support each other's and their own learning. Lisa Dorner, Marjorie Orellana, and Christine Li-Grining reported these developmental interplays between parents and children, "leading to cognitive benefits for children who are both guided by more expert others on cognitively-demanding tasks, and who get placed in the 'expert' position where they are forced to articulate their understanding for novices" (2007, 458).

To varying degrees, children reinforced their own skill sets by supporting their parents' needs. These interactions also provided natural opportunities for children to learn more sophisticated Spanish and social understandings from their parents' examples. Likewise, since cognitive development is a lifelong project, parents who actively engaged with their children around brokering tasks had natural opportunities to build their own understandings of US culture, to grow more familiar with spoken and written English, and to become more comfortable with a range of media forms, over time. Through scaffolding, children and parents could therefore facilitate each other's development of various literacies—including traditional reading, writing, and speaking in English and in Spanish and media-related literacies—while they were engaged in identifying and connecting with local resources they needed. There were three forms of scaffolding these families engaged in frequently, which I refer to as "teachable moments," "joint media engagement," and "family triage."

Teachable Moments for Language Learning

Family scaffolding around children's brokering provided natural opportunities for language learning and exchange for both parents and children. A number of parents used these interactions as teachable moments to introduce their children to new words and concepts in Spanish and, when appropriate, to relevant cultural knowledge.[12] For example, Virginia said, "Sometimes I'll write something and my daughter will correct it for me. She'll type it on the computer for me. And that way, I learn some English, and she learns more Spanish. And we'll also sit together to watch movies in English. . . . [I]t can move so fast; there are words I don't understand, so she will translate for me. I have really learned quite a lot."

Parents often found their children most receptive to language learning when it was naturally embedded in everyday activities. Milagro (age thirteen) said, "I guess learning more Spanish is just something that happens while we're doing other things. . . . We'll be talking, saying this and that, and I'll say, 'What does this mean?' and [my parents] will explain it. Then when they say it next time, I'll understand it." Milagro went on to say that the same often happened in reverse; if she used an English word her mother was unfamiliar with, she would ask Milagro to explain it to her, thereby expanding her English vocabulary.

Evelyn (age fifteen) said she often corrected her grandmother's speech, such as when Anabel said "shoeses" rather than "shoes" by erroneously applying Spanish language structures to English. Her grandmother welcomed these corrections and said she found them helpful. In general, these teachable moments fostered mutual learning that parents and children viewed positively, provided that they were embedded in mutually appreciated exchanges. Children often resisted when parents overtly attempted to teach them more Spanish, as I witnessed in interactions between Ana and Luis (age eleven). Likewise, children who corrected their parents in less gentle ways received a more chilly reception to their efforts. Victoria (age twelve) said that sometimes her dad would hear her talking to her sister in English and would jokingly join, affecting an "American" style of speaking. "When he does it, I'm like, 'Don't do that.' And he'll be like, 'What? I'm trying to learn English.' And I'll say something like, 'That's not English. It's *something*, but it's not English.' That makes him mad."

Joint Media Engagement

Many parents and children found that teachable moments occurred in the context of media interactions, like watching television together. Children of immigrants are more likely to engage in shared media activities with family members, as compared with their native-born counterparts. A representative study of adolescent children with parents from Central America, Mexico, the

Dominican Republic, and China found that only 20 percent of respondents watched television "mainly alone" and that co-viewing was most likely to occur with family members (J. Louie 2003).[13] By contrast, a general study of US teens during the same period found that more than one-third of teens watched TV "mainly alone" and that co-viewing with friends was more frequent than among children of immigrants (Rideout et al. 1999). These findings suggest that media connections may be even more integrated into immigrant family systems than those of native-born families.

These shared media experiences are examples of joint media engagement, defined as "spontaneous and designed experiences . . . when there are multiple people interacting together with media" (Takeuchi and Stevens 2011, 9). These interactions are opportunities for family scaffolding, in that "[joint media engagement] can support learning by providing resources for making sense and making meaning in a particular situation, as well as for future situations" (9). In essence, joint media engagement simultaneously provides opportunities for family members to learn from each other, as well as to engage media content that familiarizes them with local news and resources that can help solve collective problems.

For example, Alicia (age twelve) and her father watched the local news in English sometimes, and he would ask her to broker words he didn't understand. In return, Alicia said, "He explains [what the news event means] to me." In these instances, Alicia provided her greater understanding of English, while her father provided his adult interpretation of the events' significance. Together, they constructed a shared understanding of local news that, over time, helped increase their collective familiarity with the community.

Similarly, Aurora's father, Tulio, said, "I bring home [the *Los Angeles Times*] and I tell Aurora, 'Come look at this' . . . and she tells me things about what it says as I read. It's good for one to find out about these things." Tulio explained that his and Aurora's joint media engagement provided opportunities for him to read aloud in English and have her correct his mistakes and for him to teach her equivalent words in Spanish. They would discuss the events being covered in the articles they read. He would also connect that content to relevant aspects of Mexican history, news, and culture to teach her about "Mexican traditions like the Mexican independence and Cinco de Mayo—things like that. . . . [My daughters] are interested when I tell them about [these] things." In these interactions, parents and children fluidly exchanged expert and learner roles. These multifaceted learning experiences increased familiarity with both English and Spanish, two sets of cultural resources, various media formats, and the local community.

Which family members were primarily cast in expert and learner roles depended on the particular media device. For example, interactions around the computer generally placed children in more expert roles since parents were usually unfamiliar with computers and the Internet. They relied on their children to take the lead in searching for and locating online content—which, more often than not, was not available in Spanish, meaning that they again needed their children's help. They could, however, help their children understand what they found online. Milagro (age thirteen) said she and her father would look up his medications online and discuss potential side effects. These experiences were part of how she became so fully versed with his various health concerns, which in turn enhanced her brokering for him in medical contexts.

Evelyn (age fifteen) and her grandmother Anabel would go online together to map directions. Evelyn said, "She likes to know exactly where she's going, so we discuss it together and look at the different ways to go." She also helped her grandmother connect with the website for *Prensa Libre*, a prominent Guatemalan newspaper, so that she could keep up with events in her home country. Anabel would read and explain the Guatemalan news to Evelyn, especially when "things [were] happening [there]."[14] Virginia and her daughter Regina (age fourteen) went online together to look up meanings of words and concepts, discussing them together. Regina took the lead on other online tasks, like finding directions, bus schedules, and locations of local services and resources, after first discussing with her mother what she needed to find.

Juana (age thirteen) was the only child who reported learning computer-related skills from a parent. Eduardo, her stepfather, was the only parent who was currently pursuing higher education, taking college courses toward a computer maintenance certification at night. She said that he used the computer even more than she did. "When I need to do a project and I have to do it by computer, I ask him how to do it, and he shows me, but the next day I forget [and he'll show me again]." However, he often needed her help too, primarily with complex content in English: "With him and the computer . . . [I'll think], okay I know you'll need my help, so I'll go be right there for him. He doesn't usually have to call me. Because I know that there's going to be parts that don't make sense. He'll say, like, 'I was going to call you!' And I'll say, 'Well, you know I'm here.'" Juana's description emphasized the interchangeability of expert and learner roles between herself and Eduardo.

Telephones were another device that frequently engendered joint media engagement.[15] As mentioned previously, parents often screened phone calls on the answering machine, using these automated records to direct children to make return calls. Phone calls from local healthcare offices and other services were almost always in English, as were calls from schools.[16] Only one family specifically reported a local institutional connection (a doctor's office) whose staff consistently contacted patients in Spanish. When children returned calls or initiated contact with English-speaking service providers, they did so with their parents' direct involvement. Victoria (age twelve) said, "When, like, a person that doesn't know Spanish calls, my mom puts [the phone] on speaker, and when the person tells it [in English], she tells me to translate." Parents and children would either jointly engage on a phone call, as Victoria described doing with her mother, or they would adopt a back-and-forth format where parents were close by so that children could confer with them at each step of the phone call. When calls were routine, sometimes parents and children discussed the issues beforehand, after which children made the call independently and reported back to their parents. This practice was more common with older children than younger ones.

Joint media engagement generally engendered cooperation among family members but also had potential to cause conflict. Prior research on Maghrebi-origin families in France (Hargreaves and Mahdjoub 1997), migrants from the former Soviet Union in Israel and Germany (Elias and Lemish 2008), and Indian- and Mexican-origin families in the United States (Durham 2004; Mayer 2003) all documents how joint media engagement can incite family conflicts and inflame parental fears about losing control over their children.

Victoria (age twelve) said she and her mother would argue when Victoria did not understand the content of a *telenovela* or adequately explain an English-language program to her in Spanish: "Yeah, she gets mad. Ohhhh, she gets mad. She'll [be] all, 'You're a Mexican and you don't even know Spanish for that word.' ... She's like, 'You're looking at too much [English-language] TV. You're on MySpace and stuff.' And I'm like, 'I don't even go to MySpace.'" Victoria's retelling of this conflict reflected her mother's perceptions that Victoria's media connections were eroding her links to her culture of origin, to the point where she questioned her Mexican authenticity. In turn, Victoria's retort, "I don't even go to MySpace," reflected her resistance to her mother's version of events. Since joint media engagement was integral to children's brokering activities, the potential for both cooperation and conflict implicit in brokering activities more generally was also evident in how families engaged media together.

Family Triage

To this point, I have described scaffolding activities that parents and children engaged in together. These were not the only forms of collective learning that occurred in these families, though they were the most effective. I refer to the forms of scaffolding that parents did together when they had to manage without their children, and that siblings did when they had to manage without their parents, as family triage.

Both these scenarios—parents scaffolding without children and children scaffolding without parents—produced less complete understandings and less confidence about the best ways to proceed. I refer to these instances as "triage" because they were always urgent stopgap measures to deal with an issue temporarily until it could be addressed through scaffolding that involved both parents and children. For example, Marta and her husband would confer with each other or consult a Spanish-English dictionary if they had to talk to their Korean landlord when their children were not home to assist them. When Alicia (age twelve) returned home, she would go with her parents to talk with the landlord or contact him via phone, allowing the family to move beyond the basic understanding her parents had managed on their own.

Triage was a less effective form of scaffolding because it involved redundancy in some skill sets and large gaps in others. Parents managing alone lacked their children's facilities with English, US cultural norms, and media literacy. On the other hand, siblings managing alone lacked adult understandings of how to address a situation and were generally reluctant to make any real decisions without their parents' permission. There were also situations outside the home, such as in medical settings, where siblings' attempts at triage were externally limited because minor children are not legally recognized as family decision-makers. Family triage reflected how much more effective family strategies were when they drew on the collective strengths of both parents and children.

STABILITY AND CHANGE IN FAMILY SYSTEMS

As systems, these families all negotiated forces of both stability and change. Scaffolding activities were an important catalyst for family change that affected (and were affected by) children's brokering. However, scaffolding did not occur uniformly across these families; enduring social arrangements of family members could enable or constrain these activities. For example, children's brokering and family scaffolding were clearly enabled by retained parental authority and by cooperation between siblings. On the other hand, family fractures caused by illness, addiction, abuse, and divorce usually constrained children's brokering because energy spent compensating for these difficulties sapped time and energy from efforts to develop community connections.

Parental Authority

Although they often interacted with adults on their parents' behalf, brokers felt the limits of being socially positioned as children in adult interactions. Therefore, when parents retained their roles as family leaders and decision-makers—and, specifically, when they did so without negating or undermining their children's efforts—they enhanced children's brokering efforts. That children relied on and often expressed an explicit desire for parental authority highlights that many were acutely aware of their youth and inexperience. When I asked Juana (age thirteen) whom she consulted to ensure she understood what she had to broker, she said, "My parents . . .'cuz they're the people I'm most confident in, to teach me how to do something right." These findings belied assumptions in the immigration literature that as children become "experts" on American culture, they inevitably undermine traditional parent-child authority structures, causing parents to lose control and their children's respect (Buriel and de Ment 1998; Menjívar 2000; Kam 2011). In these families, parents maintained their children's respect by retaining their authority.

Parents' authority was also a reassuring presence in times of conflict. Graciela (age thirteen) recalled a phone call with one of her mother's employers that devolved into an argument: "I was arguing between adults and I was like, 'I'm a kid here!' [*laughs*]. And it was kind of awkward for me. But then, like, I knew what to say because my mom was right there and said he can't do anything [to me] by the phone." Parents' authority was an enabling social arrangement because it emboldened children's brokering and facilitated family scaffolding activities.

Sibling Cooperation

Parent-child cooperation clearly facilitated children's brokering; in some families, siblings developed cooperative arrangements as well. Even though most families had one primary child broker, their efforts could be supported by a sibling who had different skill sets and experiences. For example, Victoria (age twelve) was the fifth of eight children. She explained the roles she and her eldest sister, Maricela (who was married and no longer lived at home), played in their family as follows: "When a person doesn't know Spanish, my mom . . . tells me to translate it because I'm the better translator than any of them [living at home] . . . except for my sister Maricela. She does it the best, [but] she doesn't live here. . . . So, I don't make the phone calls. Maricela is the one who makes them because there are a lot of things [my parents] don't want me to hear sometimes—or that I can't understand."

Victoria's mother viewed her as more helpful and skilled than her other siblings who were still living at home—but not as skilled as her elder sister, who was twenty-four at that time. Victoria described a cooperative arrangement where she did day-to-day brokering as needed, but Maricela took on tasks that were anticipated, that required sensitive information deemed inappropriate for young ears, or that were beyond Victoria's actual developmental levels.

As younger siblings became more experienced with age, the balance of responsibility between siblings often changed and transitioned accordingly. These changes were counterbalanced with stability, as elder siblings often remained involved in brokering tasks, even if the degree of that involvement lessened when they left home and began working full time. That Maricela continued to be so involved in brokering tasks despite being out of the house, married, and a mother herself also demonstrated how stable and persistent social arrangements around children's brokering responsibilities could be (Buriel and de Ment 1998).

Milagro (age thirteen) and her older sister also had clear divisions of labor that consciously drew on their different capabilities: "The real important things [like health insurance forms], we let my sister do because she's more experienced. . . . [A]ll the doctor's appointments, prescriptions and stuff, I do it. . . . She's always helped us economically, and I do the translating and stuff at the house. . . . [My parents and sister are] working, so I try to make it easier for everybody. . . . It's easier for me [to be at home] than for my sister 'cuz she's always liked to work, and I've always liked being [at home]." These synergistic divisions of labor allowed both sisters to contribute to the family's resources in accordance with their strengths. Karen Pyke's (2005) study of Korean and Chinese college-age children of immigrants similarly revealed that cooperation among siblings with different skill sets could pool their complementary strengths in service of family goals.

Family Fractures

Some families' social arrangements limited the likelihood that members would engage each other to solve problems cooperatively, thereby making children's brokering efforts less frequent and less effective for addressing family challenges. Social arrangements that fractured family life tended to turn families inward, meaning that children's efforts to simply hold things together constrained their abilities to broker resources that could help their families through those trying times.

Two fathers had had long-term struggles with alcoholism. Julio (age seventeen) and Maria's (age nineteen) father used to drink heavily, reaching a point where he would drink anything with alcohol in it, including mouthwash. Julio's recollections of family life before his father's sobriety also hinted that his father had also been physically abusive when he was drunk. Alejandro, Milagro's (age thirteen) father, broke down in tears describing his alcohol addiction and the harm done to his family and his health. Both families described tremendous strains that alcohol abuse, secrecy, and shame had placed on family relationships and finances for many years.

Illness had similar inhibiting effects on family social arrangements. Alejandro has been out of work for over a year, dealing with complications from his diabetes. Milagro's after-school activities were circumscribed by explicit family expectations that she would devote that time to caring for her ailing father; she said, "Most of my time, I just give it to my dad."[17] Luis (age eleven) faced similar pressures in helping his family handle complications related to his younger brother's epilepsy. Frequent absences from school and incomplete homework constrained his chances of making and maintaining meaningful connections with his teachers and peers.

Divorce had constraining effects on child brokering in some families but enabling effects in others. In two families, men had informally adopted their spouse's children from previous marriages, effectively re-creating an integrated family. They experienced each other as family. Carlos and Liliana (age sixteen) always referred to each other as "my daughter" and "my dad"; the same was true for Juana (age thirteen) and her mother's husband, Eduardo. Children in these families had only temporarily suffered the potentially detracting effects of separation or divorce. Both Liliana and Juana also reported unusually low levels of conflict when they brokered for Carlos and Eduardo, as compared to the tensions that sometimes attended brokering for a biological father in other families.[18]

Outcomes of divorce were obviously not always positive. In some households, the fractures to post-divorce families were profound. Single parents, like Hilda, worked even longer hours to make ends meet, relying on their eldest child as a surrogate partner to help them care for younger siblings. These responsibilities limited the time and energy that parents and children had, both independently and collectively, to locate and communicate about local resources and opportunities. These families were most likely to be in survival mode, getting by with minimal community interaction. In Virginia's case, divorce had also been coupled with (and, in part, caused by) sexual abuse. The trauma Regina (age fourteen) had suffered at the hands of her father was inadvertently revealed in my interview with her (see appendix). In this family, the financial fallout that accompanied all divorces was coupled with emotional setbacks that profoundly affected Regina's daily functioning and made her fearful in community interactions.

Stability, Change, and Family Integration

In sum, these families negotiated tensions between change and stability. Enduring social arrangements made some families more predisposed to scaffolding activities that fostered family change through members' mutual learning and development. Family scaffolding was influenced by the quality of parents' and children's independent strategies and skills that each brought to these activities. Scaffolding was most effective when characterized by competent, cooperative communication among family members, including teamwork among siblings, and by enabling social arrangements, like parents' maintaining their authority to define and address family needs. Family dynamics that facilitated more rewarding scaffolding activities were also more likely to enable children's future brokering efforts. For example, retained parental authority in scaffolding events reflected the kinds of proactive parental strategies that were powerful models and support for children's brokering efforts.

Families with members who were less adept communicators were also most likely to have reported family fractures, though it is not possible to know whether this is a causal or correlational relationship. Scaffolding between parents and children was less common in these families, in which parents were also more likely to exhibit avoidant independent strategies. Taken together, children in these families had less of a framework to support their brokering efforts, which in turn tended to be less frequent, more anxiety producing, and, often, less effective for accomplishing the goals for which they were deployed.

Of course, not all families fit neatly into one of these two descriptions. For example, Milagro (age thirteen) had a mother who modeled proactive behavior, while her father was more avoidant and dependent. Milagro's efforts to make the considerable number of community connections her father needed to maintain his health were, on the one hand, limited by her father's fearful inaction but, on the other hand, enabled by her mother's proactive example and by Milagro's cooperative brokering with her older sister. Milagro also had sources of support in other family systems, which were very important for the success of her brokering efforts.

Brokering beyond the Family System

Other family systems in the community could influence children's brokering efforts. Some children could depend on extended family members and friends who supplemented their knowledge and modeled behaviors that helped them learn new skills and strategies. These sources of support were real advantages for young brokers fortunate enough to have them. Children also often provided support beyond their own families, as many of them routinely brokered for their parents' friends, extended family, and neighbors.

Social Support for Children's Brokering

Children seldom reported that their own friendship networks were sources of brokering support. Many had no idea if their friends helped their parents, and even those who did seldom discussed their experiences with each other. When I asked children to think about the reasons for these silences, they generally attributed them to protecting their parents' privacy or to their desire to have one area of their lives that family responsibilities did not permeate. In either case, these silences negated natural opportunities for children to learn from each other's strategies and to pool lessons learned through their different experiences.

Milagro (age thirteen) was one of only two child brokers who discussed brokering with her friends: "We talk about [brokering]; it just comes up in the subject [that we're talking about]. Like my friend Lola, she helps a lot in her house and stuff like that, and we just talk about what we do. . . . [W]e exchange ideas and stuff like, 'Oh, probably next time you'll want to ask more about this or that,' or something like that. Even though it doesn't always seem like it, we're always learning something [from] each other."

Because most children did not discuss brokering with schoolmates, their extended family and family friends were more likely sources of support. Juana's mother was very close to a neighbor with a nine-year-old daughter. The two women often pooled their resources by making doctors' appointments at the same time so that Juana (age thirteen) could broker for them both, with the nine-year-old (who was also Juana's main source of brokering support) helping where she could. Rolando (age seventeen) depended on an eleven-year-old cousin for help with brokering and with his own homework. These sources of support were limited since younger peers were even more likely to face developmental and linguistic constraints than the brokers who solicited their help.

Evelyn and Aurora both had more favorable support structures. Evelyn (age fifteen) had an aunt who had immigrated as a teenager and had attended high school in the United States. She was able to help Evelyn's grandmother with brokering tasks that were beyond Evelyn's capacities. Aurora (age sixteen) had a twenty-seven-year-old cousin who supported her: "Yeah, he helps me with . . . I call it 'grown-up stuff' that I just don't get. He comes and helps [my parents]. . . . [F]or me, it's car insurance and banking stuff that's really hard. When my cousin comes, I'm usually there so I can see what he explains and how. . . . [T]hat way, if in another case the same thing comes, at least I can help my dad better than I did that time." Evelyn's aunt and Aurora's cousin provided support with brokering tasks that exceeded the girls' current capabilities. These relatives also modeled successful brokering strategies that, as Aurora's comments indicated, could provide scaffolding for young brokers to develop skills and confidence to handle similar situations independently in the future.

Most children I interviewed, however, did not have reliable sources of brokering support. The majority depended on scaffolding with their parents and on their independently developed strategies, like looking words up in a dictionary or going online. Children who only depended on individual-level and family system–level resources generally found brokering activities more challenging than children who had sources of support beyond their own households.

Children Brokering across Family Systems

Regardless of whether they themselves had support beyond their family system, many of the children I interviewed were resources for younger brokers in other families. Most also regularly brokered for their extended family and neighbors, ranging from sporadic help to consistent aid that required considerable time and effort. Neighbors and parents' friends usually approached brokers' parents to solicit children's assistance, rather than asking children directly. This was consistent with Cecilia Menjívar's (2000, 214) observation that Salvadoran parents in San Francisco would "lend out" their children to neighbors and friends as a way to repay or obligate favors from other community members. In Greater Crenshaw, children's brokering routinely facilitated community connections for parents' peers who did not have children or whose children were still too young to help them.

A number of children assisted other adults by brokering school materials for them or helping their children with homework. Hernando (age twelve) helped his six-year-old cousin with her homework and translated notes and newsletters she brought home from school for his aunt. Teresa (age fifteen) helped a neighbor's son with his homework every day and accompanied the neighbor to school meetings to broker for her. Aurora (age sixteen) helped so many of the neighborhood kids with their homework that one parent had bought her a whiteboard for her "lessons" as a token of his gratitude.

Many children routinely brokered mailed items and wrote checks on behalf of their neighbors, aunts, uncles, parents' friends, and church members. If children found a mistake in a bill, they also had to call the billing department to resolve the problem. Aurora (age sixteen) routinely accompanied neighbors to pay bills at local utility company offices or to appointments when they did not anticipate that staff would speak Spanish. Graciela (age thirteen) was one of a few children who called employers on behalf of her neighbors, but she was the only one who also accompanied them to interviews for new housecleaning jobs. She admitted that she found it "awkward" to have to discuss and negotiate salary for them because "that's adult stuff." Despite her discomfort, she would make an effort to appear "real serious" so that potential employers would speak to her like an adult, a strategy she thought was more likely to foster favorable outcomes for her neighbor.

Child brokers' desire to, as Graciela said, "just help out" extended the considerable commitments many already had to their own families. That their assistance was requested so frequently by relatives, friends, and neighbors reveals just how homogeneous their parents' social networks were, as well as how critical children's brokering capabilities were for making connections to heterogeneous resident networks and diverse community resources.

Brokering Heterogeneous Connections

Many child brokers facilitated conversations between their parents and their English-speaking, predominantly African American neighbors. Juana (age thirteen) reported that she often translated pleasantries between her mother and African American parents outside her middle school. Liliana (age sixteen) brokered for her landlord uncle as she helped him collect rent and discuss maintenance issues with his African American residents. Luis (age eleven) brokered between his mother and an elderly African American neighbor who came downstairs each afternoon to "check up" on the family, as she phrased it. Luis helped her too; when she came downstairs for her daily visit during our first interview, she informed him that her cable was out, again. He immediately jumped up to reset the connection, apologizing for his absence when he returned five minutes later.

While children's brokering could facilitate meaningful connections between their parents and African American residents—whose long tenure in the area made their local knowledge a particularly valuable resource for newer, immigrant families—this potential was seldom realized. Aside from Luis's mother, only one other parent had regular interactions with African American neighbors that went beyond occasional casual greetings or smiles. Overall, interviews revealed that children's brokering was more likely to reinforce strong ties to other Latino immigrants than to develop connections to non-immigrant neighbors.

Bridging, Bonding, and Community Building

Strong ties to homogeneous networks are important sources of social support, but can have limited utility for facilitating social leverage. Silvia Domínguez (2011) documents how social support from homogeneous ties can, however, help individuals to not only "get by," but to "get ahead" as well (de Souza Briggs 2003). In some of these families, it was clear that children's brokering could be a form of community building that facilitated social leverage in both ad hoc and sustained ways.

When Carmen was first married, she and her husband had rented a one-room apartment behind her sister-in-law's house. Her sister-in-law's children were a great help to Carmen during those years, helping Carmen care for her children and brokering for her frequently. Her nieces filled out forms for schools, WIC, and Medi-Cal.[19] They also accompanied Carmen to parent-teacher meetings when Luz and Teresa started school and helped her girls with their homework. At the time of my interviews, Luz and Teresa, now teenagers themselves, helped Carmen's friends and neighbors answer their mail and complete their insurance and Medi-Cal forms. Teresa (age fifteen) also tutored a neighbor's son after school and accompanied the mother to school meetings.

Carmen's story revealed that social support given and received through homogeneous networks had more than survival value. The brokering her nieces had done for her and that her girls now did for others went beyond the explicit invoking and returning of favors that Robert Putnam (2000) would classify as "specific reciprocity" between individuals. Putnam described "generalized reciprocity" as this: "I'll do this for you without expecting anything specific back from you, in the confident expectation that someone else will do something for me down the road" (2000, 21). Carmen's nieces helped her without expecting to personally recoup their investment, and her daughters paid back her "debt" by brokering for other community members.

Generalized reciprocity was evident in many of these families, as children reported frequently brokering for strangers. Gabriela's son had made her stop the car the week before our interview so that he could translate for someone he saw struggling to speak to a police officer at the scene of a car accident. Other children reflexively offered their services in and around the community when they recognized that someone needed help. These casual acts of community building were the generalized reciprocity that Putnam (2000) claims to be the cornerstone of civil society. By brokering where needed, these children helped build social trust among community members, even if on a modest and ad hoc basis.

These acts of community building with other immigrants could also help children locate local resources. Milagro's occasional brokering for a neighbor had deepened her family's relationship with them, culminating with Alejandro and his wife deciding to attend a weekend church retreat with that couple. This retreat had been a turning point; Alejandro said the events that weekend convinced him it was time to face up to his addiction. The members of that church group, all immigrant Latinos themselves, had given him nonjudgmental support and had connected him with a local Alcoholics Anonymous chapter, where he drew support from other Latino immigrants who were also in recovery.

This story reflects how homogeneous social networks can, on occasion, facilitate links to local resources that constitute critical social leverage for a family that sorely needs it. It would be a distortion of facts to claim that Milagro's brokering had directly led to her father managing successfully to address his alcoholism. However, this story does reflect how children's community building efforts can have important, if unintended consequences. By helping where she was needed, Milagro provided the social lubricant that led to a particularly advantageous set of connections for her family.

Milagro's story echoes others in this chapter that showed how closely linked familial domestic activities were to their community connections, as well as how important home-based interactions and learning experiences were for families' local encounters. The preceding discussion also demonstrates that children's brokering activities, far from being independent activities, are embedded in and influenced by the social arrangements and communication patterns that shape their family lives. In the next chapter, I document how the strategies that children and their families developed and honed at home were deployed, with varying levels of success, in their interactions with local healthcare and social services institutions.

❀

CHAPTER 5

GATEWAYS TO FAMILY WELLBEING

The healthcare and social services environments these families encountered in Greater Crenshaw were critical to addressing many of their basic, and often urgent, needs. These institutions were also spaces where families accessed resources and services that could provide them a measure of security and social mobility. I discuss healthcare and social services together because they were generally intertwined in families' lived experiences. For example, when complications from diabetes forced Alejandro to quit his restaurant job, his doctor encouraged him to apply for disability benefits to which he was entitled. His daughter Milagro (age thirteen) helped him fill out the paperwork.

The institutions where I conducted interviews and field observations provided one or more of the following services to Greater Crenshaw families: pediatric and adult healthcare, health insurance assistance and coverage, prenatal care and nutrition assistance, parenting classes, after-school enrichment programs, individual and family counseling, and neighborhood safety programs. These locations ranged in size and complexity from a pediatrician's private practice to community clinics and local offices of state- and federally funded programs (see chapter 2 for more details on these sites). In all of these institutions, service professionals reported that children routinely accompanied their parents in order to broker for them.

Children's brokering attracted greater scrutiny in healthcare settings. The California legislature debated AB292 in its 2003 and 2004 sessions, which would have forbidden child brokering in healthcare settings and censured institutions with loss of state funding for violations of this policy. While AB292 did not ultimately pass, many healthcare institutions statewide moved to preemptively ban or curb child brokering in their facilities—without providing additional professional interpreters to replace them. In the absence of alternatives, children continued to broker these interactions anyway. Although children's continued assistance was treated like an open secret in Greater Crenshaw healthcare facilities, they brokered in settings where their efforts were either formally forbidden or seen as problematic.

ENTERING LOCAL HEALTHCARE AND SOCIAL SERVICES

Families came to local healthcare and social services agencies through referrals from other institutions, by word of mouth, or because their children's brokering activities at home had helped them identify locally available services. Parents' preferences also influenced which institutions families entered and the kinds of interactions children helped them negotiate there. Parent interviews revealed a consistent distinction between characteristics they preferred in social services providers and those they preferred in healthcare providers.

Mothers were particularly likely to prefer social services providers who were Latinas, like themselves. This preference helped explain the effectiveness of Women, Infants, and Children's (WIC) community-based hiring practices. Ms. Dorsey, a regional administrator there, said, "We just post the job announcement on the door of the clinic. . . . Ninety percent of WIC, both in terms of participants getting through the door and the hiring, is word of mouth." Since many parents had connected with WIC through prompting by their own peers, they implicitly trusted WIC and its personnel from the start. Furthermore, WIC's community hiring practices facilitated mothers' communication with "peer professional" staff, who were generally low-income, immigrant parents like themselves. Children still often assisted parents in interactions with English-speaking staff. In general, children found brokering at WIC quite easy because peer-professional staff members were nearby if they needed assistance and because their mothers were more comfortable and confident at WIC than in many other local settings.

On the other hand, most parents liked medical professionals who were different from themselves. While Spanish-speaking doctors were rare, parents who had encountered them still expressed a preference for "real American doctors," as Marita phrased it.[1] Parents' stories of past medical encounters revealed that they equated medical professionalism with social differentiation. For many, doctors who were not Latinos signaled that their families were receiving authentically American healthcare. Alyshia Gálvez's (2011) study of Mexican women's experiences in the US healthcare system revealed motivations for these preferences. She found that many expectant mothers viewed "access [to] a well-equipped, hospital-based prenatal clinic . . . as a privilege associated with immigration" and considered new technologies and forms of care superior to traditional methods of health maintenance practiced in their country of origin (Gálvez 2011, 7). For immigrant parents who viewed the US system as a reward of migration and settlement, "American" doctors were an important element of that experience.

For example, Gabriela and her two children had moved to Los Angeles from Mexico to join her husband nine months before we met her. Her son had been placed on medication in Mexico for a condition she declined to disclose. A pediatrician in Greater Crenshaw had suggested new avenues for treatment. Gabriela had been "amazed" by the number of tests he ran and the precision with which they seemed to be conducted. She was enthused about the experience, saying, "Back in Mexico, they were so careless with exams and lab work; the doctors are so much better trained here."

Even though Gabriela had not yet had time to evaluate whether all these tests had, in fact, improved her son's condition, having access to a doctor capable of such treatment strategies appeared to already be a reward in itself. However, as Gálvez points out, low-income migrants like Gabriela and her family do not enjoy most of the advantages the US healthcare system offers. Rather, they become subjects of a public healthcare system that grants them access to emergency care and clinics that are often understaffed and oversubscribed. Parents' preferences for medical professionals who could not speak Spanish only increased the challenges these interactions presented, for their child brokers in particular.[2]

Children's brokering experiences, and the kinds of resources their families secured as a result of their efforts, depended heavily on the specific institutions and providers that families encountered in the community. Mario Small (2010) found that the characteristics of particular childcare facilities in New York directly affected what kinds of resources mothers were able to access, both in and beyond that organization. Contrary to the presumption in the social capital literature that individuals will consciously "invest" in institutional ties they perceive to be advantageous, Small found that mothers' connections were usually serendipitous. He reported that mothers were motivated to find a trusted place to care for their children; discovering that they could access a wider range of resources through these facilities provided them, as Small said, with "unexpected gains" (2010, 4).

The same was true in Greater Crenshaw. Parents and children generally entered local healthcare and social services offices with narrowly defined needs. Some institutions were more likely to be resource brokers than others, whether by virtue of an institutional mandate or by the personal initiative of a particular provider (see chapter 2 for more details). When children brokered interactions with these institutions or staff, they helped facilitate links to resources that could result in unexpected gains for their families. Such serendipitous experiences could be great enablers for children too, because brokering a connection to one institution could be parlayed into multiple institutional linkages, with little or no additional effort on their part.

Not all families were so fortunate. While child brokers and parents had agency within their institutional encounters, insofar as they made choices between the options presented to them, their choices were often circumscribed by the dynamics and structures of particular institutions. These environments influenced what families were able to access and understand from their interactions with providers, as well as what they decided were the best ways to move forward from these encounters.

Understanding how children's brokering influenced their families' interactions with local healthcare facilities and social services requires accounting for the perceptions and motivations of child brokers, parents, and providers. Providers' conscious and unconscious decisions directly affected whether parents and children could effectively deploy the individual and collective strategies they had developed at home in these interactions. As a result, how providers received these families also affected what resources they were able to access through these encounters.

INSTITUTIONAL STAFF AS GATEKEEPERS

Many of the healthcare and social services providers in Greater Crenshaw were formal gatekeepers to services and benefits, in that they determined eligibility for available resources. As such, these "street-level bureaucrats" had powerful influence over the implementation of institutional policies through everyday decisions they made on the job (Lipsky 2010). Small noted, "While organizations may have a global purpose, the people who compose them may be motivated by separate or additional objectives and beliefs, resulting in a collection of actors with multiple purposes" (2010, 16). Reflecting on these different motivations and purposes, Celeste Watkins-Hayes (2009) found that street-level bureaucrats in welfare offices deployed their racial, gendered, and class identities in interactions with clients; some engaged in "racialized professionalism" to promote the needs and interests of co-ethnic welfare recipients.

I did not observe healthcare and social services providers in Greater Crenshaw engaging in racialized professionalism, as I saw in schools (see chapter 6). This distinction might be explained by my focus on healthcare and social services providers who were not fluent Spanish speakers, since I was primarily interested in providers who depended on child brokers to interact with immigrant parents.[3] The providers cited in this chapter were primarily white and African American. The majority of doctors and senior administrators were white and commuted considerable distances to work. Since doctors, in particular, seldom shared racial, class, or geographic identities with Greater Crenshaw residents, these forms of social distance seemed to promote relatively evenhanded treatment of different racial and ethnic groups.

However, providers at all levels viewed families with child brokers as posing unique challenges to their professional routines. These families' needs exposed limitations in institutions' resources since none of these facilities had sufficient numbers of dedicated interpreters on staff. Without adequate support, English-speaking providers found themselves on the front lines, often only able to communicate with these parents by relying on their children.

These challenges affected providers' formal gatekeeping roles because constrained communication with child brokers' families meant that they often knew less about their needs and circumstances than they did about other local families. Providers' complex feelings about these interactions influenced their gatekeeping roles in informal ways as well. Children's brokering presented an implicit threat to some providers' self-concept as competent professionals, in addition to violating their cultural assumptions about appropriate roles for children. These feelings had consequences for how they conducted themselves in interactions brokered by children. These two difficulties that child brokers unwittingly presented—by challenging providers' professional identities and their cultural perspectives on children's roles—tended to overshadow other social identities, such as class and race, though these could potentially become salient in interactions as well.

Challenges to Professional Identity

Watkins-Hayes found that welfare staff develop their professional identities through assessments of how they are situated within the organization, in the community, and in relation to the recipients for whom they are responsible. She argued, "This complex identity construction is not simply a symbolic exercise; it has consequences for clients in terms of what they receive from service organizations and when and how services are rendered" (Watkins-Hayes 2009, 189).

While the professional identities espoused by providers I interviewed were as varied as the titles and responsibilities they held, patterns emerged with regard to how interacting with child brokers and their families disrupted routine professional practices. Because children's brokering either went unrecognized or was made officially unwelcome, even providers who had undergone some form of cultural competence training had not received instruction on how to communicate through children. Most providers gamely did their best at "muddling through" these interactions with parents and children, as Doctor Garber, a white internist at Union Clinic, said. She continued, "I feel very powerless in these situations. Am I saying the right thing; am I doing the right thing?"

Providers felt anxious about relying on children to interact with their immigrant patients because they felt their ability to provide quality care was compromised. Doctor Meeren, an African American pediatrician, was resigned to these interactions being more difficult than her other consultations at Union Clinic:

> I am sort of guilty of being—having like a prejudged notion when I walk into a room. It's a pain that they don't speak English, so I walk in and go, "How are you today? What are you here for?" And they look at me and say nothing. I'll go, "Oh well, *habla inglés?*" because I make that assumption that they've been

here long enough to speak English. So it sort of centers on the kid. Some of the kids are born and raised here and been in school and they speak excellent English, and their Spanish is good. . . . [The] problem when it comes to medical translation is that they don't know [the words]. So that's when I sometimes have to pull someone from here to translate; and because they're not professional either, there are things that I'll say that, you know, they don't understand either. So I have actually a little Spanish-English dictionary that I'll use to help.

In this narrative of a "typical" interaction with an immigrant Latino parent, Doctor Meeren describes her many stages of work to address the challenges inherent in these interactions. She begins from a normative stance, in that she "make[s] that assumption that they've [parents] been here long enough to speak English." She admits to enlisting the help of children but notes their limitations. She references having to "pull someone from here to translate," referring to the frequent ad hoc enlistment of Spanish-speaking support staff to interpret, who are "not professional either" since interpreting is not part of their formal job description. When all else failed, she notes, she used her dictionary.

Doctor Meeren's narrative was defensive of her professional identity as a competent physician; she carefully documented the thoroughness of her efforts to resolve the challenges these interactions presented by noting the limitations of parents, children, and support staff, in turn. Similarly, Doctor Victor, an African American pediatrician at Kids Kare (a private group practice), admitted that speaking to parents through their children "freaks me out a bit." She immediately moved to re-present herself as a competent provider, saying: "[The children's] English skills leave a lot to be desired. It's one thing to speak in the vernacular. It's another thing not to *know* that it's vernacular. And the notes I've seen them write are something hideous. It's ridiculous" (her emphasis). These two pediatricians' defensive postures influenced how they interacted with child brokers in ways that, albeit inadvertently, could constrain their efforts.

Other providers were primarily concerned with the fidelity of particular concepts and ideas that even trained adult interpreters might find challenging. Doctor Thomas, a white pediatrician at Kids Kare, said, "It's not just language, but education. If I say, 'How frequently are you wheezing?' with the concept of 'frequently,' what I'm trying to do is understand the nature of the severity of the asthma. . . . They don't understand that frequency means some sort of ratio." Conveying complex concepts like ratios required medical knowledge beyond the reach of most (if not all) children. For parents with limited formal education, such concepts could be similarly daunting. Doctor Thomas continued, "I think there have been studies that show that children don't translate well . . . [but] older children I might use. But I don't want a free-flowing discussion. I ask specific questions, and I'm looking for specific answers. . . . I'm following a structure in my mind that I want to complete. It's not like we're sitting down and talking about how you feel. There is a structure in my mind I want to complete so that I can get an idea as to what is wrong with the child."

In his example, Doctor Thomas presented his primary concern as uncovering the details he needed to fulfill his professional obligations related to diagnosis and treatment. An expectation that families will dispassionately relay information often conflicts with the emotional and physical needs of patients and families. These motivational mismatches are frequent features of patient-doctor interaction, and many (non-immigrant) patients would disagree with Doctor Thomas's statement, "It's not like we're sitting down and talking about how you feel" (Erzinger 1999; Street 1991; Watson and Gallois 2004). However, healthcare providers' interactions with child brokers and their families involved additional layers of complexity. Mismatched motivations were attended by language discrepancies, as well as limited familiarity with US cultural norms and with the distinctive culture of the US medical system.

Children's limited linguistic and cultural sophistication, as compared with adults, was framed as problematic by many providers. Their subjective attachments to their parents also exacerbated the difficulties these interactions posed to providers' professional identities, particularly when they had to relay bad news. Doctor Garber recalled a number of harrowing stories about children's brokering over years of working in a variety of Los Angeles facilities:

> What's really hard is when you have a minor child who is the only one who speaks English and you have to talk about a really serious thing to the patient. You don't really want a kid to know all those serious things. I had a lady with breast cancer, really bad breast cancer that was penetrating into the chest wall and getting into the lungs. She was in deep, deep, deep denial about her breast cancer, as you might guess. She was sort of hoping that it was just an infection, only it was about the size of your fist by that time. So I had to use her son to say the word "cancer" to her, and she was horrified and in tears, and it was just a long, messy afternoon.
>
> [Her son] was a teenager. He was close to grown up, but I'm sure he felt very uncomfortable saying something that he knew was obvious that he knew his mother had. That wasn't news to the kid, but it was an awkward family moment because Mom didn't want to deal with cancer problems. I remember him telling me later that he was angry at me that I told his mother she had cancer. . . . I think he really didn't want to be in that position, because it was like him telling the bad news, not me telling the bad news.

Doctor Garber used this story as an example of a time when she had felt "powerless." The complex issues here—of patient-doctor communication around bad news that a patient resists hearing, of the relationship between mother and son and between son and doctor—were often augmented by providers' feelings about children's "place" and their need to protect innocents from the dealings of adults (Zelizer 1985).

Children Being Seen and Heard

In Greater Crenshaw, as Gálvez (2011, 26) had noted in New York, "Even though health care providers frequently hold progressive political and social views and express outwardly pro-immigrant sentiments, they serve as gatekeepers administering access to public benefits and schooling patients in acceptable and appropriate behaviors." Acceptable behaviors included providers' implicit conceptions of appropriate roles for children and, by extension, for their parents. Providers often found themselves in the contradictory position of being grateful for children's assistance—which they recognized as crucial to communicating with these families—while also holding value-laden perspectives on these roles. Children being seen and heard in adult spaces, privy to information that providers often felt was inappropriate for their ears, influenced providers' perceptions of their families and directly influenced children's brokering efforts.

Ms. Levande, an African American administrator who oversaw chronic disease management initiatives at Union Clinic, described the fortnightly group meetings she had run for diabetes patients there over the past decade. Since the group was run in English, most of the regulars were African American. She said, "When we first started, I had some Spanish-speaking patients coming, [but] they were kind of not really even understanding what was being said. . . . I know if I set it up for Spanish-speaking patients [too], they would come." She continued, "Last year, we had a son and mother. He would bring her and translate for her, and they both got attendance awards because he was there the whole time, so they got chosen together." Recognizing this mother-son team with an attendance award would seem to connote a welcoming environment for his brokering efforts.

However, just a few moments later, Ms. Levande said, "[Children's brokering] is one of the things we want to stop doing, because sometimes it would be hard on the kids to translate to us in a medical situation for a parent that might be sensitive, and the child shouldn't really be translating that for a parent. And you really—the kid, you don't want the kid—you know, they've got to let them be a kid as long as they can." Ms. Levande's prescriptive views on children's roles conflicted with her recognition that a lack of institutional accommodation gave Spanish-speaking patients two options: to forgo their opportunity to access to resources like this diabetes support group or to bring their children with them.

Providers' perceptions that child brokers transgressed the boundaries of appropriate childhood were further complicated by their conflicting perceptions of children's capabilities. Doctor Victor said, "I try not to [have kids broker]. . . . Asking an eight-year-old to explain the pathology isn't the best choice, from what I can tell. I can understand enough to know, like, if I said something and then the child tries and [translates wrong]. Though, sometimes, the kid and the mom might—because they are so familiar with each other—be able to help each other grasp the meaning a little more." Here, Doctor Victor minimized children's brokering capabilities, noting age as a constraint and her limited ability to check their efforts with her basic Spanish capabilities. And yet, her next comment demonstrated recognition that parent-child scaffolding may facilitate better understandings in healthcare interactions.

Doctor Meeren also recognized the collaborative strategies she had seen between parents and child brokers. She elected to imagine children's motivations in these interactions:

> If I can, I would prefer to communicate directly with the parent, but sometimes [the children] want to take on that role, and so they refuse not to translate almost, and I think they may be protecting their parent. You know, [they] want their parent to understand. I think they want to be normalized, you know . . . [and] they don't want to maybe seem that there is a difference between them and the other English-speaking families. I think they are sometimes protecting their parents; they're immigrants, and they're not able to communicate in English . . . and I will see them sort of jump on that role.

Doctor Meeren described children's active roles quite positively here, viewing them through a lens of family loyalty and as advocates for their parents. In doing so, however, she framed children as "protecting their parents," implying a role reversal from parents being the protectors of children. Perceiving parents as passive because their children were active was problematic because, instead of being recognized as a family system in which multiple members contributed simultaneously to an outcome, providers saw children's front-stage work as necessarily demoting parents to backstage roles (Goffman 1959).

Parents and Children in Healthcare and Social Services

It is against these complex institutional and interpersonal backdrops that children brokered interactions and information for their families. Children consistently reported that brokering in healthcare institutions was much more difficult than doing so in other local settings, including most social services. These families generally had limited healthcare access, which meant that children were particularly likely to broker in emergency situations where they had to negotiate complicated and sometimes upsetting information, and do so very quickly.

Even in non-emergency interactions, brokering in healthcare settings was different from brokering at home, in school meetings, or at other community sites. Healthcare facilities were usually unfamiliar locations for children. They often felt uncertain about rules and procedures and struggled with medical terminology and jargon that providers often used. These difficulties were augmented by children's anxieties about having a family member who was ill or hurt. For all these reasons, children uniformly talked about brokering in healthcare settings when I asked them if they had ever felt anxious, helpless, or afraid when they had to broker. Victoria (age twelve) described her nervous feelings in doctors' waiting rooms: "Yeah, like when I sit down I can't stop moving my feet. I'm always like this, and [my mother] like—she like pinches me or something to get me to stop."

Medical interactions were not uniformly frightening or difficult. Children whose family circumstances required brokering regularly between their parents and a specific healthcare provider were most likely to feel positive about these interactions and their abilities to contribute to them. For example, Milagro (age thirteen) was very comfortable with the internist she visited regularly with her father. She also felt that she could ask him questions if she needed to check her comprehension. Frequent contact, however, was not the same as routine contact. Luis (age eleven) brokered often in healthcare settings, but he and his family saw a revolving door of pediatricians and specialists and spent many nights in the emergency room addressing complications from his younger brother's epilepsy. His brokering experiences were therefore regular but not routine, and more challenging than the ones Milagro described. He said, "I mean, all of them, they use all these terms. . . . [I]t's just so hard for me. [They] like, load this stuff on me so I can translate it."

These families entered healthcare and social services sites where they faced the same constraints experienced by Greater Crenshaw residents more generally, in that there were limited facilities that were oversubscribed and underresourced. They also faced specific challenges in terms of how they were viewed by providers when children brokered these interactions. The strategies that families developed at home were tested in these public spaces, which in turn influenced how these strategies might be deployed at home and in other locations in the future. Healthcare contexts placed the most strain on family-level scaffolding and individual-level strategies; social services settings ranged from minimally stressful, like WIC, to anxiety-producing encounters with Child and Family Services.

In the following sections, I unpack how families' collective and individual strategies were enacted in these institutional settings. Families generally entered these institutions as a unit, rather than as individuals. They deployed collective strategies, including parent-child scaffolding and family triage, although these family sense-making efforts were often constrained by the challenges these institutions posed to parental authority. These family dynamics influenced how children engaged the independent brokering strategies they developed at home—using context to divine meaning, negotiating cultural expectations and norms, and engaging media as resources—in these settings.

Bringing the Family into Individual Care

Families' collective strategies were immediately evident in how frequently parents and children visited local healthcare and social services facilities together. Parents generally expressed a preference for having their children broker these interactions. Dedicated interpreters were rare and generally so oversubscribed that parents could not count on their availability. Instead, most facilities relied informally on bilingual administrative staff members who were called into consultations on an ad hoc basis. Many parents were uncomfortable with this practice and viewed these employees as being rushed or not really wishing to help them.

Milagro (age thirteen) reflected on the situation in a doctor's office she visited regularly with her father: "Yes, they have some Spanish speakers there, but sometimes [the receptionists] are not having a good day, and it's understandable, but . . . they're not that polite. And I've noticed that a lot. . . . They'll try to rush through things, and just try to get through as fast as they can . . . and that's the thing about my dad; he feels bad when he has to go through that, you know. He prefers for me to go over there." Milagro's description demonstrated empathy for her father. Diplomatically, she also expressed empathy for the receptionists who made him uncomfortable. Children like Milagro who recognized emotional states on all sides of an interaction and altered their communication strategies accordingly were often particularly skilled brokers.

Children's abilities to read their parents' emotional states provided parents some comfort in what were often stressful interactions. Wait times to see providers were often very long, appointments were rushed, and, unless families had a particular caseworker or physician, they often saw different providers on each visit (Fiscella and Epstein 2008; Heritage and Maynard 2006). Aurora (age sixteen) said, "When [my parents] have to say something [to a doctor], they want me to say it for them. . . . [M]aybe they feel more sure with me." Hilda explained her preference for having Sonia (age fourteen) broker for her by saying, "Those people there may speak my language, but my daughter speaks my heart." She explained that she trusted her daughter to understand what she was feeling or really trying to say and to relay that faithfully to the provider.

Juana (age thirteen) went to WIC with her mom whenever she could because even though many of the staff there spoke Spanish, she said, "My mom is more comfortable having me there to explain things the right way." She recounted a time in the past year where she had brokered her mom's appointments at the doctor and then at WIC. By the time the appointments were over, Juana had missed school. "I said to [my mom], 'Well, I couldn't go to school, but at least I could help you . . . and don't you feel weird when you go by yourself [compared to] when you go with me?' And she's like, 'Well, actually a little bit.'" While most parents only took their children out of school to broker in emergencies, in some families, emergencies were frequent enough for children to be absent on a regular basis.

Parent-Child Scaffolding

Parents and child brokers who effectively deployed their scaffolding strategies in these healthcare settings tended to communicate more confidently and have clearer understandings of their interactions. In general, children's brokering was more effective when supported by some amount of scaffolding with parents. Juana (age thirteen) described how her brokering efforts were enabled by scaffolding in Spanish with her mother and in English with her mother's doctor: "I'll try to figure out how to say it [in English] first and I'll say to [the doctor] how I think it goes and sometimes [the doctor] will be like, 'It doesn't go that way.' And I'll say, 'Okay,' and we'll work on it until we know we understand, and then I'll tell my mom. Then I'll make sure I understand what my mom says with her and translate it to English for [the doctor]." Juana described a nurturing communication context, where the encouragement of both adult women enhanced her brokering capabilities and facilitated agreement about the best ways for Juana's mother to manage her health.

By contrast, we observed Luis (age eleven) brokering for his mother, Ana, in a pre-surgical visit for his younger brother. The physician's assistant spoke quickly and used complicated medical terminology. Luis struggled to find a pause so that he could convey the information to his mother. When he finally did, he left out many details both because he was pressed for time and because his recall was compromised by the amount of information he had had to remember. In this exchange, when he struggled to explain "neurologist," Ana nodded her head quickly to indicate that she understood that part and that he should move on. My assistant's field notes revealed the general pattern between Luis and Ana during this and other interactions we witnessed: "Luis does this all the time; this was evident by how well he and his mom worked together. He knew when to start and stop [explaining], based on her facial expressions. If she nodded, then it meant that she understood what was being asked. She responded and he translated her answer. When she didn't understand something she asked him what was meant, and he repeated or tried to rephrase."

While Ana and Luis's teamwork facilitated some understanding of this preoperative meeting, the physician's assistant's communication style constrained Luis's brokering capabilities and attempts to scaffold with his mother. The limitations of this interaction were most evident when Ana tried to show the physician's assistant the medications her son was taking. We watched her shaking the vials (which experience had taught her to bring to appointments), saying "night" and "morning" in English to indicate when he took each, but it still took numerous demonstrations to reach even tentative agreement on whether he should continue to take them all. Ana and Luis frequently went to healthcare and social services appointments together on his brother's behalf. Their abilities to scaffold varied according to how accommodating different providers were to their efforts, as did their understandings of the treatment plans they were given.

Family Triage

Incomplete understandings were even more evident in instances of family triage, a term I use to describe times when parents had to manage without their children (or vice versa), when they usually would have pooled their skills to negotiate a particular interaction. In these institutional settings, it was not possible that children would have had to manage entirely without their parents. As minors, they were not legally permitted to make independent medical decisions, even if a parent was incapacitated by pain or illness. Family triage did, however, occur when children were ill and their parents did not have another ready source of brokering support.

A few children recalled times when they felt they had to calm their parents' fears and broker their own treatments when taken to a doctor or emergency room with an acute condition. Aurora (age sixteen) said, "There was this one time a few years ago that I was [so sick] I couldn't talk; I couldn't think. And [my mom] was like, 'No, help me talk to the doctor,' and I was like, 'Just tell them I don't feel good,' and my mom was getting more and more nervous. But thankfully, there was this other woman there whose daughter was sick too, and she could speak English, so she translated for my mom. And I was like, 'Thank God, finally,' because I was feeling so bad." Graciela (age thirteen) recounted a similar story from when she was eight years old. Her mother had taken her to the emergency room in tremendous pain (she was reluctant to provide details as to why). Because Graciela was hardly able to speak, Ileana was left alone to contend with her anxieties about her daughter's condition. Finally, after unsuccessful attempts to communicate with the doctor directly, Ileana found a janitor who spoke some English to help her, but the ordeal did not resolve until the early hours of the morning.

These two examples vividly illustrate what parents contended with when they had to manage medical encounters without their children, as well as the inadequate institutional accommodations for non-English speakers in these facilities. Since children often performed emotional support functions as well as linguistic ones, they made efforts through their discomfort to reassure their parents that they would be fine. However, these were harrowing experiences for parents, who had to simultaneously contend with their anxieties about their children's illness and with their inabilities to communicate effectively to address those fears.

Challenges to Parental Authority

Parents' retention of authority within the family was a critical form of support for children's brokering, in any location. Parental authority augmented children's confidence that they were brokering effectively. Demonstrations of parental authority also modeled proactive communication behaviors, which children mirrored in their own information-seeking strategies. Maintaining parental authority could therefore facilitate children's independent brokering behaviors, as well as family-level scaffolding activities.

Parents faced myriad challenges to retaining their authority when they entered healthcare and social services institutions. Few parents directly admitted it, but their tentativeness was evident in interactions I observed and in the observations their children and service providers made during interviews. Parents encountered profoundly uneven power dynamics in these environments, as providers differed from them in terms of education, language capabilities, socioeconomic status, and, sometimes, residency status as well. These differences augmented the standard power differentials between patients and providers, where the latter is framed as the expert from whom the former seeks advice and assistance (Erzinger 1999; Street 1991). Parents' limited experience with US healthcare also made them unfamiliar with the vocabulary and procedures they encountered in these sites. Although their visits with his internist were routine, Milagro (age thirteen) described how stressful visits with unknown specialists were for her father: "Yeah, we fight sometimes, 'cuz he gets nervous. And like, I understand him, but sometimes we get mad at each other, and I'm like, 'Well I'm not going to know every answer.' And then he gets mad 'cuz he needs to know. But it's just in the moment, and then it's all fine."

Some providers noted that parents were not only reluctant to ask questions, but also unsure of what questions to ask at all. Ms. Jaramillo was a third-generation Latina who spoke minimal Spanish and worked for an organization providing subsidized health insurance to under-served children. She said, "You know, I don't even know if [parents] are empowered to ask questions. A lot of it is that they don't know the system. It's really complicated, you know." Gálvez (2011) detailed how poor immigrant mothers struggled with the maze of requirements for public programs, mountains of paperwork, and the implicit understandings required for navigating sectors of the US healthcare system. The parents in Greater Crenshaw encountered the same dizzying system, and in many cases it made them more passive participants, at least from the perspective of those who provided them with care and services. Doctor Victor described her experiences working as an emergency room pediatrician in a local hospital:

> It's paradoxical. The usual story is that when you have a parent hassling a triage nurse saying their kid is really sick, 99 percent of the time there's nothing wrong with the kid. With Latino families, they're usually the mom in the corner sitting quietly with a kid turning white and blue and she says, "Well, they told me to wait." It's a paradoxical thing because the gentler they are, the more concerned I get. . . . Parents who are born here are more entitled . . . [and]

parents who immigrated recently don't want to rock the boat, don't want to make trouble, even when their kid needs urgent care. . . . [T]hey'll just sit and wait until someone notices them.

Parents employed avoidant strategies more often in healthcare settings than in social services, as interactions in the latter were more likely to be a choice than forced by an emergency. Social services were also more likely to have staff members who spoke Spanish, so families felt confident that their children's brokering efforts were more adequately supported. Of course, such accommodations depended on the nature of the social services in question and on how the family came to interact with them.

Juana (age thirteen) and her mother, Estela, related a story where resource brokering by a healthcare professional had become an oppositional process. Five years prior, Estela had fallen on a slippery sidewalk while carrying Juana's infant sister. She took Juana to the emergency room to broker for her. When the baby was almost a year old, they were back in the emergency room when the baby became ill. A doctor, having read about the first visit in their file, found a bruise on the baby's knee. She called a social worker downstairs, who did not speak Spanish. The social worker proceeded to ask Juana, who was nine years old at the time, a series of questions to assess if her parents were abusive. "Then they took [Juana] away to ask her questions away from me . . . [and] it felt like hours. They didn't ask me if they could talk to her. They didn't even look at me," Estela said. She phoned her husband, who left work immediately to come to the hospital. His relatively strong command of English allowed him to make demands that his wife could not. He insisted that Juana not be asked any more questions until a bilingual social worker was found so that he and Estela could participate in the conversation. Juana could not even bring herself to talk about this experience in our interview.

An interaction like this one would be traumatic for any family, and perhaps the social worker and doctor would tell the story quite differently. Recalling the event in this frame does, however, reflect some important dimensions of how these families interacted with complex US institutions. One dimension is that Estela's and Juana's limited understandings of institutional systems made them totally unprepared for this kind of interaction and ill-equipped to handle it effectively. The second is that both Estela and Juana had to struggle to understand the experience on their own; the doctor could not speak directly to Estela and could not ask Juana to broker when her family was suddenly being scrutinized for evidence of domestic violence. Finally, the tenuousness of the resolution they described was striking. If Estela had not married a man with different linguistic and cultural proficiencies from her own, this family would have had no advocate in a rapidly escalating situation that could have had deleterious consequences.

CHILDREN'S INDEPENDENT STRATEGIES

Children were well aware that their parents' limited language skills, education, and income made their brokering assistance essential. Their parents' limited demonstrations of authority, particularly in healthcare settings, were a challenge for children who felt expected to demonstrate courage and proactivity even when their parents did not. Children generally applied the same brokering strategies they did at home in healthcare and social services sites: extracting meaning from contextual cues, negotiating cultural norms, and engaging media as resources. The institutional environments in which they did so and the providers they encountered there greatly influenced how successful these strategies ultimately were.

Context and Meaning: Being Able to Ask

Children's primary opportunities to extract meaning from context occurred during conversations between their parents and service providers. Children listened carefully to these professionals, using statements around an unfamiliar word or idea to deduce what it could mean. This was a relatively successful strategy in social services interactions because the vocabulary and ideas in these conversations were generally quite straightforward. In medical situations, however, I witnessed doctors and other personnel inadvertently making it more difficult for children to understand what they were saying. By using complex medical terminology when simpler terms would have sufficed, failing to provide adequate explanations of complicated ideas, and not checking children's comprehension by asking if they understood, doctors' instructions and explanations were often well beyond child brokers' capabilities. When providers' communication styles were unaccommodating, children's usual strategies for extracting meaning had little or no utility.

What mattered most was what children did—or did not do—next in these situations. Children whose parents modeled proactive communication styles were more likely to ask questions when they did not understand what providers had said. Milagro (age thirteen) said, "Sometimes it's not a typical word and I don't know how to translate it either from English to Spanish or Spanish to English, but I try my hardest . . . [and] I ask the doctor or my dad for another definition or another way that they can give me clues, and most of the time I get it." Many children did not directly engage assistance from providers and parents as Milagro did. They were often reluctant to directly question authority figures, anxious that asking questions would make them appear less competent.

They were more comfortable clarifying that they had understood their parents' meanings than questioning providers. However, they often did not have the requisite knowledge to prod parents for more information about a medical condition, as a professional interpreter might (Hsieh 2007; Willen 2011). There were also times that children refrained from prying into their parents' answers, either out of respect or embarrassment at hearing private information.

Although children had different motivations for limiting the questions they asked providers and their parents, these choices all made misunderstandings more likely. When I asked Doctor Meeren if children asked for clarification when they needed it, she said,

> No. They struggle . . . even to the point where they'll translate it wrong. [I will say] "No, that's not what I said. Do you understand?" They don't like to admit sometimes that they don't . . . and they'll say it again, and I'll go, "No, that's not what I'm saying." I think they feel sort of defeated if I go and get a translator and they feel that they couldn't help their mom understand as they should have. When I try that, I don't do it in a negative way. I say, "It's okay, you know, let me go get someone else to help us."

For many children, admitting they needed help was more than embarrassing; it was a defeat, as Doctor Meeren had surmised. Aurora (age sixteen) said, "Sometimes . . . I'm just like, 'I don't understand what you're saying. . . . Can you explain better or say it in other words, describe it to me so I can better translate it to my parents.' And they try to, but sometimes I just don't get it. . . . I feel sad 'cuz I can't help my parents; I try to understand the doctors, but I can't [sometimes]."[4] Acutely aware that their parents were depending on them, younger brokers were particularly likely to feel that asking for help meant they were not living up to their family responsibilities.

As Marjorie Orellana and her associates observed, brokers were also aware of their social positioning as children operating in adult situations and that "these factors may affect how they and their families are viewed and treated, as well as how entitled they felt to ask questions, make demands, or speak on behalf of their families" (Orellana, Dorner, and Pulido 2003, 522). Luis's behavior in the waiting room for one of his brother's doctor visits clearly illustrated these constraints. His mother told him to go to the counter and ask if they had been called while they were in the pharmacy and, if so, to demand that their names not be moved to the bottom of the list. Luis walked to the counter and asked only if their names had been called but did not request his family not lose their priority to be seen. Ana could obviously see his reticence and understood just enough to march him back up to the counter to make her request in full. Luis was clearly uncomfortable and made the request in a small voice with downcast eyes, with none of the forcefulness of his mother's wishes.

Some children felt more comfortable asking questions, and older brokers were more likely to make enquiries of their parents and of providers, indicating that relationships within the family system change as children get older. Occasionally, younger brokers also asked questions; Graciela (age thirteen) was a notable example. As discussed in earlier chapters, Graciela's mother strongly encouraged her to take initiative with her brokering. When I asked her how she ensured she had understood doctors' instructions correctly, she giggled and said, "Because I just won't let them leave until I know I got it right." Few children felt entitled to engage with providers this way, but those who did increased the chances that they would broker difficult information successfully.

Negotiating Cultural Norms

Implicit in whether children felt they could ask questions and how insistent those requests could be were the cultural dimensions of their brokering experiences. Children worked hard to finesse interactions where cultural expectations could conflict and adversely affect their families.[5] Children often had to negotiate knowledge related not only to US culture and their families' culture of origin, but to the culture of the institution where the interaction took place. Barbara Sharf (1993, 36) noted, "Doctors and patients do not talk with one another in a vacuum. These encounters occur within professional, institutional, political, and socio-cultural contexts that should be taken into account." With varying degrees of success, children attempted to account for these various contexts (see García-Sánchez 2014).

When these efforts required pleasing oppositional parties, brokers admitted that they occasionally altered the meaning of messages. Aurora (age sixteen) said, "Sometimes I think, 'That's not how you say it,' but I don't really tell them nothing. I just let them talk and then I say it in my own words." Her family had recently had a problem with their health insurance where their coverage was not being accepted by a doctor's office. Her parents were very upset and directed their frustration at the office staff and doctors. Aurora altered their speech in accordance with her understanding that the problem lay with the insurance company, not the doctor's office itself. Her approach resulted in the office manager taking responsibility for clearing the problem personally. In this case, Aurora negotiated multiple forms of cultural knowledge to craft a message that facilitated the outcomes her family ultimately desired.

Other forms of cultural knowledge were equally challenging; these children had to negotiate what it meant to be an appropriate child in interactions that often brought conflicting expectations to the fore. As discussed previously, child brokers challenged many providers' cultural expectations that children should not operate in adult spheres, have access to adult information, or have to "work" (Bourdillon et al. 2010; Orellana 2009). For parents, it was critical that their children broker in ways that still accorded them appropriate levels of respect and deference.[6]

Some providers inadvertently made it more difficult for children to maintain this delicate balance between adults' expectations of them. I witnessed interactions where doctors directed their first question to the parent, but only addressed the child once he or she started brokering (see Orellana 2009, 74). Parents felt slighted when they were effectively excluded from the discussion, and their children felt caught between helping as needed and maintaining their parents' sense of dignity in these instances. On the other hand, providers who only addressed the parent and effectively ignored the child brokering the interaction also challenged children's sense of their "place." Feeling removed from the conversation made children even less likely to reassert themselves in the discussion when they had questions.

Many children were adept at recognizing adults' emotional states, those of their parents in particular. For many parents, having their children broker sensitive, embarrassing, or adult matters for them was very difficult. In these situations, children had to manage their parents' reticence in culturally appropriate ways, while also managing their own feelings about certain kinds of information. After all, Mom's gynecological exam or Dad's prostate cancer screening may be considered "routine" medical visits, but both make children privy to information that parents and children would prefer not to share with each other. Some parents and children were better at managing these feelings than others. For example, Juana (age thirteen) went with her mother to the gynecologist. She also accompanied a neighbor who did not have a child old enough to help her. Juana managed her embarrassment by framing the experiences as "educational," saying, "It's okay if I know [about gynecological visits] 'cuz one day I'm going to have to know it anyway, right? . . . And they're not [embarrassed for me to hear it] 'cuz they want me to learn."

Juana treating these interactions as learning experiences helped her appear appropriate from both her mother's and the doctor's perspectives. Like Juana, many child brokers managed differences between parents' and providers' cultural expectations by foregrounding their desires to be helpful, dutiful children. Providers who recognized these avowals tended to be more accommodating, as children acquiescing to parental demands is a relatively consistent expectation across cultures (even if, in this case, what children were acquiescing to was considered inappropriate by providers).

Reflecting on her years of pediatric practice, Doctor Meeren commented, "I think they are used to sort of taking on that responsibility and just speaking in English and translating, and sometimes they will even—we'll be in a conversation, and they will still be trying to tell me whatever the mother is saying in English. . . . I think they believe that is their responsibility or maybe they've been given that responsibility. . . . [U]sually the oldest or the older children will take on that responsibility and do it automatically. I don't hear the parents say, you know, tell her this for me." Children felt pressure to appear compliant with adult demands coming from both sides. Victoria (age twelve) said, "My parents and the people there, they expect me to know. They expect me as a Mexican [to understand Spanish] but also to know English. They expect me to know it straight up and to help them." Child brokers strongly identified with their helper roles; managing the fine lines of appropriate behavior to do so effectively was often hard work.

Media as Resources and Paperwork as a Gatekeeper

Institutional interactions were inevitably accompanied by reams of documents required for receiving or maintaining benefits, services, devices, and medications. Many parents had trouble completing these forms independently, even in Spanish. These documents were gatekeepers that determined families' eligibility for many of the most valuable resources and services available to them, like food assistance and insurance coverage.

For all these reasons, and because mistakes could result in their families losing out on resources and services they sorely needed, children approached brokering these documents with trepidation. Evelyn (age fifteen) lived with her grandmother Anabel and found the paperwork for her many prescriptions stressful: "To me when [my grandmother] needs me to order pills, that's the worst 'cuz I think, what if I say the wrong name and they give her something else? . . . Yeah, even though I've done it for a while I still feel like, you know, it's the first time." Alicia (age twelve) recalled being afraid when her father sent her to the pharmacy to pick up prescriptions on her own. She was worried that she would "mess up the words" and get the wrong medication.

Children highlighted prescription-related brokering as particularly anxiety-inducing because, in addition to requiring specialized medical vocabulary, parents often had children handle these tasks on their own. As such, children had to have a working knowledge of their families' health insurance and compensation plans because making a mistake—either by accepting the wrong prescription, or incurring considerable cost by accepting a drug not covered by insurance—weighed very heavily on them. Even children who usually asked for assistance from English speakers were unsure of how to phrase their questions related to health insurance and prescriptions, since these were such complex subjects.

So complex, in fact, that even doctors had trouble navigating them. Doctor Zimba, an African-born pediatrician in private practice, said that even for parents who had managed successfully to subscribe their children to state-subsidized low- and no-cost health insurance programs, they were required to constantly navigate paperwork in order to keep it:

> No, they don't understand how the system works, and then I think a lot of times . . . they feel they can't ask for change. I don't know if they know they have a lot of choices. . . . They call me and say, "Well, why is my one kid's [primary care doctor] changed," or they'll say, "Why am I not with you this month?" I called the [insurance provider myself] and they said, "Oh, they have forms they have to fill out." If they don't fill it out in a timely fashion, they drop them or change them, and this is news to me too.

Doctor Zimba was deeply dissatisfied that insurance technicalities limited her abilities to stay connected with her patients and their parents. Her comments indicated that, like many of her colleagues, she too was unsure how the system worked and therefore could not advise families or champion their efforts to understand their benefits. Doctor Thomas had similar perceptions of how little parents knew and similar admissions about how little he did, too: "I think they understand close to zero, or very little [about insurance coverage]. . . . You know, I can sort of identify with that myself, having a million papers sitting around here. A significant number of [families] are terminated . . . [and] a lot of the time they don't even know. There's not a lot of understanding of what's happening."

Eligibility paperwork was a perfect storm. No one—not doctors, parents, or children—felt they had a working understanding of the labyrinthine requirements and documents needed to fully access services and resources that were, in theory, available to these families. Chapter 4 described how paperwork and the language required to complete them posed considerable challenges for these families. These challenges were magnified in institutional settings, where expectations of qualified assistance were, particularly in medical settings, seldom realized. Families were often not able to secure as much guidance from administrative staff or providers with these forms as they felt they needed.

Children described times when parents had become anxious or angry when they were not able to complete these forms easily. The squabbles parents and children had over these documents did not necessarily lead to negative outcomes. Many children said that their own and their parents' anxieties motivated them to work especially hard on completing these documents, seeking out reference books, dictionaries, office staff, and even Internet resources (when available in institutions' waiting rooms) to ensure that everything was filled out correctly. When these efforts paid off, the pride and happiness children felt about these accomplishments were that much greater.

This pride was clearly evident in Milagro's (age thirteen) description of her father's recent hospitalization for eye surgery, when she had been "in charge" of all the necessary paperwork: "My mom was there, but she didn't know nothing; she really needed someone to figure out [everything]. . . . I had all the information on my dad, and like everything . . . paperwork, . . . little notes, appointments, his history, and, um, how he'd been hospitalized before. So I organized everything, and I'm the only one there who knows everything. . . . My mom really was [appreciative]. She even said, "If you hadn't been there I don't know what I woulda done." Milagro proactively organizing the considerable paperwork required for her father's surgery reflected her internalization of the US healthcare system's expectations around self-care and management, learned through regular visits to her father's doctors (Gálvez 2011). For Milagro, who was so invested in her role as her father's caretaker, this opportunity to showcase her accumulated knowledge of the US medical system reinforced her important place in the social arrangements her family has developed around her father's illness.

UNANTICIPATED CONSEQUENCES IN GREATER CRENSHAW INSTITUTIONS

The goals that motivated families' contact with local social services and healthcare facilities were generally narrow; they approached WIC for food assistance and a pediatrician for children's checkups. The best-case scenario was that families would also accrue unanticipated gains through those connections. Resource brokering was particularly important to these families because they remained unaware of many local opportunities unless a service provider alerted them to those possibilities. Over time, such rewarding connections could have unintended consequences, in the form of greater familiarity with individual providers, institutional routines, and locally available resources.[7] These familiarities were crucial for families to develop sustained connections to local institutions that could support their wellbeing over time.

This chapter has demonstrated, however, that unanticipated gains were far from guaranteed. These families generally encountered overburdened and under-resourced institutions, and children faced multiple layers of challenges to broker in these environments. Despite children being officially prohibited from brokering in some locations and tacitly prohibited in others, parents and providers alike indicated that they frequently depended on children to facilitate their interactions.

Children's brokering efforts were acts of expediency, a strategy of last resort for providers given few, if any, institutional resources to facilitate communication with Spanish-speaking parents. From parents' perspectives, relying on their children was partly a reaction to a lack of reliable adult options and partly an issue of trust. For parents navigating confusing and often frightening systems, relying on their children may not have been a perfect option; but, overall, they assessed it to be their best one. For children, who knew their parents could not manage without their help, brokering efforts were as much acts of expediency as expressions of love and loyalty. As such, they often placed their own needs (such as school attendance or homework completion) second to those of their families.

Encounters with healthcare institutions, even more so than social services, tended to stress these family systems. Parental authority was compromised, which inhibited both parent-child scaffolding and children's independent brokering efforts. Misunderstandings were common, ranging from misinterpreting doctors' instructions to more minor discrepancies, like thinking a provider had been condescending. Whether the provider had actually been insulting was irrelevant if the family acted on that perception by disconnecting from that institution or feeling that the provider had broken trust with them. Whether instances

of miscommunication were obvious or minor enough to be almost impercep-
tible, they all carried potential to fray what were already fragile ties to local institutions and the resources they provided.

The next chapter addresses families' connections to local schools. I document
how children brokered their parents' connections to their and their siblings'
schools, as well as how their established roles as their family helpers could compromise their connections to the educational opportunities and resources that
schools could offer them.

CHAPTER 6

SHORTCHANGING THE IMMIGRANT BARGAIN?

As community sites, no institutions are more closely tied to parents' aspirations for their children than the schools. Providing children with broader educational and occupational prospects is often a major motivation for parents' migration. Their children's educational attainment is also viewed as a pathway toward repaying their parents' sacrifices.[1] These repayments may be literal, in that they can more easily help support their families with a professional salary than with earnings from low-skilled work. Education can also provide emotional payback made manifest in parents' pride in the opportunities their migration has made available to their children.

These parental expectations, and children's motivations to meet them, have been coined by Robert Courtney Smith (2002) as the "immigrant bargain." Vivian Louie (2012) found that for parents, the immigrant bargain is rooted in their optimism about opportunities the United States offers for social mobility, coupled with their pessimism that their own accents, limited English proficiency, and other markers of foreignness make them unlikely to realize these opportunities themselves. They therefore transfer their ambitions for social mobility to their children. Her findings suggest that children who "win" the immigrant bargain share their parents' optimism and faith in the American education system. They are also buoyed by support from parents, siblings, and non-family actors who act as their mentors, champions, and guides.

Vivian Louie concluded that children's educational successes resulted from "individual agency, family agency, and institutional supports *combined*" (2012, 173 [italics in original]). The immigrant bargain is therefore a moral contract between parents and children that requires institutional, non-family support to be successfully enacted. For children growing up in homogeneous family and social networks in Greater Crenshaw, schools were their best chance for locating adults who could alert them to opportunities for educational advancement and help them navigate the vagaries of the US school system. A compassionate teacher or administrator could become a mentor. An instructor in an afterschool program could improve children's mastery of their schoolwork, increasing their grade-point averages and enhancing their college eligibility. The majority of Louie's Dominican- and Colombian-origin informants had had at least one such role model who was pivotal in their school success; about half her sample named two or more (V. Louie 2012, 101). While children of low-income immigrants can gain a great deal from these kinds of relationships, they often find it extremely difficult to locate individuals who can fulfill these roles (V. Louie 2012; Stanton-Salazar and Spina 2003).

This chapter builds on Smith's and Louie's work by exploring how brokering responsibilities affect children's chances of winning the immigrant bargain. The moral contract represented by the immigrant bargain relies on an interdependent family system, since parents' sacrifices are redeemed in the successes of their children. Earlier chapters have detailed how children's brokering responsibilities also reflect and rely on family interdependence. While success in school and in life was how these children planned to uphold the immigrant bargain in the long term, the everyday help they provided by brokering was how they realized the immigrant bargain in the short term.

And therein lay the rub. Brokering when parents needed them often resulted in incomplete homework, foregone after-school and weekend programs, and school absences. By spending less time on campus both during and after the school day, child brokers had fewer opportunities than their classmates for contact with adults who might become their mentors and role models. Incomplete homework and missed school days could directly contribute to lower grades and limited mastery of school-related material. Many children's time was consumed not only by brokering regularly for parents at home and in local institutions, but also by serving as tutors and guides for younger siblings, cousins, and neighbors. Younger children therefore benefited from brokers' trial-and-error movements through the US school system, even though these activities regularly redirected brokers' time and energy away from their own schooling. Keeping the immigrant bargain created a catch-22 for these kids because the brokering activities that satisfied their short-term family obligations often circumscribed the kinds of meaningful connections to schools that would help them win the immigrant bargain in the long term.

Child brokers' relationships with schools were more multidimensional than those with other local institutions because the majority of their interactions there were independent of their parents. The remainder of this chapter therefore unfolds in three parts. The first details how children's brokering responsibilities influenced their school connections and the kinds of relationships they developed with teachers and other personnel. Since family responsibilities could constrain children's school experiences in a variety of ways, the second section identifies mismatches in teachers' and parents' values, expectations, and behaviors. Children had to navigate these gaps and contradictions as they tried to balance family responsibilities and school commitments. These aspects of children's relationships to schools influenced how they brokered for their parents on campus, as detailed in the final section.

CHILD BROKERS AS STUDENTS

Daily interactions with teachers and other school personnel can develop into relationships that dramatically influence children's educational trajectories in under-served schools. Ricardo Stanton-Salazar and Stephanie Spina (2003, 250) have noted, however, that such connections are "structured around fortuity and individual access, not group access," for low-income Latino students; the young people in Greater Crenshaw were no different in this regard.

Although Tyler Middle School was significantly better resourced than Bellum Middle School, the same community issues pervaded both campuses and affected teacher-student relationships.[2] Teachers were generally new to both the profession and the community. Most were sympathetic (or at least resigned) to the time constraints that multiple jobs and childcare concerns created for working-class parents. They were generally unaware, however, of how the home lives of students with immigrant parents differed from those of other students, as revealed in the surprised questions many asked about these families during our interviews. Since most teachers did not know much about immigrant families, and children volunteered little about their family circumstances and responsibilities, teacher-student relationships were often rather superficial and therefore more vulnerable to misunderstandings.

Angela Valenzuela's (1999) study of a Latino-majority high school in Texas uncovered how misaligned teacher-student expectations created "subtractive schooling" environments. Teachers fulfill their professional obligations in demonstrations of "aesthetic caring" for students by teaching them the material and skills necessary for normative progress through the curriculum. They expect students to exhibit aesthetic caring by mastering these materials and skills. Children I interviewed said that they often went to school tired, distracted, or with incomplete homework because of their brokering responsibilities. Without knowledge of their home lives and responsibilities, some teachers inferred that these behaviors were due to a lack of student interest or effort.

Teachers knew little about children's home lives partly because children only volunteered information to teachers they already trusted. Like Angela Valenzuela's (1999) informants, child brokers expected teachers to demonstrate "authentic caring" by showing respect for and interest in them as individuals—not just as students—before entrusting them with details about their lives. Valenzuela found that students required authentic caring from teachers before being willing to show them aesthetic caring. Conversely, teachers who perceived a lack of aesthetic caring from students were disinclined to demonstrate authentic caring.

These mismatched expectations, Valenzuela argues, produce subtractive schooling experiences for students.

While my interviews and field observations revealed that students and teachers demonstrated a range of authentic and aesthetic caring behaviors, certain school conditions affected the likelihood of mismatched expectations (see chapter 2 for more details). Campus safety issues, in particular, made teachers feel as if they directed more energy toward discipline than education, limiting their connections with "good" students. Some teachers consciously limited their interactions with students to curricular content as a way to avoid being too close to the risks of campus violence. Children felt this distance in teachers' emphasis on "teaching to the test," which discouraged all but the most motivated students and made it difficult to develop deeper relationships with teachers.[3] For most children I interviewed, high and low achievers alike, their teachers were simply presences in their lives—not usually overtly negative, but not overtly positive either.[4]

How Child Brokers Demonstrated Aesthetic Caring

Since teachers generally emphasized aesthetic caring in the classroom, students who did likewise could develop positive relationships with them. Child brokers were able to demonstrate aesthetic caring more easily in some subjects than others. Language proficiency was a major factor, as students generally had difficulty with text-heavy subjects. Eighteen respondents said history was their weakest subject, and twenty-one said math was their strongest.[5] Rolando (age seventeen) explained by saying, "History, it's just sentences." He had migrated from Mexico less than a year earlier, so he struggled with the cultural references and language of instruction in his US history class. He said, "I didn't learn nothing [in my history class]. . . . The teacher was just writing in [sic] the blackboard all the time. . . . Yes, I was copying all the sentences there, but I didn't learn." The greatest mismatch between students' and teachers' expressions of aesthetic caring occurred in subjects like history and English, especially if teachers relied on the textbook rather than more interactive, demonstrative methods to engage students with content.

On the other hand, math gave child brokers an opportunity to display skills and knowledge with minimal language constraints.[6] For the same reason, many parents helped their children with math homework, making it the only subject where there was, as Ms. Rosenfelt (a Jewish math teacher at Tyler) described it, a "triangle" of communication and support between teachers, students, and parents. "You need the triangle," she said. "If you lose one of those three points, you have a flat line." Teachers recognized that math was usually children of immigrants' strongest subject. Ms. Rhodes, a white English as a Second Language (ESL) teacher at Bellum, said, "Math is easier for many of them because it's a universal language. You know, there's not too much reading involved." Math classes were therefore opportunities for teachers and students to recognize mutual aesthetic caring.

When teachers came to know high achievers as individuals, they were more able and motivated to open doors to other opportunities for them. For example, Liliana (age sixteen) had attended a troubled middle school until a teacher there told her about a new charter school opening near her home. The teacher helped Liliana complete the application, knowing that she would have had to broker these forms for her parents if left unassisted. Liliana was in a position to benefit from this opportunity because her teacher's support, coupled with her high grades, made her eligible for admission and signaled her aesthetic caring.

Developing close relationships with teachers and other adults on campus required regular opportunities for contact. Child brokers had fewer opportunities to interact with teachers outside their classes because they seldom attended after-school programs. Juana (age thirteen) said, "I can't stay after school because I have to help my little sister with her homework and, like, I need to help my mom if people are talking to her and she doesn't understand." Chapter 4 described how children's responsibilities to their families, neighbors, and others in their parents' peer networks generally occupied their afternoons. Even on afternoons when they had no family responsibilities, many children were not allowed to stay late because parents worried that it was unsafe for them to walk home alone.

Since children had few, if any, sources for homework assistance at home, after-school programs could offer much-needed support. While some child brokers were high achievers, many were failing (or in danger of failing) at least one class during the time I spent with them, and thus could have benefited greatly from such interventions. Even for students with less acute concerns, teachers were often more relaxed and accessible in after-school roles than during class. After-school programs gave teachers and students opportunities to get to know each other better and for teachers to potentially become more meaningful members of children's support networks. However, only five of the child brokers I interviewed participated in on-campus activities after school, even irregularly.

How Teachers Demonstrated Authentic Caring

Teachers generally described children of immigrants as quiet, obedient students; given how much time teachers and administrators spent as disciplinarians, they looked favorably on these traits. Being quiet in school, however, held many of the same risks as in healthcare and social services settings—child brokers were more likely to be ignored or overlooked than the more demanding students. Feeling distant from teachers made them even less likely to volunteer concerns or to admit when they needed assistance. Stanton-Salazar (2001, 13) had similar findings with regard to Mexican-origin high school students; "while the most obviously disengaged students disrupt classes [or] skip them . . . most disengaged students behave well in school and generally attend class. Yet researchers suggest that beneath the surface, this silent majority experiences a lack of psychological investment in learning, a lack of intellectual mastery of the curriculum, and a nagging sense of disconnection, if not alienation, from the core social fabric of the institution."

Past experiences had taught longtime teachers that children of immigrants were particularly unlikely to voluntarily disclose information to them. These teachers had learned to ask them gently, and directly, if they felt something was going on. Children sometimes deflected these inquiries to protect family privacy. However, demonstrations of authentic caring from trusted teachers encouraged children to open up to them. Ms. Rosenfelt said:

> I know when a kid is overburdened or overwhelmed by having to take care of everything. See, teaching sixth grade is different than teaching seventh and eighth because I have them for blocks every day for two hours. . . . I get really close with them, so I know when something is wrong and I ask what is going on. . . . And with parents, they never show when things are hard. They never react. That's why I ask. I know that sometimes they just can't find other sources of support, that their kids are absent [from school] because they have no one else to help them. They are very grateful. They're really grateful that I show that I care. I've been doing this a long time. Even if I don't speak Spanish, kids are kids and parents are parents, and it's rough out there in this community.

Child brokers who were or had recently been Ms. Rosenfelt's students singled her out as exceptionally empathetic. She demonstrated authentic caring, and her long tenure in the community and school made her a particularly useful resource broker for students and their families. She also noted that child brokers who did not actively seek assistance had parents who exhibited the same behaviors, reflecting her nuanced understanding of parent-child communication patterns in these families. While Ms. Rosenfelt did not speak Spanish, her innovative pedagogical approaches (detailed later in this chapter) helped her to make meaningful connections to her students and their families. She drew on common experiences by saying that "kids are kids and parents are parents" to express how she fostered the reciprocal warmth that forms the foundation for authentic caring (see also Angela Valenzuela 1999, 61).

Other teachers and administrators at Tyler also emphasized commonalities to encourage closeness and trust with these students. Ms. Rhines, the ESL coordinator, drew on her own immigrant identity in interactions with students and parents. The identity work she did to connect her experience migrating from Barbados to these families' experiences was particularly important because she was an ESL coordinator who did not speak Spanish. She told me, "I speak love, honey, and that's the only language these kids need." Ms. Walker was a Teach for America teacher at Tyler who had grown up in Greater Crenshaw.[7] She is African American, but saw social class as her unifying identity with these students.

"Black or Latino, I understand these families. My mom worked graveyard shift, and she wasn't always able to make my parent-teacher conference night. I know these parents care about their children's education even though they can't come in for meetings. I understand it. I know how these parents struggle to make it."

Celeste Watkins-Hayes (2009) described how service providers invoke their social identities in performance of their professional responsibilities. She found that welfare providers drew on "their dual status as both community insiders and agents of the state to build relationships with clients and direct them toward these goals," describing this identity work as "racialized professionalism" (Watkins-Hayes 2009, 151–153). At Tyler, teachers like Ms. Rhines and Ms. Walker invoked nonracial social identities they shared with students and families to achieve these same aims.

I frequently witnessed racialized professionalism at Bellum, but it was visible only between African American teachers and students, since Latino teachers were conspicuous by their near-absence from both campuses.[8] Repeatedly referred to as the "last African American–majority school" in the district by teachers and administrators, Bellum had many more African American teachers and administrators than Tyler.[9] In the hallways, in meetings with parents, and in other campus activities, African American teachers connected with African American students by drawing implicitly or explicitly on their common racial identity.

In a parent conference, Ms. Wagner, an African American math teacher, chastised an under-performing student by saying, "Girl, can't you see you breakin' your daddy's heart?" to the nodding approval of her father. These familial forms of advice-giving were common forms of racialized professionalism; I heard administrators tell young men to curb their language by saying, "Wait 'til I tell your momma how you talk here" or "You treat that young woman with the respect an African queen deserves." African American students clearly understood these admonishments as demonstrations of authentic caring. I do not think these teachers and administrators at Bellum communicated differently with Latino students on purpose. However, a lack of common cultural (and sometimes linguistic) ground with Latino students meant African American teachers and administrators were more professional than familial in their interactions with Latino students.

Where Authentic and Aesthetic Caring Converge

Child brokers' feelings about school were clearly influenced by features of their school environments, including their perceptions of how invested their teachers were in them and their success. Since children's brokering responsibilities were what marked them as different from their classmates, occasions when teachers demonstrated that they knew about and valued children's brokering skills were opportunities for convergence between authentic and aesthetic caring.

Both campuses had minimal Spanish-speaking support for teachers, so it was common practice for teachers to enlist child brokers as informal helpers when new immigrant students arrived and were placed in their English-only classrooms.[10] Children's brokering capabilities became a valuable classroom resource in these cases. Enabling teachers to communicate with new classmates allowed child brokers to show aesthetic caring by facilitating new students' learning (and often their own in the process). And teachers who showed appreciation and respect for children's brokering capabilities demonstrated authentic caring. Mr. Todes, a white assistant principal at Tyler, said: "When I was still in the classroom, these kids were great helping each other out as classmates . . . you know, to show them [what to do]. They made a huge difference to those kids and to me as their teacher." Classroom brokering was a way for teachers to validate children's brokering skills and make these students feel more valued in the classroom. Graciela (age thirteen) described assisting teachers by saying, "I feel pretty proud that I can, you know, do that for them."

Not all teachers welcomed children's bilingual capabilities into their classrooms equally, and the conditions in which students demonstrated their brokering skills mattered a great deal. Victoria (age twelve) compared the reception her brokering abilities had received from two teachers:

> VICTORIA: For fifth period I have Ms. Painter; she doesn't know anything about Spanish and, like, if you correct her, she embarrasses you bad. . . . She embarrassed me once because I corrected her in class. She made me cry.
>
> VK: You corrected her in class or you corrected her in a meeting with your mom?
>
> VICTORIA: No, in class because she had said—she tried saying "stupid" in Spanish and she said "burro," like a donkey, and I put my hand up and told her: "It's not burro. It's burra." And she got mad at me and was like, "Who is asking you? You don't have to correct me like that." And I got mad, and I tried not to cry, [but] then I was. I was crying and everything, and then she grabbed me from the shoulder and said, "You know I'm just playing with you."
>
> VK: Are there other teachers who don't speak Spanish but are more appreciative when you help?
>
> VICTORIA: Mr. Marcus, he's my gym teacher and my homeroom teacher, he—when he needs help with Spanish, I say, . . . "It's okay. I'll translate." And he's always, like, "Thank you, Victoria," and I tell him he's welcome. Whatever he needs, he tells me and I just tell whatever he needs them to know, the parent or student or whatever.

What Victoria described were two very different receptions for her brokering abilities. While Ms. Painter viewed Victoria's correction as a challenge and disciplined her publicly, the same set of skills facilitated reciprocal exchange of goodwill with Mr. Marcus.

As Marjorie Orellana (2009, 79–94) noted, context matters a great deal for how behaviors are treated on campus; talking in class, for example, is viewed as participation in some instances and as interruption in others. The same is true of children's brokering abilities, as Victoria's experience clearly demonstrates. Ms. Painter interpreted Victoria's attempt to assist her as an impertinent interruption. By emphasizing her authority, backing down only when Victoria began to cry, Ms. Painter broke trust with Victoria and potentially with other students who witnessed the incident. On the other hand, by demonstrating appreciation for Victoria's assistance, Mr. Marcus conveyed that the skills she used at home were also valued on campus.

MATCHES AND MISMATCHES BETWEEN SCHOOL AND HOME

There were other ways in which alignments or misalignments between child brokers' home and school experiences could either facilitate their connections to schools or further distance them from campus activities, practices, and opportunities. Schools, like other US institutions, are imbued with cultural values, including expectations for how students and their families will interact with them (Heath 1983; Lareau 2003; Thorne 1993). These norms include active parental involvement in children's schooling, such as assisting with homework, encouraging children's enrollment in after-school programs, attending parent-teacher meetings, and participating in parent-teacher associations and other organizations. Vivian Louie (2012, 69–70) notes that "such practices, either based in schools or at least visible to them, represent the norms of middle-class families, and, historically speaking, of white middle-class families." For a number of reasons, these immigrant families developed collective strategies that often deviated from schools' standard prescriptions.

Teachers perceived immigrant parents as being minimally involved in their children's schooling, although most recognized that parents were constrained by work commitments, language, and their own limited educations. Parents were invested in their children's educations, but not necessarily in ways that were visible to teachers and administrators. Elder siblings were often very involved in their younger siblings' schooling, although these contributions were also not visible to school personnel unless brokers attended meetings on campus with their parents, or in their stead. Elder siblings' active involvement was a natural extension of their brokering responsibilities, as parents depended on their help when younger children's homework and school-related decisions exceeded parents' own capabilities. Furthermore, brokers' own experiences at earlier grade levels made them relatively expert resources for parents to consult about their siblings' school performance and activities. For these reasons, child brokers not only played large roles in their siblings' school successes and failures, but also were entrusted with making more independent decisions about their own schooling.

These patterns—parents' under-involvement, siblings' over-involvement, and children's independent decision-making, relative to US cultural norms—had potential to place these families at odds with the expectations of teachers and administrators at Greater Crenshaw schools.

Parents' Involvement in Student Learning

US schools' emphasis on parental involvement insinuates that family influence on learning flows only downward, from parents to children. However, these parents and children learned the school system together. Since child brokers were often the eldest child, their experiences were usually their families' first encounters with the US education system. The lessons parents and children learned together more often benefited younger siblings than child brokers themselves. Parents uniformly said that they were more involved, more informed, and more comfortable navigating the school system for their younger children than they had been for their elder.

Parents were most able to help with homework—a form of parental involvement that schools recognized and encouraged—when their children were in elementary grades. Most parents had less than an eighth-grade education and became less able to assist with homework as their children advanced through school, though curricular content they had learned with elder children helped them better guide their younger ones (Valdés 1996; Zarate 2007). Virginia was typical in this regard: "When [my daughter] was younger, I helped her a lot, but now she doesn't even ask me because she knows that I can't help. But yes, I help all that I can. . . . I help my son more with his homework [now]." Successive school years brought not only more advanced schoolwork, but changes in school environments. Parents found that local elementary schools had more Spanish-speaking teachers and resources than the middle or high schools, which also made it easier for them to interact with schools early on.

There were two circumstances in which parents were able to assist children with homework beyond their own levels of formal education, both of which reflected how scaffolding by parents and children encouraged mutual learning. When children had assignments related to Latin America, parents relayed information to their children in Spanish, providing homework assistance while taking advantage of teachable moments for language learning. For example, Hernando (age twelve) said, "It was Mexican History Month and I told [my mom] I wanted to do [my report] on Emilio Zapata. So she told me all about him and how he lived and everything. Then we rented a movie at the library, and we saw it, and I really liked it, and I wrote a report on it. Then I took a book out the library and drew a picture of him for, like, ten points extra credit."

Since such assignments were rare, math was the content area where parents could more consistently assist with homework. Milagro (age thirteen) said, "In math, most of the time I go to my dad. He's really good in math, and, like, numbers are numbers, so I don't have to explain too much." Besides being less language-dependent than other subjects, math gave Mexican-origin parents, in particular, a serendipitous advantage because the Mexican math curriculum is more advanced than that of the United States. A Mexican-origin parent with a sixth-grade education could generally understand his or her children's math homework for at least a year or two beyond the same grade in the United States (Zuñiga and Hamann 2006). Furthermore, a number of parents taught their children problem-solving strategies out of math textbooks from their own school days. When I expressed surprise at hearing that Mexican textbooks were being used by yet another family, Juana (age thirteen) shrugged and said, "I guess my dad just really loves math. He came here with what he could carry when he came, but he brought his textbook with."

Parent-child interactions around math content tended to be mutually positive experiences, in that parents enjoyed actively participating in their children's learning, and children enjoyed both the help and the confidence that being able to provide it engendered in their parents. As mentioned previously, child brokers overwhelmingly said math was their favorite subject and the one in which they usually received their highest grades. This was the one content area where parents could consistently provide the kinds of assistance valued by US schools, and these contributions were visible to teachers. A few teachers had initially been mystified when children used methods they had not taught in class to complete long division problems and solve algebra equations. Once they understood, most teachers rewarded a correct answer, regardless of how students had calculated it, as a way to reinforce that parents' participation was welcomed.[11]

But math excepted, parents had difficulty meeting schools' expectations for their direct involvement in and guidance of their children's school experiences. Language-based subjects were very difficult for parents, even if children translated the assignments for them. US history was the most unassailable of all because both the language of instruction and the content's cultural referents were unfamiliar to parents who had grown up elsewhere. Parents' abilities tracked with their children's strengths and weaknesses by subject area, showing that parents and children can encourage each other's learning when content is accessible enough to scaffold shared meanings. That child brokers generally performed well in math and poorly in history and (to a lesser degree) English reflected how valuable homework assistance from qualified adults could be. Children's difficulties with text-heavy subjects were also consistent with how challenging brokering tasks that required mastery of formal English were for many of them.

Many of parents' investments in their children's schooling were largely invisible to teachers. Parents tried to make sure their children were not being distracted from homework by siblings or media, that their handwriting was neat, and that their work looked complete. They also provided emotional support by encouraging their children to persevere and work hard. Many used their own experiences to explicitly enact the immigrant bargain; Marina said, "I tell my children, get an education so you don't have to work like a donkey, like I do," and Carmen told hers, "I work with my hands so that one day, you get to work with your head" (see also Holmes 2007). Parents made these admonishments to encourage their children and to remind them that their academic commitment was viewed as a demonstration of family loyalty.

These reminders of the immigrant bargain were not the only way that parents intertwined morality with education. Many parents perceived a mismatch between their moral values and those rewarded by US schools. Leslie Reese found that immigrant parents in Los Angeles distinguished between the education their children received in US schools and their own *educación* in Mexico. The latter term connotes not only academic knowledge, but also lessons in what it means to be a good person, such as showing respect for one's elders and maintaining close family ties (Reese 2001; see also Valdés 1996). Parents took teaching their children moral standards and appropriate behavior very seriously because, as Marita said, "Here [in the United States], children are handed out privileges and no rules." A number of parents criticized neighbors whose children "fell off the path," as Paula said, viewing wayward offspring as a sign that their parents lacked moral fortitude. Many parents felt they had to maintain their traditional values as a counterbalance to the American individualism they viewed as corrosive to family unity. Teaching these traditional values, combined with the forms of support they were able to provide for their children's formal schooling, was what parents felt they could do to make their children "successful" adults.

Siblings and Schooling Success

Since parents could offer their children limited educational guidance, one way they reinforced the value of family unity was having elder children help their younger siblings to navigate US schools. Vivian Louie (2012) noted that many children of immigrants who had successfully pursued higher education had elder siblings who had helped pave the way for them to do so. These siblings were role models and guides, having learned—sometimes through missteps that cost them opportunities for their own advancement, sometimes through their own successes—how the US school system worked.

Most child brokers were the eldest in their families and contributed heavily to their younger siblings' schooling. A few brokers had elder siblings whose experiences provided them with valuable advantages. These two family positions—being the guide or being the guided—offered important insights into inequalities that can exist and persist even among siblings raised in the same household.

Child brokers who were the eldest played extensive roles as tutors and teachers to younger siblings, neighbors, and family friends (see Orellana 2009, 56). They helped younger children with homework, read to them, and corrected their writing and speech. Graciela (age thirteen) had started talking with her four-year-old sister exclusively in English and coached her on sounding out letters when they read together; "I want her to be really prepared for pre-K, you know? It's really hard to start and not, like, know any English at all." Graciela was determined that her little sister be better prepared for school than she had been. These activities also coincided with what schools expected in terms of family preparation for youngsters' literacy development. In addition, Graciela helped her brothers with their homework and would help her mother check her younger brother's homework each night before bed.[12] When I asked her who helped her with her own homework, she shrugged and said, "I help myself." She did so by referring back to her books or by calling a classmate.

Many brokers who helped their younger siblings had no one readily available to help them with their own homework. While teaching others can enhance both participants' learning (Dorner, Orellana, and Li-Grining 2007, 458), the material that brokers covered with their siblings was often many grade levels below their own schoolwork. For brokers who, unlike Graciela, were not excelling in school themselves, assisting younger siblings diverted time and effort from their own homework. Aurora (age sixteen), who tutored so many neighborhood kids that one father had bought her a whiteboard for her "lessons," was struggling to pass some of her own classes. Her relative expertise made her a strong tutor for children in lower grades but was not enhancing her own schooling. Since teachers seldom knew how much time these students devoted to tutoring younger children, their own middling performances were often erroneously seen as a lack of aesthetic caring. Aurora's afternoon lessons also helped her develop organizational, presentational, and other valuable skills, but these developmental byproducts of brokering were seldom recognized in formal schooling contexts.[13]

Younger brokers were often the beneficiaries of their elder siblings' firsthand experiences with the school system. Milagro (age thirteen) was in her eighth-grade year at Tyler and zoned for an under-performing high school. She would not be going there, however, she said, "Because my sister is figuring it out, how to put me in Jackson High. She thinks it will be a good environment for me." Jackson High was in a wealthier Los Angeles neighborhood and well known for its specialized programs and quality teaching. Her sister had arranged with a cousin, who lived in the residential catchment area, for Milagro to list that address on her admission forms—an unofficial but common strategy for enrolling in the city's more sought-after schools. Her sister's efforts were not unique; Milagro's two best friends would not be attending the high school they were zoned for, either. She explained, "They have older sisters, and I think they're like my sister; they try to look for a better environment. And we all have different strengths—like, one is into art, the other is really good in math—so our sisters are helping us look for places that will help us get even stronger."

In assessing their younger siblings' needs and helping them access more advantageous high school environments, these three sisters assumed roles that traditionally fall to parents. They had been entrusted by their parents—who deemed them better equipped to do so—with navigating the complex district rules in their stead. Elder siblings' efforts therefore appeared independent, but they often involved parents' active counsel and direction. Juliana (age nineteen), Marina's eldest daughter, had just started her first year of university. Marina said, "Now she knows how it all works—the financial aid, the admissions, and everything. My little one [Aracely] doesn't find school so easy, but at least she'll have her sister to help her make it when it's her turn."[14] These family dynamics are important because they reflect potential for social mobility within a single immigrant generation.

Not all elder siblings could offer advantages like Milagro's sister or Marina's eldest daughter. When children were very close in age, they had less to leverage. They were also more likely to express sibling rivalries than collaboration. Victoria (age twelve) said her older sister Yessenia (age fourteen) would withhold homework help from her: "When I ask Yessenia for help because she's, like, the only brain in the family, she tells me, 'Did you ever help me with my homework when I was in the sixth grade?' and I'm like, 'No, I was in the fourth grade when you were in the sixth grade.' 'So, you didn't help,' she'll say. So I just try solving it. I try remembering. I close my eyes and I'm like, what is this about? If I don't remember, sometimes I call my friends to see if they know."

The other sibling inequality that featured prominently in these families' stories revealed more profound differences in what brothers and sisters could hope to accomplish in the United States. At least one elder sibling in many families had migrated in early childhood and therefore did not enjoy the security and benefits of legal US residency that younger siblings did (Menjívar and Abrégo 2009). These inequalities could affect sibling relationships in many ways, including their growing awareness as they progressed through school that college and its promises for social mobility were closed to them, even as they were open to younger children in the family (Abrégo and Gonzales 2010; Gonzales 2011). As a parent to one of these mixed-status families, Marita wanted her younger, US-born children to pursue higher education because "they're not incapacitated like their brothers and sister" by their legal status. In some ways, US-born siblings in these families had the burden of fulfilling the immigrant bargain twice—to redeem not only the sacrifices of their parents, but also those of the elder siblings who helped them succeed while having to live in the shadows themselves.

Were Brokers Really on Their Own?

Elder siblings often helped compensate for parents' limitations by guiding younger children's educational trajectories, but few had similar guidance for their own decisions. Vivian Louie (2012, 85) argued that children were essentially on their own to determine their educational pathways, such that "the inherent authority relationship between parent and child was inverted with migration." However, children's taking the lead did not necessarily mean that family structures were inverted or otherwise disrupted. In much the same way that kids took the lead in brokering media content if they were more familiar with the device than their parents, children's greater familiarity with school environments meant parents often trusted their initiative in these contexts.[15] Orellana (2009) noted that even in non-immigrant households, such as those headed by single parents or where there are large numbers of children, elder children being granted early responsibility for younger siblings or themselves can be a normalized strategy that does not invert family roles. Orellana (2009, 11) found that as long as children feel supported, early allocations of responsibility can signal trust in and recognition of children's competence (see also Domínguez 2011, 38).

The kinds of support that children needed were dependent on the decisions they had to make. Some child brokers dealt with routine educational challenges, such as a poor grade on an exam or difficulty mastering a particular topic, head-on. More often, they avoided handling these issues. As discussed previously, school environments and family responsibilities made it difficult for these children to develop trusting relationships with teachers that would have encouraged them to seek help when they were having difficulties. Troublingly, children who did not ask teachers for help were also unlikely to reveal their struggles to their parents; prior research had similarly shown that low-achieving Latino adolescents talked less and less with their parents and became increasingly disconnected from their schooling (Weisner et al. 2001).

Julio (age seventeen) was failing two classes and in danger of failing a third. He told his family very little; his parents often only became aware of problems when administrators called because he was on the verge of another suspension for fighting. He also felt alienated from his teachers; if he approached them for help, he said, "[They] will think I'm even dumber." Julio became increasingly disconnected, left to make his own decisions without adequate support from either home or school to encourage his feeling competent to do so. Having observed his parents' avoidant behaviors with regard to their own community connections, Julio was in an inert state, seemingly waiting for an adult to notice that he was in distress, but unable to actively seek out assistance.

Vivian Louie (2012, 103) found that young adults who had attended better-resourced schools with well-supported teachers were more likely to have had educators with time and energy to fully invest in them. In Greater Crenshaw, teachers did not enjoy such institutional support, so it usually fell to children to advocate for themselves to teachers or other school personnel when they needed help. Making demands of adults was a formidable prospect to many of these children. Those who were doing well in school were more likely to approach teachers and proactively resolve minor difficulties with schoolwork before they become major problems. These children were often directly encouraged to take these actions by their parents, who were generally more engaged with their schooling than parents whose students were struggling. Higher achievers generally knew where to find help and how to ask for it; they were also certainly made braver by their parents' support for these efforts.

Still, supporting children in resolving educational challenges was easier for parents than helping them identify educational opportunities. Parents largely left the latter to their children, reasoning that they would be alerted by their children if and when their assistance was needed. Talking with Juana (age thirteen) elicited one limitation of this strategy. She was earning straight A's and had been offered admission to the gifted magnet program within her middle school. The problem, she told me, was that going to the magnet program would track her to a different (and superior quality) high school from the one her friends would attend. It became clear in our conversation that Juana intended to opt out of the considerable opportunities the magnet track offered so that she could remain with her friends.

Children like Juana who navigated their educational trajectories with limited parental intervention revealed just how little their parents knew about the opportunities that US schools could offer students. Juana could easily present her choice to her parents in a way that downplayed the benefits of the magnet track and minimized their resistance to her decision. Whereas parents more familiar with the system would probably counter their daughter's adolescent desires to prioritize her friends over her long-term interests, Juana's parents were not familiar enough with the school system to be able to make such assessments.

Children's control over aspects of their own and sometimes their siblings' educations should be placed in larger context. Their brokering responsibilities already reflected that these parents expected their children to take responsibility for themselves earlier than other parents did (Buriel 1993). When parents could support their children's efforts as needed, their early independence did not necessarily carry undue risk. Parents were often successful in supporting their children's efforts to resolve their educational difficulties in proactive, timely ways. Their strategies were more limited when it came to educational opportunities. Without elder children who might familiarize themselves with opportunities such as magnet programs, families were heavily dependent on teachers and administrators who took the initiative to alert them to these avenues for social mobility. The final section of this chapter details parents' direct experiences with their children's schools and how children brokered these interactions.

PARENTS ON CAMPUS

Children's brokering in schools generally resulted in less vivid memories and less strong emotions than brokering in other local institutions—healthcare settings in particular. Juana (age thirteen) said, "It's different because I know the people at school, and I kinda know what they're going to say [in the meetings]." Brokering in schools was usually less challenging because children were familiar with school environments and personnel. Meetings also tended to follow a predictable format. While some vocabulary and concepts were challenging, children generally felt they could convey most information accurately. Children could also build on their own school experiences when they brokered meetings about younger siblings. In many cases, they had gone to the same schools; some had even had the same teachers.

Trips to campus were generally less comfortable experiences for parents. Even at better-resourced schools like Tyler, parents reported trouble locating Spanish-speaking adults. Beyond their language constraints, many parents felt undermined by their limited formal education and unfamiliarity with the US school system when they talked with teachers (see Valdés 1996). These feelings deepened as their children progressed through middle and high schools, surpassing most parents' own levels of formal education. Some parents applied their home country norms about schooling and did not attend meetings with teachers unless a child was in trouble. Interactions for lesser reasons ran counter to their perceptions of teachers' and parents' realms of responsibility.

However, what parents considered respectful distance could be viewed by teachers as non-involvement or disinterest. Ms. Watkins recalled learning how immigrant parents' views on their roles could contrast with her own: "When I first got here, I remember one parent telling me, 'You know, where I come from, we esteem the teacher very highly, and their word is true when it comes to us. If the teacher says, "A," we believe "A," and, you know, if they say, "B," we believe "B." So, teaching is your job. My job is to parent.' And, you know, I totally respected that. It totally opened up my eyes."

In the same way that teachers could amend their perceptions of parents' motivations and behaviors over time, some parents learned that regular interactions with teachers in the United States reaped rewards for their children. In some cases, parents had been prompted to these actions by their children; for others, influential interactions with elementary school teachers had paved the way for their continued involvement in subsequent grades. Parents who had been in the United States since adolescence were more likely to have adopted schools' expectations for involved parenting, as compared with parents who had arrived later. Carlos fit this pattern, having migrated to the United States as a teenager. He walked his five-year-old son into his classroom each morning to greet his teacher. He often did the same with Liliana (age sixteen), much to her adolescent dismay.

Parents who had completed high school or attended college in their country of origin were the most likely to make regular visits to campus. Gabriela, a college-educated mother from Oaxaca, Mexico, had been in the United States for nine months. She went to her daughter's middle school weekly and her son's elementary school almost daily to check on his progress in an English-only class-room. She actively supported and modeled language learning at home: "We have a competition every day to see who can learn the most new words and teach us all how to use them." Her knowledge of formal education systems was also evident from her having sent the children's school records with her husband (who came to Los Angeles ahead of the rest of the family) so that he could locate the best schools in the area and have them enrolled prior to their arrival. Gabriela felt her education and professional experience were resources that could provide lever-age for her children in their new schools, compensating for her limited English proficiency and current occupation as a janitor.[16] Gabriela said, "My boss says he doesn't think of me as a janitor. It's not how I think of myself either."

Research on children's educational outcomes generally accounts for par-ents' occupational status in the United States, but not in the country of origin (V. Louie 2012, 81). Many teachers, however, recognized the impact that parents' pre-migration educational and occupational experiences had on their interac-tions with their children's US schools. Ms. Rhines, Tyler's ESL coordinator, said that the immigrant parents she saw all wanted their children to "do better than they did. But, for some, 'better' means just getting more years of school than their parents. So, if you leave school in tenth grade and your parents only went to fifth, that's better. For others, it's everything the US can offer, the best out there. I don't know if those parents are always, *always* the educated ones in the countries where they came from, but they know what the goal is right when they get here, that's for sure" (her emphasis). Ms. Hernandez, the ESL coordinator at Bellum, made similar observations: "The most active parents, the ones who come to our [bilin-gual parent group] meetings, are usually mothers. The one leader, I remember that she was educated. She was a teacher in Mexico. So I think she knows how important it is to be involved, and she is not scared to come into a school even if she doesn't speak English."

Teachers' observations revealed considerable diversity among a popula-tion of low-income, immigrant Latino parents often presumed to be homo-geneous. Parents who had pursued higher education and held professional occupations prior to migration were more likely to demonstrate the forms of parental involvement that were recognized and valued by teachers and admin-istrators. Among parents with more limited education and nonprofessional backgrounds, age at migration seemed to matter; parents who arrived earlier were more likely to have adapted to US schools' expectations than those who had arrived later. Even for parents with these relative advantages, interacting with school personnel was not easy; these experiences required a great deal of courage, as well as assistance from their children.

Motivations for Campus Visits

Parents' trips to campus were generally prompted by some form of communication from the schools, whether by phone call, newsletter, or other print materials sent home with children. Some schools had automated calling systems that informed parents if their child had been absent, had been late to class, had incomplete homework, or had otherwise misbehaved. While parents appreciated any form of outreach, particularly in Spanish, some felt that these messages should tell parents what they were expected to do with the information. "Do I need to call the teacher? See the teacher? Just say thank you to the machine? I never know, and usually my daughter will have to explain to me," said Ruth. While these systems provided parents with some information, they facilitated rather passive, limited forms of communication.

Parents' visits could be prompted by a phone call from the classroom. When child brokers ran afoul of class rules, teachers often had them call their parents to inform them of their own misdeeds during recess. This approach had double utility from a teacher's perspective: these calls made the children directly accountable for their behavior, while also resolving the language barrier that prevented teachers from calling parents themselves. Ms. Rhodes was one of the teachers who used this strategy: "If it's just something small in class, like you were talking too much, I will have them call their parents and explain. . . . I'll say, you know, 'Hello,' and I'll ask, you know, '*Habla español?*' . . . and I'll say, 'Okay. *Un momento.*' I give the phone to the kid, and I say: 'Okay, you need to tell your mom that you're talking too much in class and didn't do your work.' I can understand enough to know if they said it or not. I mean, if it was really serious, I could try [to] find an adult to do it."

Given that Ms. Rhodes's primary alternative (since few adults at Bellum spoke Spanish) was the automated phone system, having children call home at least allowed parents to interact with teachers through their children. This approach was more likely to result in a shared understanding of what the child had done and what teachers expected parents to do about it. Furthermore, since parents expected child brokers to take early responsibility for themselves (Buriel 1993; Buriel and de Ment 1998), they usually felt that their children being directly accountable for their behavior was appropriate. It is worth noting, however, that other students were not held to this standard. If a child with English-speaking parents misbehaved, teachers called their parents directly. Children's brokering skills, coupled with schools' limited linguistic assistance to teachers, meant their missteps were treated differently from those of their classmates.

School newsletters and other print material sent home in children's backpacks also prompted parents' campus visits. Aurora (age sixteen) noted that although the newsletters she brought home were bilingual, "information about what's going on in school is mostly in English. And then stuff, like, that we're getting out early this day, or there's not going to be school this day, is in Spanish [and English]. And report cards are just in English too." There were discrepancies between reports from administrators and parents on this issue; Ms. Nelson, an African American assistant principal at Bellum, insisted that all materials were sent home in both languages. Parents and children said otherwise, and I saw examples that reflected Aurora's observations—English-only materials generally contained more technical information, news, and opportunities than bilingual missives did.

I am not implying that schools intentionally limited Spanish-speaking families' access to valuable news and resources. Rather, schools' shortages of fluently bilingual staff made it difficult to translate everything that had to be sent home to parents. Information and news that required contextualization for immigrant parents rather than direct translation were usually only available in English. Ms. Hernandez said, "It's really hard to break all that information down [in Spanish], and even if, like, they send memos out . . . most parents who read it probably think, 'I don't understand.'"

In short, phone calls and print media from school were intended to keep parents informed or bring them to campus. However, because of institutional limitations and inadequate accommodations for non-English speakers, child brokers' families often had less access to these news sources and opportunities than children from native-born families. Furthermore, addressing these limitations often fell to children, who had to broker print materials from schools that arrived in English or decontextualized Spanish—even though these documents had often come home in English precisely because they contained complicated information. In the case of phone calls about their performance, children were often effectively conscripted into brokering by their teachers, who had little access to Spanish-speaking adults who could assist them. With these phone calls, and to a lesser degree with the automated calling systems, children were doubly positioned in that they were both the subject of the message and the medium through which these messages were transmitted (Orellana 2009). These complex roles were even more apparent when children brokered face-to-face interactions between parents and school personnel.

Children in Parent-Teacher Meetings

Children usually participated in parent-teacher conferences either as the focus of the meeting or as the elder sibling, cousin, or neighbor of the child in question. The expectation that children of immigrants had the language capabilities to broker parent-teacher interactions was so normalized that when Marita recently attended a meeting with her son Isaac (but without her primary broker, Victoria), his teacher was visibly surprised to find that Isaac did not speak enough Spanish to broker for them. Marita said, "All [the teacher] could say was, 'Now what? Both of us don't speak Spanish. What are we going to do?'"

Orellana (2009, 79) described child brokers as being "multiply positioned" in these meetings, in that they were both the reason for the meeting and the means by which adults in that meeting communicated with each other. A number of teachers espoused student-centered approaches to learning that emphasized children's leadership in their own learning and stressed accountability for their own behavior. Teachers who engaged these approaches were most likely to view children's brokering as a natural extension of the participation levels they expected from all students during parent meetings. For example, Ms. Rosenfelt had been a pioneer for student-centered parent conferences at Tyler; an assistant principal noted that other teachers had followed her example with considerable success. While Ms. Rosenfelt used this approach for all her students, it worked particularly well for brokers and their families; she said:

> Basically, the kid runs the conference. They sit with their work. They explain to the parent why they got this certain grade. . . . I really do like the kids to accept responsibility for what good things they've done and for the bad things they've done. For the parents to understand what the kid is doing, for the kid to understand why he is getting a D, and for the parents to understand why he is getting a C and not an A. It's ownership, for the kid and for their parent. The kid translates so I can talk to their parent. . . . They don't edit. I can tell. I do have that—certain words I am listening for.

Though much is made of children's potential to mislead or lie to either adult when brokering school meetings, teachers and parents generally felt that children acquitted their brokering responsibilities honestly, even though they occasionally needed some prompting to provide all possible details. Ms. Hernandez said, "They don't lie, no . . . but they might be reticent to say something. So the parent might prod, and so you might hear them add something; but they—I haven't heard them twist anything. Like, they say, 'I have detention.' And [the parent asks], 'Why do you have detention?' And then you hear a silence, and 'Because I didn't do my work in class.'"

Overall, I found that children were more likely to downplay their successes than their failures.[17] Graciela (age thirteen) said it was easier for her to translate criticism (such as talking too much in class) than praise. If a teacher was too effusive, she said, "Sometimes [my mom] won't believe me, or she'll get mad—you never know the reaction." Praise forced children to make what Orellana (2009, 82) called "transcultural moves," evaluating the expectations of both adults and making appropriate cultural adjustments to messages. If teachers described students' accomplishments in glowing terms, children knew that their parents would think it inappropriate for a child to talk that way. Children therefore downplayed their teachers' words to align with parents' expectations of appropriate self-presentation. Juana (age thirteen) even couched her explanation of this practice in self-minimizing language to me, to ensure her presentation of self was appropriate. She said, "Sometimes I get nervous, 'cuz I don't know if [the teacher is going to say] something good or bad, or if I'm gonna get in trouble. Sometimes my teacher can tell I'm nervous and she'll say, 'Don't be nervous; you're doing fine; you're, like, the best one in the class.'"

Many child brokers appeared to have more experience relaying teacher criticism than compliments. Alicia (age twelve) said that she felt "ashamed" when she had to tell her mom she was not doing well or had not completed assignments. When I asked her if she was ever tempted to soften her teacher's message so that her mother would be less angry with her, she looked at me wide-eyed and shook her head vigorously. "Even if I wanted to . . . she'd know. And I'd get in so much more trouble if she started thinking I, like, lied [to her]." Others made similar reports; parents may not have been comfortable speaking English, but many knew enough to follow the gist of teachers' messages. All parents actively followed nonverbal signals like tone, body positioning, and facial expressions, so they did not rely entirely on their children to understand the proceedings. Teresa (age fifteen) giggled and said, "Sometimes it's so tempting to change what the teacher says [to my mother], but she—she would figure out the truth in, like, a minute."

Teachers and parents generally felt that they could monitor children's brokering via nonverbal cues or a few familiar words in the other language. Most teachers spoke positively about their interactions with Latino parents, despite the language challenges. Many teachers associated these parents with familiar tropes about Latino immigrants' stable families, collectivist orientations, and work ethic. While these tropes were romanticized generalizations, they did align with school values. Teachers also noted that immigrant parents, like their children, were more likely to take responsibility for their child's poor performance than to blame the teacher. Ms. Rhodes said:

> We sit around the table, because I don't want them to feel like [I'm superior], because I think Latino culture already does that. They already put teachers up [on a pedestal], which I appreciate, because the parents look at their kid and say, "What are you doing?" You know, they don't look at the teacher and say, "Why are you screwing up?" I have never really had an interaction where I felt like communication didn't happen, and the kids are usually very appropriate in that situation. They know that they've got two people looking at them, and they have to do what's appropriate. I think the parents tend to know enough of what I am saying, and I know enough of what they are saying.

While children brokered school meetings with their own teachers most often, many also accompanied their parents to meetings for their younger siblings. Some also went to broker meetings with other relatives, parents' friends, or neighbors who had younger children. Here, as with their own meetings, brokers felt bound to relay meanings accurately, though they were less conflicted about relaying criticism and praise that was not directed at them. Most younger children understood that elder brokers had to be honest, though Teresa (age fifteen) said, "Sometimes my cousin gets so mad at me; he says, 'Why'd you have to do me like that? I got in so much trouble 'cuz of you.' But I just tell him, 'If you didn't do stupid things, then the teacher wouldn't have nothing bad to say about you.'" Teachers who did not subscribe to student-centered approaches sometimes preferred to have an older sibling broker their interactions with parents. Their command of both languages was likely to be more sophisticated, and these teachers felt that siblings would relay information more objectively.

None of the children in these families routinely went to meetings with teachers in place of their parents, though teachers reported that as a fairly common practice. Mr. Todes, an assistant principal at Tyler, discussed his prior experiences as a classroom teacher: "A lot of the older siblings were really good, and they took, I think, education maybe a little more seriously [than their younger siblings]. . . . Many parents were working three jobs and were tired and they didn't know what to do with their kid, but they were very supportive of me and the school and everything I was trying to do. So talking with the older brothers and sisters helped; it never steered me wrong."

Children brokering in school meetings was generally viewed positively by teachers and seldom presented direct challenges to their professional identities. Since teachers had sustained daily contact with children at a particular developmental stage, they held fewer assumptions about children's capabilities than healthcare and social services providers who were obliged to accept children's help to communicate with parents. Furthermore, the popularity of student-centered learning approaches meant many teachers' professional identities were actually enhanced by children taking active roles in meetings with their parents.

Some teachers also successfully deployed the professional skills they used in the classroom to communicate more effectively with immigrant parents. Ms. Walker said, "I make sure I look the parent in the eye when they talk. Just because they don't understand English, it doesn't mean that I am not regarding them as the authority figure." This practice contrasted sharply with many healthcare providers, who often effectively removed parents from interactions by only addressing children once they began to broker.[18] Ms. Walker's techniques for teaching English to non-native speakers were useful in parent meetings as well: "I like speaking to [parents] in person, because as an ESL teacher I have learned to be extremely animated and act everything out that I do. So when they come in, it is so much better [than speaking on the phone] because I can act out how their kid acted in class, or I can show them the work. I can definitely show them the numbers because numbers are, you know, multilingual, and that they clearly understand."

While brokering in parent-teacher meetings rarely challenged teachers' professional identities, few teachers connected children's brokering abilities with the limited aesthetic caring many of them appeared to demonstrate through incomplete homework, fatigue in class, and frequent absences. Neither children nor parents were likely to tell teachers otherwise, and teachers seldom asked. Teachers did not make these connections in part because, although they found children's brokering helpful, they viewed these skill sets as largely extraneous to the requirements of the formal curriculum.

Brokering an Education?

In contrast to prior research, I found that children who were performing well in school seemed to do so in spite of their brokering responsibilities, not because of them.[19] This apparent contradiction is explained by differences in focus and methodology. Research claiming a positive relationship has focused squarely on how brokering affects children's educational outcomes. Considering children's school-related activities in context of what they do at home and in other community sites revealed that family responsibilities spread children's time and energies thin. Any educational gains they may make as a result of having to broker are therefore still sub-optimal. In addition, prior studies have often depended in whole or part on surveys completed in school, wherein the child is the individual unit of analysis (and data are self-reported).[20] These measures cannot account for the interactive nature of brokering activities or for intra-family variation, including differences among siblings that findings in this chapter suggest are critical to understanding school performance.

These tendencies toward a school-based focus and to a particular set of methods have made it difficult for researchers to differentiate between skills students may acquire and hone by brokering at home and in the community, on the one hand, and how these skills or activities are received by schools, on the other. Brokering activities can help children develop important skills with relation to reasoning, problem-solving, public speaking, and so on. These skills are valued by schools—when they are developed through the formal curriculum. Because teachers at Bellum and Tyler knew so little about what child brokers did for their families, their informal gains were seldom recognized at school.

Furthermore, while teachers appreciated children's brokering between them and new students or parents, they viewed these activities as largely extraneous to materials that students were expected to master to be successfully promoted to the next grade. Children brokering in the classroom or after school could therefore further strain their already limited time to focus on their own learning. The skills that successful brokering could build did not always manifest in forms that demonstrated the aesthetic caring recognized as "success" in standardized evaluations of their school performance.

These contextual factors are critical to understanding how children's brokering efforts in the short term affect their long-term development and opportunities for success. Vivian Louie (2012) found that being able to win the immigrant bargain required agency at the individual and family levels, bolstered by support beyond the family, particularly from adults related to schools. These three dimensions mirror the three levels of family systems theory—that is, individual, family system, and intersystem levels—described in earlier chapters.

At the individual level, children's brokering in schools was different from their brokering in other community sites because the skills they developed in and through these settings—in terms of increased literacy, learning strategies, and so on—directly influenced the quality of their brokering in every other setting where they engaged these skills. Furthermore, brokering at school was different because of how much time they spent with teachers independent of occasions when they acted as brokers, which was not the case in healthcare facilities and social services. Children could therefore draw on more multidimensional relationships with their teachers and schools when they brokered interactions. In optimal cases, exchanges of aesthetic and authentic caring with teachers could support children's brokering efforts and their intellectual development. When their daily experiences with teachers were a mismatch of aesthetic and authentic caring, interactions they brokered between parents and teachers were similarly strained.

At the family level, parent-child scaffolding around school content was limited mainly to their joint engagement with math homework and content. The positive outcomes families reported related to math—higher grades; more positive affect from parents, children, and teachers alike; and greater mastery of the material—demonstrated how powerful parent-child scaffolding was for their mutual learning. Beyond scaffolding, parents' modeling and encouragement could help children manage everyday crises but was less helpful for identifying educational opportunities, since parents were unlikely to know what options were available. As a result of these constraints, family-level strategies often involved parents depending on children to make or heavily inform education-related decisions for themselves and their younger siblings. Brokers' involvement in their siblings' schooling demonstrated the value of accounting for intra-generational differences in educational outcomes, because brokers' familiarity with the school system often benefited their younger siblings more so than to themselves.

Brokers who enjoyed access to school-related opportunities tended to be those who had encountered adult supports beyond their family systems. Access to enrichment programs, magnet schools, and other educational options was usually enabled by a particular teacher or administrator who had demonstrated enough authentic caring to become familiar with that student's circumstances. These educators were therefore more motivated to assist students by acting as resource brokers when opportunities arose. These occasions were rare and were constrained by under-resourced school environments in unsafe neighborhoods and by child brokers having more absences and attending less after-school programs—programs that would have given them additional time with teachers. Schools also communicated differently with these families. Limited language resources made these students responsible for negotiating phone calls and newsletters for their parents that were often difficult to understand.

At each level—as individuals, within their family systems, and with regard to extra-family support at school—children faced constraints on their educational advancement that were directly related to their brokering responsibilities. These constraints often resulted from the responsibilities that children assumed with relation to their parents, as well as younger siblings, cousins, and neighbors, in order to win the immigrant bargain in the short term. Their difficulties in making meaningful connections to their schools, their teachers, and their schoolwork constrained their chances of winning the immigrant bargain in the long term. The implications of these findings are discussed in greater detail in the final chapter of the book, which also provides suggestions for interventions at various levels to address these concerns.

⅌

CHAPTER 7

BROKERING AND ITS CONSEQUENCES

The preceding chapters document how children's brokering influenced their families' interactions across community locations, as well as the individual and collective activities that enabled and constrained their efforts. By considering what children do across multiple sites, it was possible to assess what strategies were successful in which settings and how interactions with service providers in particular institutions affected what child brokers could (and could not) help their families accomplish. Children's brokering is an important dimension to how we understand two issues of great concern to a range of stakeholders: namely, immigrants' interactions with US social institutions, and the social trajectories of immigrants' children, because family responsibilities also have consequences for their independent choices and opportunities.

Considering immigrants' community interactions as a family project—not as something one generation does for the benefit of another, but as a collective project to which all members can make real contributions—gets us closer to understanding the complex and creative ways that families manage challenges related to migration and settlement. To varying degrees, parents and children honed their skills and strategies, learning from each other and from their local interactions over time. They made each other braver, and courage was surely needed to face the considerable difficulties they experienced making local connections to improve their current circumstances and enhance their future options. The preceding chapters demonstrate just how critical local institutions and the professionals who represented them were to determining whether children's and families' efforts and strategies ultimately bore fruit.

A family systems approach to analyzing families' experiences accounts for what the family can do as a unit, but also demonstrates how individual members' experiences may differ. Children and parents all contributed to their families' local interactions, but not always equally and not necessarily in the same ways.

Child brokers often communicated differently with their mothers and fathers, and siblings' contributions to collective strategies also varied. Elder siblings often played different roles and shouldered additional responsibilities for family functioning. These differences were most visible in the heavy investments that many made in their younger siblings' connections to and success in school.

Children's family responsibilities also influenced their own development and access to opportunities. Brokering was a way for children to honor the immigrant bargain and redeem their parents' migration sacrifices through their achievements in the adopted country—at least, in the short term. The everyday ways that children put their families' needs first helped them survive and develop innovative, collective strategies for scaffolding meaning and making decisions. Children's relatively greater fluency in English, familiarity with US cultural norms, and facility with communication technologies were crucial to these efforts; and engaging these skills powerfully demonstrated children's commitment to their families' wellbeing.

Brokering activities helped address family problems in the short term but could hamper children's chances of realizing the immigrant bargain in the long term. Children's family responsibilities affected their relationships with their schools and often reduced their chances to build meaningful relationships with educators who could help them secure a wider range of educational opportunities. The time and energy that children put into brokering often displaced time and energy to spend on schoolwork. The result was a catch-22 for children: brokering pulled them away from their schooling, and schools' resources were exactly what they required to broker more effectively and efficiently for their families as they got older. This tension between short- and long-term gains has implications for these children, their families, communities, and US society as a whole.

UNINTENDED CONSEQUENCES AND UNANTICIPATED GAINS

Conscious choices yielded both intended and unintended outcomes for many of these families, echoing others' recent findings on immigrants' experiences in the United States. Richard Alba and Victor Nee (2005, 41) theorized how immigrants' desires for a better life can have "unintended consequences" for their families; a decision to move to the suburbs, for example, can have the unintended consequence of US-born children being less likely to retain their parents' language than if they had remained in ethnic enclaves. Likewise, Mario Small (2010) described how connecting with well-resourced childcare institutions could yield "unanticipated gains" for parents who were initially motivated by achieving narrow, specific goals. In both of these cases, immigrants' strategic decisions—moving to the suburbs or choosing reliable childcare—spawned consequences beyond those they had initially foreseen or predicted.

The same was true for many decisions that these families made. Most were motivated to make community connections that could address immediate family needs. Their focus on the here and now partly reflected the particular stages of settlement these families were experiencing when I met them. Though most parents were not recent arrivals to the United States or Greater Crenshaw, most found themselves feeling "new" as their eldest children entered developmental phases that required familiarizing themselves with new schools, teachers, service providers, doctors, and local opportunities, goods, and services.

Whether families' community connections were strategic or serendipitous, unanticipated gains could result from their increased familiarity and comfort with the local area. If families were lucky, their connections yielded resource brokering by providers who were personally motivated or institutionally mandated to do so. Over time, many families' accumulated community experiences began to foster a sense of local belonging. Their community integration was, to some degree, an unintended consequence of doing the everyday things they deemed necessary to address family needs.

While families could experience unanticipated gains, there was also the possibility of unanticipated losses. Families' likelihood of securing needed resources depended a great deal on the local institutions they encountered and the interactions they had there with native-born residents and service providers. Douglas Massey and Magaly Sánchez (2010) argued that these local, interpersonal interactions are where immigrants negotiate (and often challenge) how they have been categorized by the native-born. Social integration, from this perspective, depends on how effectively immigrants broker the social boundaries that separate them from the native-born.[1]

Massey and Sánchez focused on how adult immigrants engage in these negotiations, but brokering efforts by children become many times more complicated. Child brokers who were perceived as acting independently of their parents evoked complex reactions from providers, whose expectations of appropriate childhood behaviors were challenged by these encounters. Since service providers were generally gatekeepers to institutional resources, families' access to opportunities depended a great deal on how professionals felt about having to communicate through children. While providers were committed to serving local families, their discomfort with children speaking for adults, about topics many deemed inappropriate, often constrained children's capabilities to act as intermediaries in these encounters. When these families were treated differently from other residents because their strategies depended on children's brokering capabilities, they risked suffering unanticipated losses. Furthermore, since these families often depended on service providers to alert them to opportunities and resources they did not know were available, they were vulnerable to additional disadvantages compared with residents who knew what to ask for. If families never learned of open-enrollment periods at better-resourced schools, applications for no-cost health insurance, or poverty alleviation benefits, then their limited awareness could lead to additional unanticipated losses.

The anticipated and unanticipated outcomes of these families' actions reflect the inherent tensions between structure and agency. To varying degrees, children and families demonstrated their desires to act on their environments. Many developed creative strategies to overcome disadvantages such as limitations on parental education, English language proficiency, income, and residency status, pooling their skill sets and working together to learn and interact meaningfully with their community and its institutions. They did so against considerable odds. They encountered social conditions in Greater Crenshaw that often compounded their difficulties in making meaningful connections; for example, violence and crime both on and off campus was one of many layers of structure that constrained teachers' and students' daily interactions with each other. The communication strategies that worked well for parents and children at home were therefore often sorely tested in local institutional structures that provided limited time or opportunity for families to optimally enact them.

Institutional Responsiveness to Community Change

Alba and Nee (2005) argued that immigrant-receiving societies are changed as much by newcomers as are immigrants themselves. These changes are evident at national and state levels, but even more immediately at local ones. As neighborhoods change, so too do the effects those neighborhoods have on the people who live and work in them (Domínguez 2011; Sampson 2012). Greater Crenshaw had experienced a considerable demographic shift in a short amount of time, stressing providers and resources already stretched thin to now serve a more culturally and linguistically diverse population.[2] The struggles that professionals faced in Greater Crenshaw will sound familiar to anyone who has worked in or conducted research on institutions in urban areas, which are so often oversubscribed and under-resourced. Even the area's relatively better equipped schools, healthcare facilities, and social services did not have the human and material resources to handle the challenges that demographic change had brought through their doors.

It would be impractical to suggest that large infusions of money would resolve all the challenges that families and providers experienced, particularly because the current economic climate is more likely to result in further funding reductions. Funding alone would also not resolve the challenges that families and providers faced as they tried to communicate with each other. My findings do identify points of intervention to improve families' encounters with local institutions, as well as the professional experiences of providers who work with them. Since Greater Crenshaw resembles low-income, increasingly diverse communities in other US urban centers, these suggestions should be instructive for creating change in similar locations as well.

Respecting the Family in Institutional Encounters

Child brokers and their families unintentionally posed challenges to local institutions already struggling to respond to community changes. Immigrant parents with limited English proficiency required assistance to communicate in these environments, as well as additional explanations to complete necessary paperwork and frequent checks for their comprehension of instructions. With the notable exception of Women, Infants and Children (WIC), the schools, healthcare facilities, and social services in Greater Crenshaw offered fewer language accommodations than their clientele required. Spanish-speaking staff hired as dedicated translators were rare and generally spread too thin to fully address the levels of need. The more common practice was to pull bilingual support staff into consultations on an ad hoc basis. Most parents found this practice discomfiting and undesirable, as they (often accurately) intuited that these staff members did not appreciate extra tasks being added to their workday without increased consideration or compensation. Parents preferred to bring their children to broker these interactions instead.

Parents' preference for their children's assistance over rushed assistance from adults highlights where changes in institutional practice could help improve service provision. While ad hoc arrangements seemed like an appropriate band-aid solution in under-resourced institutions, the practice often widened the chasm between families and providers, adding to parental discomfort rather than alleviating it. While budgets are stretched (and, unfortunately, may become even more so), institutional leaders should take a harder look at how failing to allocate resources to language assistance may be eroding staff morale and failing to reduce patient anxiety. Furthermore, some institutions these families frequented had implemented prohibitions against having family members, and particularly children, translate in medical settings. Since these prohibitions were not accompanied by increased language accommodations, children continued to broker in these facilities anyway.

Prohibiting children's brokering may make sense from a litigation-minimizing perspective, but such moves break trust with families who are already tentative about interacting with formal institutions. These regulations also reflect embedded cultural assumptions about appropriate communication in healthcare contexts, which are generally framed as private discussions between providers and individual patients, rather than between providers and families. This embedded emphasis on individuality strains—and, in extreme cases, invalidates—the strategies that families develop to meet these interactions' challenges as a team.

While many reasonable arguments can be raised about the limitations of children having to broker complex information, until families are presented with better resources and more bilingual doctors, they will continue to depend on their most trusted resources. As long as these resources are their children, providers and institutional management should take reasonable steps to make children's brokering responsibilities less onerous, rather than inadvertently doing the reverse. Recognizing and respecting these families' collective strategies can build trust, encourage children to ask more questions, and otherwise enhance communication between families and providers.

Supporting Service Providers

From the perspective of individual healthcare and social services providers, children's brokering often posed direct challenges to their professional identities. The discomfort many felt when they had to communicate with parents through their children revealed their own assumptions about appropriate childhood activities. These assumptions need to be revisited in any effort to improve communication with child brokers and their families. Many healthcare providers felt a particularly pervasive sense of professional failure in these interactions, but those feelings should be recognized as resulting primarily from inadequate workplace support and training. When providers feel compelled to defend their professional identities from challenges that certain recipients seem to present, it is clear that institutions have to provide more support or risk the high rates of burnout and rapid staff turnover that were so common in Greater Crenshaw.

Institutional support for employees need not be extremely costly. Support could mean providing spaces for regular, honest conversation among providers about the professional challenges they are experiencing, developing formalized best practices to guide their interactions with child brokers and their families, and providing ongoing communication skill–building opportunities.

In Greater Crenshaw, providers' schedules included little time for meaningful interactions with colleagues when they could share experiences and challenges with each other. Formalizing regular meeting times for providers to have these discussions and elicit advice and support from each other could boost morale and facilitate developing new strategies for service provision going forward. These meetings would also be safe spaces for providers to reexamine their assumptions about particular service recipients, including families with child brokers, without directly threatening their professional identities in the process.

The development of best practices to guide new providers in their interactions with diverse residents would also be an important step toward standardizing institutional practice and supporting individual providers. These guidelines should not depend on culturally laden assumptions that presume to explain "the Latino family," for example, in static, stereotypical ways. While acknowledging that all families are different, providers can be taught general guidelines as well as specific communication skills to interact more effectively with them.

Communication skills training is a critical dimension to enhancing interactions between service providers and local families. Few providers had more than perfunctory training on effective communication with non-English speakers, and none had received instruction on how to handle interactions that included child brokers. Many providers unconsciously focused all their attention on children as soon as they started brokering, effectively cutting their parents out of the conversation, or did the reverse by speaking directly to parents and not engaging children. This communication pattern reflects that providers had been trained to address individuals, not families, as well as their assumption that one family member being active in an interaction necessarily meant that the others were passive.

Skills training should include learning how to: appropriately balance attention between both parents and children; adjust one's rate of speech and use less complex terminology whenever possible to better facilitate children's understanding; pause frequently and provide time for children to relay information to and from their parents; check frequently for comprehension and encourage children to ask questions; and display verbal and nonverbal cues of empathy to put parents and children at ease and encourage them to clarify when needed. These communication practices cannot resolve all misunderstandings and miscommunication, nor can they fully compensate for gaps in children's language skills or understanding of sophisticated concepts. However, these practices make it more likely that parents, children, and providers will be able to scaffold shared understandings together. Successful scaffolding can also enhance children's brokering capabilities in both the short and long term, ultimately making their responsibilities less stressful and more effective.

Supporting Educators

For child brokers, disconnects between home and school could exacerbate the tensions between their family responsibilities and their full participation in educational experiences. Most teachers were minimally aware of their students' family responsibilities. Since children were unlikely to spontaneously reveal private information, teachers often erroneously attributed incomplete schoolwork, absences, and obvious fatigue to students' lack of caring.

Veteran teachers were more likely to have nuanced understandings of their students' family circumstances, but this knowledge was hard-won through years of experience. New teachers were overrepresented in these schools and less likely to have developed such understandings. High staff turnover at these schools also meant that many families started anew with freshly minted teachers at the beginning of each academic year. Schools must prioritize providing better support for both their veteran and new teachers in these regards. Long-time teachers will need assistance to adjust their practices under the pressures of increasing community diversity. New teachers also have to be better prepared for how students' lives outside the classroom can influence their learning. Such training should be integrated into new teachers' formal certification requirements.

Schools could provide support via the strategy-sharing meetings, development of best practices, and communication skills trainings that I suggested for healthcare and social services providers. Teachers were less likely to view children's brokering as a threat to their professional identities than were healthcare providers, mainly because these activities could be integrated into their student-centered approaches to learning. Some teachers also reported that the demonstrative strategies they used during class were very useful for communicating with immigrant parents. Formalizing opportunities for educators to share these kinds of communication successes with colleagues is a particularly promising way to develop best practices that reflect specific community needs.

However, many teachers still had incomplete and often stereotypical perceptions of these students and families, and children were unlikely to correct these misperceptions.[3] Like other local providers, teachers and administrators must consider how their own presumptions can influence their interactions with particular students. They must also guard against treating child brokers differently from their classmates.

Validating Children's Brokering on Campus

Low-cost strategies can provide teachers with opportunities to learn more about students' brokering responsibilities without adding another uncompensated expectation to their workdays. For example, school nurses often make health-related presentations to students. These might include occasional instruction on how to communicate effectively with doctors, which would provide a space for child brokers to discuss what they do to help their families. Sharing these experiences would do more than break the silences that most children kept about their family responsibilities. Legitimizing what children do for their families, within school grounds, could provide powerful and relevant learning experiences for them and simultaneously increase their sense of belonging to their schools.

Signaling to children that their brokering capabilities are valued also requires recognizing these activities as congruent with school objectives. Children developed skills through brokering that were relevant to school contexts but seldom recognized there, such as being able to balance a family budget when they help parents pay monthly bills. Integrating applied assignments into the curriculum can reinforce skills all students need to learn and can have particular utility for brokers in further developing their skill sets. Likewise, application forms and formal paperwork were universally difficult for child brokers. Since schools are charged with developing students' abilities to communicate in formal English, projects and assignments that emphasize these comprehension strategies can be especially important and immediately useful to children who broker for their families.

The preceding recommendations are intended to be practical, in that they do not require enormous outlays of time, effort, and funding to be effective. These are suggestions to help providers do what they are already doing—endeavoring to serve increasingly diverse, complex populations—without adding additional burdens to already over-scheduled days. Implementing these kinds of changes requires institutional leaders to review current practices and expenditures and adjust to routines accordingly, to enable staff members to do their jobs more effectively and facilitate families' access to resources. A particularly urgent institutional priority relates to the paperwork required for most services and resources. These documents created trouble for families by limiting or precluding their access to opportunities they qualified for, or by requiring service providers to go beyond their formal responsibilities by providing additional assistance. While Spanish is the most common language spoken among US immigrants today, simply translating documents into Spanish is not enough (Shin and Kominski 2010). Giving examples, having instructions in clear and easily followed language, and providing more contextual information would better arm parents and children to understand what is available to them and would make it easier for them to access it.

COMMUNITY BUILDING AND FAMILY CHANGE

While some may perceive parents' dependence on their children as proof that these parents have no desire to learn English or otherwise fully invest in living in the United States, their children's help should be seen for what it is—a family's most effective strategy for managing their challenges at a particular point in their collective evolution. Parents did not expect to depend on their children's help forever, at least not to the same degree. As children grow, develop, and change, so do their parents. Changes experienced by individual family members ultimately influenced the nature of the family system itself, as well as how these families interacted with their local community.

Interviews with Graciela, Luis, Liliana, and their parents in 2011, four years after completing the study, provided a glimpse into how time had changed three of these twenty families. Their experiences may or may not be representative of the other families in this study or of immigrant families with child brokers more generally. Their stories do, however, provide insights into how these families' dependence on children's brokering had evolved, as well as how child brokers themselves had changed as they entered late adolescence and young adulthood.

Parents' Changed Community Perceptions

Parents in all three families reported feeling more comfortable with English, more familiar with the community, and more capable of handling community interactions on their own than had been the case four years prior. Liliana, now twenty-one years old, said, "My parents, I think they're more comfortable in the neighborhood now. . . . [T]hey're more confident now; they're more open. My mom used to be scared; now if someone speaks to her in English, she's not so afraid to reply. Back then, she wouldn't even try to understand. . . . I think they've started depending on themselves more for things now." As their child brokers became older and more independent, parents found that raising younger children in the same community was less stressful. Since parents had the benefit of their experiences with their elder child (or children) to draw on, they felt less pressure handling new stages and needs in the lives of younger children.

Family Stability and Family Change

Parents' needs had changed in part because their children had changed. In all three families, parents said that they practiced English more now with their younger children, who were less fluent in Spanish and therefore demanded different kinds of scaffolding efforts from their parents. Liliana said, "I think it's because my little brother speaks a lot of English, and then he speaks to her in English, not in Spanish. And I've noticed that even if she doesn't respond in English, she knows what he's telling her. . . . I was so used to her not knowing English that I always speak to her in Spanish. . . . [N]ow I see the more he speaks to her in English, the more she understands, and if she doesn't get [the meaning of] something, she asks me and I tell her . . . and then next time she's like, 'Oh, that's what that means.'"

The child brokers in these families had changed too; Luis, now sixteen, was the only one of the three still living at home and therefore available to help out on a daily basis. Liliana's husband was serving overseas in the US Navy and she now lived an hour away from her parents. Graciela, now eighteen, had a toddler son and lived with her boyfriend's family about ten minutes from her mother's house. While both young women continued to broker for their parents, they helped less frequently and for a smaller range of tasks.

In part, their brokering responsibilities were more limited because they no longer lived at home; Ileana said she depended on her eldest son more now that Graciela did not live with her. But Ileana had also become more capable of managing simple interactions in English on her own. Graciela said, "I went with her [to work] recently . . . and [her employer] told her to do something, and she was like, 'Okay, that's fine.' I was like, 'What?!' And she said, 'Oh, you know, she told me to go and clean this,' and I said, 'Oh, well, I guess you don't need me now, huh?' Yeah, pretty much the basic things that she wouldn't understand before, now she does." In her interview, Ileana mirrored her daughter's perceptions, saying, "I feel that I understand more, yes, because before, it was really hard for me to communicate with people. . . . I would call my children . . . and say, 'Hey, the lady needs to tell me something but I don't understand her,' but now that no longer happens. I can communicate more. . . . Sometimes they leave me notes and I go around sounding them out and I see what letters they are, and then I put them together. Now I understand."

While parents' English comprehension had improved, they still depended on their children, particularly for more complicated tasks. When Carlos reflected on the past four years, he said, "Ah, yes, there have been changes. It has been hard. Liliana was key because I had not learned my English so well, so for a phone interview, for a complaint, it was hard [for me to do it independently]. I only used her a little, but she was key. . . . I [have] stopped needing help with lots of things, but she is still needed for important things, like before signing any important paper." Liliana also noted that mobile phones allowed her to continue to help her parents even though she lived further away; "Sometimes my mom will call me and say, 'I received this letter and there's some words I don't know,' . . . so I tell her to spell them out for me and I write them down and then I can tell her what they mean. Obviously, the hard words she didn't understand are the ones that gave the meaning to the letter, so I can help her to understand those things to know what the letter means."

Every family system is characterized by tensions between stability and change; changes in individual family members' abilities over time had made parents at least somewhat more independent of their children than they had been four years prior. However, embedded, stable family arrangements meant parents continued to double-check their understandings with their children when they had the opportunity to do so, even though they now managed simpler tasks on their own.[4]

Since he still lived at home and his brother's health was still a major worry for the entire family, Luis still brokered frequently for his mother, Ana. They both reported that Luis helped less as he got older, though they both felt his brokering was more effective now. He reflected:

> I think I help less now, because I have less time. Sometimes when I get home I check the mail and help her with the letters. Sometimes she has phone calls for me to make. . . . But, oh, it's a lot easier, yeah. Now, I can translate better than I could before. The only thing is the different medicines [for my brother still] get me confused, but, yeah—other than that, it's not bad. It's a lot easier for me. . . . I would have to say it's because I have learned different ways of translating. I have Spanish courses now that have really helped. I know more. I learned better strategies for how to use both languages now. . . . I see words and I can usually translate them, and that's something I couldn't do before. It would take me quite a while to translate a whole paragraph. And now that I'm older, it's easier to ask questions [to doctors] too. You get more respect.

Luis was able to see changes in his brokering capabilities resulting from the more sophisticated language proficiencies and comprehension strategies he had developed over time. His capabilities had been further enhanced by the advanced

Spanish classes (including two Advanced Placement courses) he had taken while in high school. Being older also imbued him with a greater sense of confidence; the shy eleven-year-old I had met initially was now a sixteen-year-old young man. He was more comfortable asking questions and felt he was treated with more deference by providers as he became increasingly capable of interacting like an adult.

Managing Closeness and Independence

Within family systems, individual members manage needs for closeness against their needs for differentiation. These tensions had also shifted as family circumstances had changed over the intervening four years. Liliana's early marriage and move out of Los Angeles had resulted in greater independence from her family of origin. The same was true for Graciela, who had become a mother herself and moved out of the house. Both young women still worked hard to maintain a sense of closeness to and continued interdependence with their families. They still communicated with their parents numerous times a day and visited them often. They were still able to broker for their parents, albeit less frequently. Both also contributed financially to their parents' households whenever they were able to do so.

Luis was still living at home and in the throes of adolescent desires for more independence than his family responsibilities allowed. It wasn't easy. His family needed his help in taking care of his younger brothers and with brokering tasks on a daily basis. Since he slept on a twin mattress in the living room that doubled as a couch, he also had almost no privacy. He said, "Yeah, sometimes I wish I had to help less. I don't know. I don't know why. It's just like I don't want anyone to bother me. Because I have so much stuff going on in my head, and then . . . I think, why do I need to do this? I have other things I could do better than this stuff, you know." I asked him if he ever tells his mom that he cannot or does not want to broker for her. He replied, "Not really. Because she needs me. . . . I guess the way I was raised, it's not good to say no."

Ana could read his occasional resistance now, though she attributed it to his heavier load of schoolwork as he progressed through high school. She had to manage on her own sometimes when appointments were only available during school hours because, she said, "Right now, no, because I don't want him to miss school. I don't want him to [miss classes] because right now it's the hardest three years for him, so unless it is gravely important, no."

WHAT CONSTITUTES SECOND-GENERATION SUCCESS?

Interviews with Graciela, Luis, and Liliana also provided insight into their own trajectories since we had followed their progress four years prior. A great deal had changed in the interim. The educational trajectories of Graciela (age eighteen) and Liliana (age twenty-one) had been influenced by other choices they had made with regard to early motherhood and marriage, respectively.

When we first met Graciela, she was thirteen, earning straight A's at Tyler Middle School and involved in a range of educational enrichment opportunities both on and off campus. She had also just been accepted into the next freshman class at a competitive magnet high school in the area. In the intervening four years, she had graduated from that high school and recently started her first year of a liberal studies degree at California State University, Los Angeles. She was living with her boyfriend's family, who helped her care for the son she had had at fifteen.

Graciela's pregnancy had been a shock to her family and particularly to Ileana, who had talked repeatedly and openly with her daughter about birth control and pregnancy prevention. Graciela said, "My mom was like, 'Well, I know I'm not gonna stop you from doing it, but at least I can help by giving you birth control pills. I can take you guys wherever you want to go, you know, to get checked or anything,' but then I was always scared of what she would say or think if I actually asked for it, you know."[5] When the pregnancy was revealed, Ileana encouraged Graciela to have an abortion: "She had scheduled the appointment and she was telling me, 'Well, you know what, this is better for you guys because a kid is only going to hold you back from what you want to achieve.' And I thought, well, it might be a good idea, but it just wasn't the right thing for me. And later on, she understood." While Ileana had accepted what had happened, she was reluctant to revisit the topic in our discussions with her.

With the help of her boyfriend's family and her mother, Graciela had managed to stay in school for the full term of her pregnancy and had missed less than two weeks of classes when her son was born. In her senior year, she had taken the initiative to contact the university she now attended and make enquiries about admission, grants, and scholarships. She appeared to have made a rather smooth and fully funded transition into college in that first semester. She was enjoying and performing well in her classes and felt that although having a child meant she was achieving her goals more slowly, she was still on track:

> I'm hoping to become a teacher within four and a half, five years. I know I can't do it in four years. It's gonna take me a little bit longer, but I want to be a teacher. I want to teach somewhere where there are a lot of minority students . . . I want to keep them motivated, you know? If it's third grade, fourth grade, fifth grade, I want—you know, I wanna push them to see it's important to have an education and not just fall back like other people. I get that from my mom because she's always like, "You know what, if you don't go to school, you'll end up cleaning houses. You'll end up doing all these things that you don't want to do." So I mean, I wanna love what I do, and I always wanted to be a teacher.

While Graciela had in fact talked about becoming a teacher even at thirteen years old, she admitted that having a child had curtailed her original college plans; "Before I had him, my dream school was [UC] Berkeley," she said. She dismissed that aspiration by saying that she would not have moved so far from her family, anyway; "Seeing that my mom is here and her situation, I would have stayed here. I wouldn't dare go anywhere else because of my mom." While she may have been saving face by claiming that she would have stayed in Los Angeles, Graciela still clearly framed success as making her mother proud and helping her whenever she could. Though her young life had taken some unexpected turns, she still endeavored to uphold the immigrant bargain.

Liliana had married at twenty, but had not had children and had no immediate plans to do so. After graduating from her charter high school, she said, "I kinda took a break from school for a few months. I kinda wanted to go to school, but my friends who were going were just, like, taking classes over and over it seemed, and it didn't seem like it was getting anywhere, so I figured I'd go for something fast, and that was medical assisting." She admitted that her parents had been taken aback by her choice not to pursue a bachelor's degree, but she was resolute that she had no regrets about her choice. "I think I had graduated and I was ready to work. . . . I mean, I knew school could help me in the long run, but I was ready to do something in that moment. . . . But yeah, I am going to go back to school at some point. I don't want to be a medical assistant forever. I want to be a registered nurse." After completing the nine-month training course, she had no trouble finding employment; her bilingual capabilities made her a highly attractive candidate.

She had met her husband, two years her senior, three years ago. When we spoke, he was on active duty in the US Navy and deployed for his second tour in Afghanistan. "They say this is his last time there, but we're not quite sure. . . . When he had just got back the first time, how do I say it, . . . it took him awhile, he was sleeping a lot, and he wanted to be home all the time. He didn't like going out much because he hadn't been home for so long. He hated remembering that he had to sleep in the cold and he just wanted to be where he was comfortable." They decided to get married between his deployments: "The first time, we thought, let's see if we can get through the deployment together . . . and we went through this situation where we couldn't talk to each other for eight months and we made it, you know? So when he came back we decided that we were going to get married."

Liliana's husband was in the US Navy, and Graciela's boyfriend was in San Diego in basic training for the Marine Corps. She said that they had opted not to marry so that Graciela would be able to stay in Los Angeles, where her support system enabled her to attend university. She said, "We talked about it and I think he is not holding me back from what I want to do, and I won't be holding him back from anything he wants to do either. Once we're both done, it'll be better." Both young women framed their partners' choices as the best of their options; Liliana described her husband joining the navy as an "escape" from his home in Texas, where his brother and sister had already become embroiled in gangs and drug dealing. Graciela hastened to tell me that while "school wasn't his thing," her boyfriend wanted to make more of himself and the Marine Corps offered more advancement opportunities than the kinds of jobs available to him in Greater Crenshaw.

Luis had also started framing his future choices as potentially including the military. When we met with his mother, she begged me to talk him out of considering enlisting in the US Air Force. She was so upset that he might forgo or delay college that she had threatened to go back to Mexico if he did so. They both seemed to know that she would not act on that threat, regardless of what he did. When I asked him about the air force, he told me that recruiters from different branches of the military had come to talk to students in his high school. He said, "I mean, I'll apply to as many colleges as I can, but if it doesn't work out, then I am going to the air force. I wanna—I don't know. It's just interesting. The adrenaline flowing through your body is a nice thing. I want to fly." When four more years of school was compared with learning to fly planes, the latter clearly captured Luis's imagination. While he described the air force in terms of the exhilaration and freedom of flying, attending college was framed in terms of duty. Luis worried about disappointing his parents. When I asked him what would disappoint them, he answered, "If I don't go to college. I'm planning on going. . . . I mean, they say to me, whatever you do is good enough. It's just that I guess I would be the first one out of my whole family to go to college. So I want to make that a priority. I feel pressure about it, but it's from them and from me too, I guess."

Luis's anxieties about his chances of being admitted to college and what campus life would involve are common concerns among young people beginning the formidable application process required for higher education. For low-income young people of color (and for young men in particular), attending college often means being the first in one's family to do so.[6] Breaking new ground carries additional uncertainties and challenges. Luis was attending a magnet high school that provided more direction about college admission processes than most local schools did, but he remained unsure about the mechanics of turning his abstract desires to attend college into a reality. The road to college seemed lonely and unchartered. On the other hand, Luis saw military service as offering a collective experience: "I always had liked the idea of trying to join something, but I didn't know what yet."[7]

It is not altogether surprising that Graciela's, Liliana's, and Luis's lives were all being directly influenced by the possibility or realities of military service. Recruitment rates among low-income young men of color are rising steadily; according to the most recent available data, Latinos comprised 17 percent of military personnel in 2010, up 4 percent from four years earlier (US Department of Defense 2010). That the military appeared to provide more realistic pathways for social mobility than higher education for the young men affiliated with all three of these families raises profound questions about equal access to opportunities for self-determination and advancement.

Graciela, Liliana, and Luis all had lessened educational expectations as compared with four years earlier. Both young women had already achieved more academically than their parents, but less than they and their parents had initially imagined they would. In Graciela's case, early motherhood had led to her selecting a fine local university but had precluded her applying to the top tier of universities she had initially been aiming for. Liliana had opted to delay university indefinitely to complete a technical-training course that put her more immediately into the workforce. Luis's trajectory remains to be seen in the coming years, but he was already considering possibilities other than college.

While these three young people's educational and occupational trajectories are still works in progress, the brokering assistance that they had provided and continued to provide to their parents is an important part of understanding their experiences. Both young women planned to work in the kinds of institutions where they had brokered for their families as children. Liliana already worked as a medical assistant and routinely engaged her brokering skills as part of her professional duties. Graciela was in the earliest stages of training to become a teacher and was specifically interested in working with minority students. The bilingual capabilities and other brokering-related skills they honed as children and adolescents had equipped them to begin populating California institutions with personnel who can address increased local population diversity. Of course, only time will reveal if young people like Graciela, Liliana, and Luis will ascend beyond the introductory ranks of their professions to positions of institutional leadership.

While immigrant success in the United States is popularly considered as an individual achievement that results from pulling oneself up by one's own bootstraps, support at different levels facilitates what may appear to be solo efforts at first glance. Immigrants' efforts to build a sense of community are a collective effort; individuals' actions are buoyed by family support and by meaningful relationships with local institutions and the professionals who work within them. The same is true for educational attainment and social mobility among the second generation; their own hard work is greatly influenced by their siblings, parents, and adults beyond the family who can help guide and support them.

These families' experiences reinforce recent findings highlighting social resources that have traditionally been overlooked in research on immigrant families. Parents' educational attainment and professional experiences prior to migration, regardless of their occupational status in the United States, are two important examples (V. Louie 2012). Similarly, elder siblings' experiences and input into their younger siblings' development suggest intra-generational social mobility that has largely gone unexplored and will be a fruitful area for future research.

Finally, focusing on immigrant families' communication dynamics can explain a great deal of the diversity in their community experiences. The family home has long been a "black box" in immigration research; scholars acknowledge that family interaction is an influential variable for a range of neighborhood effects and outcomes but seldom focus on the specifics of their communication practices.[8] Communication norms that were modeled by parents and negotiated by child brokers structured the collective strategies they developed by building on successive community experiences. Parents' and children's scaffolding activities facilitated mutual language development in English and Spanish, as well as their capabilities to interact with providers, communication technologies, and other local resources. The diverse communication practices and strategies documented among these twenty families reveal considerable range and creativity in how they addressed local challenges. Immigrant settlement is a family project that has consequences for the collective and for its individual members. Children's brokering should be recognized as a critical component of how that project unfolds.

APPENDIX

Challenges of Departure

Qualitative researchers, ethnographers in particular, often focus on how to gain "entry" to a chosen field of study. Explaining how access to a particular community, site, family, or individual was negotiated is integral to how researchers establish their bona fides and the quality of their reported findings. It is also part of how researchers self-reflexively account for how their personal characteristics (gender, race, migration history, and so on) influenced their study, while simultaneously establishing the distance required for engaging in empirical analysis. These details are important tools for readers to assess both the researcher and the presented findings.

Much less has been written about the challenges of leaving the field (LeCompte 2008). Whether departure refers to leaving the field at the end of one's research, at the end of a stage of a study, or from a single interaction, these experiences tend to, as Ariana Mangual Figueroa (2013) has noted, reassert many of the inequalities between the researcher and the researched that are embedded in the research process. Reflecting on her own experiences of departure, Mangual Figueroa (2013, 129) says:

> Narratives of entry presuppose that the research site is a bounded geographical location that the ethnographer can, and ultimately must, leave at the completion of the study. Our failure to account for how researchers leave the field—how they can responsibly extricate themselves from an ethnographic situation that binds the researcher and the researched . . . is a troubling area of silence. Aside from occasionally observing that it's hard to leave the field, ethnographers rarely reflect on those issues we are best positioned to consider at the conclusion of our fieldwork. . . . We might ask: have we acknowledged and fulfilled our responsibility to the communities who have welcomed us? Have we—both in our own opinion and in the opinion of the participants—fulfilled the commitments we made at the beginning of the study?

This appendix describes challenges I faced in departures from the field. Figueroa's questions, posed above, speak directly to the inherent difficulties of fieldwork in intimate settings like family homes. Some of the challenges I faced were resolved; others were not. I hope my discussion in the pages that follow will further contextualize the findings I presented in the preceding chapters. I also hope my experiences will be instructive for future researchers, since students should be disabused of the notion that fieldwork is a tidy and cleanly organized process as quickly as possible. I discuss problems of departure in order of magnitude, beginning with the challenges of leaving interviews that take unexpected turns, the challenges of reciprocity in ongoing relationships, and, finally, the challenges of ending a research project. Before doing so, I briefly summarize my experience of entering Greater Crenshaw and of becoming acquainted with the families who were my informants, to contextualize the challenges of departure that follow.

EXPERIENCES OF ENTRY

My entry into Greater Crenshaw was facilitated by a number of factors. I was already familiar with the area from my work as a research assistant for the Metamorphosis Project.[1] As part of these prior efforts, I had already connected with supervisors at the Women, Infants and Children (WIC) office in Greater Crenshaw, where I later conducted field observations; it was the WIC site that most interviewed mothers were currently affiliated with or had used when they had children under age five. Survey data collected via the Metamorphosis Project made it possible to identify parents whose children brokered for them frequently. These parents were contacted by my research assistants Benedicte (Beni) and Michelle to invite them to participate in interviews (chapter 2 provides more details on the research design).

Beni is the US-born eldest child of Mexican-origin parents, and Michelle migrated to California with her mother and younger sister from Mexico City when she was ten. Both Beni and Michelle were advanced undergraduates at University of Southern California (USC), fluently bilingual, and had been their families' primary brokers as children. Their commitment to this project greatly contributed to its success, as their abilities to genuinely empathize with parents certainly built trust and facilitated open communication. Either Beni or Michelle accompanied me to every parent interview, all of which were conducted in Spanish.

I am not a native Spanish speaker, but months of language immersion in Guatemala had made me capable of conversing quite easily with parents. My Spanish was not perfect, however, and I would explain to parents when we met that I was still learning Spanish. I asked them to forgive my mistakes and invited them to correct me, so that I could continue to learn. These admissions visibly put parents at ease and generally prompted discussion between us about how difficult it was to learn a new language as an adult. Though there were unquestioningly many differences between me and these parents, the fact that we were both language learners helped to make our interactions a little more level. Parents were generally very patient and accommodating if I made mistakes in Spanish.[2] On the other hand, some parents jokingly admonished Michelle and Beni if they made (very occasional) mistakes, clearly making comparisons between them and their own children in a way that they did not do with me.

Like other researchers, I was aware that my appearance was salient to these interactions. That Michelle, Beni, and I were all women definitely facilitated the confidences we had with many mothers. As I mentioned in chapter 3, this gendered dynamic also certainly constrained how men conducted themselves in parent interviews (and probably affected whether they were willing to be interviewed at all). Just as these parents were marked by their language and accents, they marked me by mine. Some parents noted my lack of accent in Spanish and attempted to guess where I was from (since I am South African and I learned Spanish in Guatemala, apparently my Spanish does not carry that telltale American twang). I was initially taken aback when the first (of four) parents asked me if I was Jewish. When I asked why they thought so, they explained that the only Spanish speakers they had seen before with features like mine were the Jews in Mexico City. Certainly, as much as I was there to understand their experiences, these parents were also trying to place mine.

Although some children were initially reticent in our interviews, most opened up quickly. Many children had been present for at least some portion of their parents' interview and so were familiar with me and had noted that their parents were comfortable talking to us, which no doubt made them more willing to sit down with me. Marjorie Orellana (2009) noted that children often view researchers as teachers, a dynamic I felt in some of my interactions with younger brokers and seldom when talking with adolescents. I went to all interviews, whether with parents or children, in jeans and a T-shirt rather than formal clothing. Combined with looking young for my age, my more casual attire and demeanor helped older brokers in particular to see me as less of a *maestra* (teacher) and as more of a student, as evident in their comments and questions about life as a college student. I did not encounter noticeably gendered differences in terms of which children were most likely to open up to me, though my relationships with children in the families we shadowed to their interviews certainly deepened over the time we spent with them.

Departing the Interview

Parents and children varied in terms of how much they chose to reveal to us, on what topics, and over what periods of time. As Orellana (2009, 127–142) noted in her own methodological appendix, it is particularly critical that researchers give children room for silence, since the relationship between an adult researcher and a researched child is particularly asymmetrical.

I began these interviews expecting that there would be times when private information was divulged that we had not asked for. Parents revealed information about their residency status and other details about difficult experiences in their lives. I noted in chapter 5 that Alejandro was in tears as he described the damage his alcoholism had done to this health and to his family. Other parents were similarly emotional in recounting painful memories of migration. Many had left behind beloved relatives who had since become ill or passed away, and they felt overwhelming guilt that lacking legal residency or adequate funds had made it impossible for them to return to care for them or to pay proper respect when they died. These admissions and expressions of trust were not taken lightly by my research assistants or me, and we found it natural to validate these experiences and provide comfort as needed.

In one instance, the secret divulged was so unexpected that I faced a problem of departure from the interview itself. My meeting with Regina (age fourteen) began like many others; we had previously interviewed her mother, Virginia, and knew that she was divorced from Regina's father. Nothing in our rather lengthy interview with Virginia had led us to expect that anything other than routine conflicts had prompted the dissolution of her marriage. As I did in all my interviews with children, I asked Regina about how she helped her mother with various household tasks and brokering responsibilities, and then asked her if she had helped her father as well. She burst into tears, revealing through sobs that her father had sexually abused her for years and that the revelation of his abuse had set in motion her parents' divorce and a restraining order preventing him from having contact with either Regina or her younger brother.

Unwittingly, it was my own phrasing of the question—so carefully considered when I wrote it, so that it would encompass my own definitions of brokering but also leave room for children to include other forms of "help" they exchanged with family members—that set off this chain reaction. Regina's father used "help" as his code word for his acts of abuse. I was in shock, totally unprepared for the consequences of my seemingly innocent question. My first thought was how I would possibly explain this to Virginia, who was in the other room, if she walked in and found her daughter crying.

As if on cue, Regina's younger brother walked in, comically shook his head and said, "Oh no, not *again*," and ran back out the front door to play with his friends again, unaffected. I hugged Regina until she calmed down, repeatedly telling her how sorry I was and that what had happened to her was not her fault. I asked her if she wanted to continue the interview. Somehow, at that moment it seemed very important to me *not* to leave. I felt ending the interview myself would reinforce that the injustice done to her had somehow marked her and made her less worthy of being spoken to. She wanted to continue, and over the next forty minutes I think we both found our footing again. By the time I left the interview, I believe she was back on emotionally stable ground.

Since the abuse had ended and Virginia, with the help of a priest at the Catholic school her children attended, had taken steps to legally protect her children from all contact with her ex-husband, I did not have to take steps to report Regina's admission (as I would have if she had divulged ongoing abuse). As a young researcher, this was a lesson in the challenges that emerge unbidden in fieldwork. With the benefit of hindsight and more research experience, I have come to the sad realization that those of us who research families are inevitably going to encounter stories of sexual and physical abuse in some of the households we enter.

These situations present dilemmas that may be even more difficult for those of us who study immigrant families, as opposed to native-born families. While researchers are legally bound to report evidence or suspicion of family abuse in all cases, if one or more family members are in the United States illegally, making that phone call may also set deportation proceedings in motion. How can a researcher uphold the basic ethical standard to "do no harm" in such a situation? Does suspicion of abuse warrant that phone call; or, when dealing with mixed-status or undocumented families, must one be absolutely certain that abuse is occurring before alerting authorities? These questions of what one does in departing an immigrant home should be covered in methodology classes long before students could encounter these issues firsthand.

DEPARTING EARLY INTERACTIONS: THE CHALLENGES OF RECIPROCITY

Any methodological guide to ethnographic research will advise readers that access to a community, family, or individual is a process, as trust and confidence may be negotiated and renegotiated over time. My experience was no different; parents and children became more comfortable talking with me, Beni, and Michelle over multiple visits to their homes and, for the case-study families, over periods of months. These deepening relationships brought to the fore contrasts between the families' and our perspectives on what we were doing there and what families could expect from us.

Other researchers have written at length about what constitutes adequate reciprocity between researchers and informants; after all, when respondents open up their lives to you, what can they expect in return? As Mario Small (2010, 225–226) points out in the appendix of *Unexpected Gains*, there are two schools of thought on this dilemma: "Some researchers believe it is unconscionable to fail to provide aid; others . . . believe that doing so will undermine the aims of the project, since one is unable to understand how people truly manage their circumstances."

When we first met with families and introduced them to the study, part of the informed consent procedure was making them aware that we were interested in the roles that children played in their households. For the families we approached after their initial interviews to ask if we could shadow them to their appointments over subsequent months, we explained that we wished to observe their children as they brokered their families' community interactions. Parents therefore knew what our focus was, even if many were unsure why we were interested in behaviors they took for granted as a normal element of their household routines and family relationships.

As Guadalupe Valdés (1996, 9–10) found in her research with Mexican-origin immigrant families, parents and children reconstituted our roles into ones that fit their preexisting categories. As such, some parents viewed us as readily available, additional brokers once they discovered we could speak Spanish. As parents came to know us better, some made requests for assistance during home visits or via phone calls to Michelle or Beni when school newsletters came home in English or they had trouble completing paperwork. These parents' strategies were completely practical; after all, here were three young women who were college educated and bilingual (if overly curious) who, they felt, could surely broker more effectively than their children. In short, some parents attempted a strategy of including us in their support networks, either to supplement or to obviate their children's assistance.

These bids for assistance of course created a conundrum for us. From a strategic standpoint, refusals to reciprocate could threaten the often-fragile trust we had developed with these mothers (fathers did not make these requests of us). But since we were there to document how children brokered, warts and all— when they got it right, what strategies they enacted when they were struggling, and when they made mistakes—replacing them in these interactions would have been counterproductive to the aims of the project. And yet, from an ethical perspective, choosing to simply document families' hardships when we were in a position to assist (even temporarily) ran counter to my motivations for pursuing this project in the first place.

The compromise I settled on was that if families asked us to broker documents for them during an interview, we would decline by explaining that we were there to understand how their children performed these roles. In some cases, this explanation prompted children to broker the material while we were there, which may not have been a totally spontaneous brokering event, but given how hard those are to observe (see García-Sánchez 2010; Orellana 2009, 139), these experiences gave us valuable insights into how children engaged these tasks. We also agreed that if parents with whom we would not be pursuing a longer-term relationship contacted us for assistance, Michelle or Beni could accommodate their requests if they had the time to do so.[3]

Reciprocity became even trickier business with the families we shadowed to their appointments. We found it difficult to explain—not only to parents and children, but also to ourselves—what benefits accrued from us sitting and taking notes on a child's struggles to broker from the corner of a doctor's examination room. Such experiences brought the inequalities of the researcher-researched relationship into uncomfortably sharp relief. For Beni and Michelle, who had brokered for their own families as children, sitting on the sidelines was even more difficult than it was for me. I remember Michelle commenting, after a doctor's visit with Luis's family, that she was physically tired from the effort it took *not* to jump in and help.

Our compromise for these interactions was explained to families in advance. While we would not broker in place of their child, we promised that if they made a mistake or omission that would alter the course of a conversation, we would step in to help (and, obviously, we would have stepped in even earlier if they made more serious errors). Parents and children were satisfied with the safety net this compromise provided. Knowing we were there and could help if needed may have altered children's brokering to some degree. However, when I compared the brokered interactions I witnessed serendipitously in Greater Crenshaw schools, healthcare facilities, and social services offices with interactions where brokers were aware of our presence, our safety net did not seem to affect their activities. This compromise also allowed us to show families the goodwill and reciprocity we felt was appropriate for us to demonstrate.

There were also challenges to demonstrating more formal reciprocity. A grant from USC's Urban Initiative allowed me to offer families incentives for participating in this project. Parents were given a $50 gift card for agreeing to be interviewed; children were given a USC T-shirt, since I was mindful that parents might be uncomfortable with my giving their children money. Parents and children were generally delighted with T-shirts that showed an affiliation with their local university. Families who agreed to have us shadow them to local appointments received an additional $100 gift card, and they received the same when we revisited them in 2011.

While most parents were grateful for the financial assistance and recognized it as an appropriate demonstration of gratitude, a few parents initially protested, saying that they only wished to help us. These magnanimous refusals generally evolved into acceptance after we reiterated that the gift card was not money out of my own pocket and was supplied by the university. The mother who always seemed genuinely willing to refuse financial incentives was Ana, Luis's mother. Considering that we spent more time with her family than any other, she more than deserved what was a paltry sum, relative to the amount of time she gave us. And yet, each time—even in the very first meeting—she had to be convinced to take the gift card, that it would be useful for her family. She said that having us visit with her and listen to her was, for her, all she wanted. Given the tremendous stresses in her life and the sadness that enveloped this family as they struggled to keep Julio healthy, I believe (and hope) that our visits were a source of support and comfort for her.

Departing the Field (or When You Think You Have)

By the second half of 2007, I had completed my interviews with parents and children, as well as our visits with case study families to local institutions.[4] Having concluded this part of my study, I became more involved with assisting Luis and his family. I made peace with this more activist role by only entering it after I had concluded the family stage of my fieldwork.

At the time, Luis was attending Bellum Middle School, which also housed a magnet middle school for gifted children. Luis mentioned that he had tested for and been found eligible for admission to the magnet program. Somehow, the paperwork required for the transfer had never arrived in the mail. Ana had promised to go to the school to enquire, but then Julio had gone through a period of poor health that had sidelined all other responsibilities. I went to Bellum and spent two hours with the magnet program administrator, retrieving the necessary paperwork and having him explain to me how the process worked. Even as a native English speaker with graduate degrees, the process was far from transparent to me.

The advantages of attending a magnet school made the process a particularly important one to understand. For students in Los Angeles Unified School District, particularly those at the district's most under-served schools, magnet schools offer considerable opportunities. By virtue of how points are allocated in the system, graduating from a magnet middle school essentially guarantees admission to magnet high schools, which teachers at Bellum and Tyler felt provided superior preparation for attending a four-year university. Students in magnet schools have the benefit of smaller classes, more subject options, and, often, excellent teachers. Magnet schools generally have fewer problems with gangs and school violence, though they are certainly not immune to these problems.

Michelle came with me to explain the paperwork and process for matriculation into the magnet middle school program to Luis and his parents. We outlined the differences between his current middle school and its magnet program, and what the trajectories were in terms of high school and college admissions. I made it clear that the choice was theirs and that I only wanted to ensure that this opportunity—for which Luis had already been eligible—became a real option for him. They discussed it as a family and agreed to make the change. Luis matriculated into the magnet program halfway through seventh grade. After this interaction, Michelle and I kept in contact with Luis and Ana a few times a year, ensuring that he was continuing to do well in school. There were times we lost touch for longer than a few months; their phone was routinely disconnected, but since the family did not move, we only had to go knock on their door to make contact again.

I certainly did not anticipate when I concluded all my fieldwork that I would re-interview families again in 2011. I decided these interviews were necessary during the process of writing this manuscript. Since the book would focus on how children's brokering affected families' local interactions and their own developmental trajectories, following up with a handful of families to see how their individual and familial trajectories had manifested over time seemed like an important part of the story this book could tell. The goal of those 2011 interviews with Luis, Graciela, Liliana, and their parents was to assess both family change and child brokers' development during the intervening years. What Alessandro Duranti (1997) termed the "participant-observer paradox," wherein the researcher affects the activities she observes by participating in them, was very apt in this case.

There can be no question that I influenced Luis's development by intervening in his schooling. Had I known in 2007 that I would attempt those follow-up interviews four years later, I may have been more guarded and self-conscious about how involved I became in Luis's schooling, though I suspect I would have done the same thing anyway. For one thing, I did not go searching for alternative schooling options for him; he had already been accepted to the magnet program, so all I did was facilitate the paperwork. And second, given the potential payoffs to Luis for attending magnet middle school and high school programs, I have no regrets about helping to facilitate the considerable success he has had in both.

But, the conundrum remains. Where is the line between researcher and social worker? How involved is too involved? These questions are not new. There has, as Duranti observed, always been a tension between participant and observer roles. Over time, the challenges to observation being the primary mode of fieldwork have mounted. In recent years, "academic advocacy," "action research," and similar buzzwords have emerged as calls to action across a range of disciplines. The common thread across these concepts is a commitment (to varying degrees) to partnering with community members rather than entering a site, collecting data, and leaving. For many researchers, these forms of community engagement involve advocating for community change in partnership with residents, with the view that one's findings should directly serve the community that has been under study.

However, other researchers argue that these approaches diminish the data one gathers and that advocacy makes for less rigorous, less academically valuable research. I am certainly not going to manage to resolve debates of this magnitude in a methodological appendix. Did my involvement with Luis and his family make me less objective in my analysis? Luis and I still exchange messages on Facebook and I keep up with how he is doing in school. As he enters his senior year of high school and begins his college applications, I will do my best to help him with that process, if he asks me to. I also exchange emails with Graciela from time to time. I do not deny these investments, but they certainly highlight the problems of departure.[5] Mangual Figueroa suggested one reason these experiences may be omitted from researchers' accounts: "Are we afraid to concede failure? Recounting challenging encounters with participants during a study's closure . . . would mean relinquishing some of the narrative control of the ethnographer—namely the power to represent our research in a positive light, smoothing over the tensions that emerge between the researcher and the researched" (2013, 142).

There is no doubt that the desire to present one's work as clean and coherent may make it tempting to omit struggles like those I have detailed above. Numerous ethnographers have argued eloquently that attempting to remove the self from one's research does not ensure objectivity, since researchers are always present in their work. Self-reflexivity and honesty are, I think, the keys here. I therefore present my challenges of departure, so that readers may decide for themselves whether these disclosures affect their perceptions of my findings. I hope these experiences contribute to the frank discussions other scholars have started about their experiences in the field.

I also hope these discussions will support the ongoing evolution of what it means to be a researcher. As the conditions in which scholars do their work continue to change, the responsibilities and commitments one makes and honors are changed in the process. Researchers, myself included, increasingly endeavor to write for varied audiences simultaneously, either due to personal motivations or because university faculty increasingly find themselves redefining and explaining their relationships to society at large. Rigorous research can contribute to scholarly, policy, and public discourses—and can do so while also contributing to the lives of participants who have made such work possible. To honor those commitments, we need to squarely face the challenges of departure, because these speak directly to the struggle of what it means to invest oneself in the lives of others. To do so mindfully is critical to how researchers view themselves and to how our work is viewed by others—and, in particular, by those who allow us into their worlds, perhaps for longer and more deeply than anyone initially expects.

NOTES

CHAPTER 1 — CHILDREN, FAMILY, AND COMMUNITY

1. To protect their privacy, I have replaced all participants' names with pseudonyms.

2. I am grateful to Hanna Adoni for this reference.

3. Other examples include Berroll (1995), Cordasco (1976), Fabiano (2011), and Weiss (1984).

4. For example, see Dumas (2004), Orellana (2009), Park (2001), Pyke (2000), and Abel Valenzuela (1999).

5. For example, see reviews of research on children's brokering in the United States, United Kingdom, and Europe in a 2010 special issue of *mediAzioni* 10, retrievable online at http://mediazioni.sitlec.unibo.it.

6. For example, see Aldridge and Becker (1999) and Katz (2014).

7. For example, see Dreby (2010), Gálvez (2011), Hirsch (1999), Hondagneu-Sotelo (2001), Kibria (1993), and Pessar (2003).

8. I refer to brokers as children, regardless of their chronological age, because their identities as sons and daughters of immigrants are their most salient roles in these interactions. See Katz (2014) for more detailed discussion. According to Thorne and colleagues (2003), these young people may also remain "children" in their parents' eyes well beyond the age of majority when they legally become "adult" (for example, age eighteen in the United States) because of their ongoing family responsibilities; this again frames "childhood" as a social role as much as a demarcation of chronological age.

9. While immigrant mothers and fathers both encounter employment-related constraints, their experiences are also gendered. Service industries related to care and cleaning tend to favor women for these roles, so immigrant women may find employment in these sectors more easily than men (Pessar 2003). Long work hours do not, however, release women from traditionally gendered roles in domestic contexts. The mothers in this study still shouldered primary responsibility for tasks related to household maintenance and childrearing, even if they were working full time. Dreby (2010) noted that parenting practices among transnational Mexican parents were gendered, in that mothers were expected to maintain emotional connections and nurture their children even over long distances, whereas fathers' financial support was how they primarily showed caring.

Kibra (1993) finds similarly reified traditional gender roles among immigrant parents in Vietnamese-origin families.

10. There is a substantial amount of research on domestic tasks that children shoulder in working poor families; see Dodson and Dickert (2004), Romich (2007), and Abel Valenzuela (1999).

11. Other terms have been used to describe these roles, including *translators, interpreters,* and *"para"-phrasers*. These different terms are summarized and discussed in Orellana, Dorner, and Pulido (2003).

12. Researchers continue to debate whether the linguistic aspects or cultural aspects of brokering are most primary; my decision to emphasize neither term and instead refer to "child brokering" is discussed in greater detail in Katz (2014).

13. Also see Rueda, Monzó, and Arzubiaga (2003).

14. For example, see Durham (2004) and Elias and Lemish (2008, 2011).

15. While children sometimes strategically altered messages for their family's benefit, I found that they seldom did so for personal gain, such as lying in a parent-teacher meeting. See García-Sánchez and Orellana (2006) and Orellana, Dorner and Pulido (2003) for convergent findings.

16. Stephen Gavazzi states, "The family system is thought to be best understood through the recognition that family members (as parts of the system) interact with one another in such a manner that, over time, these interactions become patterned behavior" (2011, 35). See Katz (2010) for a discussion of how these patterned interactions among family members influence children's brokering experiences.

17. The features of a community and the characteristics of people who settle in it interact with each other and influence residents' communication patterns. This phenomenon has been described as "geo-ethnicity," referring to the interaction of community features (geo) with imported values immigrants bring to that new environment (ethnicity). Researchers at the USC Metamorphosis Project have documented significant differences in immigrants' communication patterns when they settle in different parts of Los Angeles, even when they share a country of origin and are demographically similar (i.e., when geography varies and ethnicity is held constant). Likewise, different immigrant and ethnic minority groups living in the same local community exhibit different communication behaviors as well (i.e., when geography is held constant and ethnicity varies). Some of these findings are documented in Kim and Ball-Rokeach (2006), Kim, Jung, and Ball-Rokeach (2006), and Lin and Song (2006).

18. Prior research highlights schools, healthcare facilities, and social services as the community resources that immigrant families connect with early and most often. Carmina Brittain (2003) notes that enrolling children in school is often the first local action new immigrant parents take; Guadalupe Valdés (1996) indicates that other immigrant parents inform newcomers that enrollment is a legal imperative. Parents also frequent healthcare resources for their US-born children, who are eligible for a variety of programs serving poor children. Many immigrant mothers also enroll in the Women, Infants, and Children (WIC) program during pregnancy, giving them access to a range of social services and healthcare for pre- and post-natal care and nutrition; see Domínguez (2011) and Gálvez (2011).

19. Massey and Sánchez (2010) were primarily concerned with the boundary brokering that immigrant adults do in interactions with the native-born in workplaces and how these interactions affect immigrants' identity development. The processes they describe were also evident in the community locations I studied.

20. Robert Courtney Smith (2002) originally coined the term "immigrant bargain."

21. Others, however, have documented such a connection. For example, see Buriel et al. (1998), Dorner, Orellana, and Li-Grining (2007), and Valdés (2003).

22. Robert Sampson (2011) and others have coined the term "concentrated disadvantage" to refer to the compounding challenges faced by residents living in under-served communities (see also Sampson, Morenoff, and Gannon-Rowley 2002). There is some evidence to suggest that concentrated disadvantage has differential effects on boys and girls as they grow up. Nancy Lopez (2003) and Ana Celia Zentella (1997) found that Dominican and Puerto Rican girls have higher educational attainment, bilingual proficiency, and adherence to parental cultural values than their brothers, largely because they are kept closer to home and family.

CHAPTER 2 — SETTLING IN GREATER CRENSHAW

1. Greater Crenshaw is not the formal name of this community, but rather one coined to help mask its specific location and identity.

2. See Elman (1967), Sides (2004a, 2004b), and Sitton and Deverell (2001) for more detailed histories of South Los Angeles.

3. Shelley v. Kraemer, 334 U.S. 1 (1948); Barrows v. Jackson, 346 U.S. 249 (1953). The Los Angeles Urban League documented twenty-six different intimidation tactics in a 1947 report, the results of which are included in the US Commission on Civil Rights (1960, 158–159).

4. Sanyika Shakur (2004) recounts his experiences as a Crip gang member during this time period.

5. The Watts Rebellion took place from August 11 to August 15, 1965, resulting in thirty-four deaths, over one thousand injuries, three thousand arrests, and more than $40 million in estimated property damage. Detailed accounts include Cohen and Murphy (1966) and McCone (1965).

6. For more detail and analysis on the causes and consequences of the 1992 Rodney King verdict, see Cannon (1999), Fulton (1997), and Hunt (1996).

7. Negative connotations of South Central Los Angeles are examined in Hunt (1996), Matei and Ball-Rokeach (2005), and Sides (2004a, 2004b).

8. Los Angeles became the first city in the United States to have as many Spanish-speaking households as English-speaking ones in 2000; by the 2010 US Census, 52 percent of households in Los Angeles were Spanish speaking.

9. Mexico ceded territory to the United States that became all or part of ten US states (including California) under the Treaty of Guadalupe Hidalgo, which ended the Mexican-American War (1846–1848) on February 2, 1848.

10. Ivan Light (2008) documents these shifts in Latino settlement away from traditional receiving communities.

11. Since many eligible respondents' phones had been disconnected since completing the survey at the end of 2005, the interview pool was augmented with respondents identified at the local WIC (Women, Infants, and Children) office where I later conducted field observations. Using the same inclusion criteria as for telephone-survey respondents, my research assistants identified eligible parents at WIC between October 2006 and March 2007. Screening surveys also collected demographic information to ensure similarities between interviewees recruited via these two methods. Eligible telephone-survey respondents were contacted and asked to participate in interviews between November 2006 and

March 2007. Once that pool was exhausted, eligible WIC respondents were contacted between March and May 2007 until twenty parents had agreed to be interviewed. Four families recruited at WIC were interviewed.

12. For more details on the closure of King/Drew Hospital and how it was covered in the mainstream press, see Hunt and Ramon (2010).

13. See chapter 3 for more details on family demographics.

14. According to research conducted by UCLA's Civil Rights Project, Latino and African American students are as likely to have white classmates today as they were forty years ago; see Orfield and Yun (1999).

15. Title I is a provision of the 1965 Elementary and Secondary Education Act, under which funds are allocated first to state and then to local agencies for distribution to schools and districts where at least 40 percent of students are classified as low-income, according to US Census and Department of Education definitions.

16. See table 2.2 for details. In addition, Tyler Middle School had ten Teach for America teachers the year I observed the campus; they were viewed as a valuable but temporary presence by longer-term educators and added to perceptions of rapid faculty turnover.

17. Gang initiations, in particular, were often racially motivated, as African American newcomers would be instructed to "jump" a Latino student by existing members, and vice versa. Juana (age thirteen) said, "I'm comfortable with my friends . . . with the black students; we're cool with them, but it gets weird and tense when there's fights happening."

CHAPTER 3 — CHILD BROKERS AND THEIR FAMILIES

1. There is a large literature on the invisibility of domestic work and its tendency to be gendered female. For summaries of the invisibility of domestic, feminized forms of work, see Duffy (2011) and Hondagneu-Sotelo (2001).

2. Protectiveness and intensive surveillance of female children has been documented across a range of immigrant groups; see, for example, Le Espiritu (2001), Lopez (2003), Varghese and Jenkins (2009), and Zentella (1997).

3. Pyke (2005) reports the same findings.

4. I returned to Los Angeles in 2011 and interviewed these families again, four years after we concluded our observations of their activities. These interviews are detailed in chapter 7.

5. Weston's (1997) research on the biological and chosen relationships of lesbians and gay men introduces the notion of "chosen families," in opposition to the biological or the involuntary ties that make up "blood families." The idea of voluntary, chosen family ties reinterprets the meaning of family to emphasize love "as both the necessary and sufficient criterion for kinship" (Weston 1997, 107). Weston argues that families can be based on a shared emotional and material responsibility and not just on genetic links.

6. Vivian Louie similarly reported that mothers who had been in the United States for over a decade, and, in one case, for over thirty years, still felt like immigrants and newcomers in interactions that required them to speak English (2012, 48).

7. When this survey was conducted in 2005, the federal poverty line was $22,610 for a family of five. Most public services in Los Angeles use 150 or 200 percent of the federal poverty level to determine eligibility, in recognition of the high costs of living there. At the time, a family of four living on $35,000 or less was considered a reasonable estimate of living in poverty in Los Angeles County.

8. This gendered pattern is consistent with prior research; see, for example, Orellana (2009) and Abel Valenzuela (1999).

9. Menjívar (2000) recalls similarly gendered experiences conducting her research.

10. Respondents were asked, "Where do most of your close friends and family live?" The following fixed responses were provided: "In your neighborhood," "In the Los Angeles area," "In California, but outside of the L.A. area," "In the United States, but not in California," or "In another country." Chi-square analyses revealed that parents dependent on child brokering were significantly more likely to have close friends and family in the neighborhood than were other Latino or African American residents ($p < .05$).

11. Respondents were asked: "How often do you have discussions with other people about things happening in your neighborhood? Using a 10-point scale where '1' means 'never' and '10' means 'all the time,' where would you place yourself?" T-tests revealed that families with child brokers engaged in these discussions significantly more often than other Latino residents ($p = .05$), but less than their African American neighbors.

12. Massey, Durand, and Malone (2002) document the relationship between social networks and chain migration; Hondagneu-Sotelo (1994) and Menjívar (2000) chronicle how social networks are changed as a consequence of migration.

13. Small (2010) and Domínguez (20011) both explore the limitations of low-income immigrants' social networks for connecting with local resources.

14. Menjívar also reported this practice of "lending" children to others when they had to go to an appointment or received mail they could not understand, as a means for parents to return or invoke favors or feelings of goodwill (2000, 214).

15. Respondents were asked: "Overall, how easy or difficult is it for you to get medical care for the child we've been discussing when they need it? Would you say it is very difficult, somewhat difficult, somewhat easy, or very easy?" Later in the survey, respondents were asked to make the same evaluations for themselves: "Overall, how easy or difficult is it for you to get medical care when you need it? Would you say it is very difficult, somewhat difficult, somewhat easy, or very easy?" Survey respondents were also asked: "Thinking about this child, how easy or difficult is it for you to get good advice on how to handle problems that come up in raising the child? Would you say it is very difficult, somewhat difficult, somewhat easy, or very easy?" T-tests revealed that families with brokers were significantly more likely to report difficulty accessing all three kinds of resources, compared with other Latino and African American residents ($p < .05$ for all three measures).

16. California voters passed Proposition 10 in November 1998, adding a new fifty-cent tax to the price of a pack of cigarettes. This revenue was disbursed to each county to develop health programs for underserved Californians. In Los Angeles County, these funds created First 5 LA, which provided no- and low-cost health insurance to low-income children between birth and age five. First 5 LA also helped families locate equivalent coverage once their children aged out of the program.

17. According to the US Department of Health and Human Services (2010), Latinos and African Americans are at disproportionately high risk for chronic conditions such as diabetes, hypertension, and heart disease. Obesity is a contributing factor for all these conditions, and Hispanic Americans and African Americans are 1.1 and 1.4 times more likely, respectively, to be obese than are non-Hispanic whites (Office of Minority Health 2010). Furthermore, working-age Latino and African American adults are also more likely to report gaps in insurance coverage and have less access to medical care than white working-age adults (Doty and Holmgren 2006).

18. The family interaction index (FII) includes six questions that measure the frequency of family communication in the home, as well as the frequency of talk about particular topics and family activities, using a five-point Likert scale, where response options were "very often," "often," "sometimes," "rarely," and "never." Respondents were asked: "How often does your family . . . sit down and eat together? . . . sit down and talk together? . . . discuss issues that are happening in the neighborhood? . . . discuss work-related issues? . . . participate in neighborhood and community activities as a family? . . . participate in activities outdoors together like sports, hiking, going to parks, etc.?" Cronbach's alpha for this measure was $\alpha = .75$. T-test analyses revealed that these families engaged in significantly more family interaction than other Greater Crenshaw residents ($p < .05$). For other applications of the FII, see Wilkin, Katz, and Ball-Rokeach (2009).

CHAPTER 4 — COMMUNITY BEGINS AT HOME

1. For example, see Dorner, Orellana, and Li-Grining (2007); Park (2001); and Tse (1996).

2. I am not suggesting that ethnically targeted media do not provide community information that helps orient immigrants to their surroundings. Rather, it is a question of the goals for which individuals connect with media. In these cases, parents' ethnic media connections were motivated by desires for entertainment. For details on the orientation functions of ethnic media, see Matsaganis, Katz, and Ball-Rokeach (2011).

3. Families' media environments can evolve rapidly. In 2007, devices like smartphones were less common in these families than they would likely be today, although technology ownership in low-income families still tends to lag behind that in wealthier families; see Madden et al. (2013).

4. Clark found that when parents take a "panopticon-like approach to discipline," by keeping devices in locations where children feel parents can observe their online activities at any time, children tend to monitor themselves (2005, 215); see also Tripp (2011).

5. While others have claimed that children's brokering usurps parents' authority or otherwise "parentifies" children, I, like Orellana, Dorner, and Pulido (2003), found that children's brokering was most effective when parents retained their authority. For "parentification" arguments, see Kam (2011), Menjívar (2000, 213–228), and Oznobishin and Kurman (2009).

6. Lisa Park (2001) and Miri Song (1999) both document child brokers who felt that their family responsibilities constrained their choices to move away to college or to not work in the family business. Such limitations were sometimes imposed by parents, but more often, children preemptively constrained their own choices because they believed that their parents' lives would be more difficult if they chose to break away.

7. The relationship between brokering and the immigrant bargain is detailed more extensively in chapter 6.

8. These fears are hardly unique; across socioeconomic levels, racial/ethnic groups, and national contexts, parents report concerns about risks and potential harms that their children may encounter online. On the other hand, nationally representative data collected by the Pew Center suggests that parents also believe Internet access is beneficial and necessary for their children's education. See Clark (2011); Hoover, Clark, and Alters (2004); Lenhart (2005); and Livingstone and Haddon (2009).

9. This is consistent with findings from larger studies showing that children's new media literacies are correlated with a home-based Internet connection. Sonia Livingstone

and Ellen Helsper (2007) reported that having Internet at home is associated with children's having been online for more years, using the Internet more frequently, and exhibiting more Internet-related skills. In the United States, school-age children whose parents have less than a high school diploma are significantly less likely to have Internet access at home than if their parents are college graduates (74 percent versus 91 percent, respectively). School-age Latino children trail both their white and African American counterparts in this respect, with 74 percent having home-based Internet access, versus 88 percent and 78 percent, respectively; see Rideout, Foehr, and Roberts (2010).

10. National studies by the Pew Internet and American Life Project had previously reported that schools and libraries are primary points of access for the 30 percent of lower-income teens without Internet access at home; see Lenhart et al. (2008).

11. See, for example, Kam (2011).

12. Robert Havighurst first popularized the term "teachable moments" (1953, 7).

13. Marcelo and Carola Suárez-Orozco were co-principal investigators of the Longitudinal Immigrant Student Adaptation (LISA) study, the data source for Josephine Louie's analyses (2003).

14. This was consistent with Georgiou's (2001) findings that collective media consumption becomes more intensive and promotes more intergenerational conversation when major news events occur in the home country.

15. While few families had cellular phones, some used them as mobile translation devices. Regina (age fourteen) said that her mother would often use her cell phone to have Regina broker remotely if she could not locate someone to help her at an appointment or in a store. This strategy allowed Regina to stay home and supervise her younger brother's homework while still being "on call" for her mother.

16. The only consistent exception was that some schools had an automated service to call and inform parents, in Spanish, if their child had been late, was absent, or had not completed his or her homework. These calls were considered helpful by many parents, although they expressed frustration with the lack of interactivity these calls afforded them. See chapter 6 for more details.

17. Alejandro's illness had also been a source of strain for Milagro's older sister, who had dropped out of high school to work and support the family. She had since completed her high school equivalency exam and was attending community college while working.

18. Interested readers can find further discussion of this phenomenon in chapter 3.

19. Medi-Cal is the California medical welfare program, which provides coverage for low-income families, seniors, pregnant women, and other vulnerable groups.

CHAPTER 5 — GATEWAYS TO FAMILY WELLBEING

1. Gálvez also found that immigrant parents expressed a preference for receiving healthcare in places with fewer Latino workers (2011, 84).

2. Gálvez's (2011) "subtractive health care" concept draws from Angela Valenzuela's (1999) earlier work on children of Mexican immigrants' encounters in US schools (see chapter 6). Gálvez contends that "what patients are offered is subtractive health care, a model for provisioning prenatal care that strips away and induces women themselves to shed the protective practices that have enabled them to have positive outcomes in the years immediately following their migration. The practices that epidemiologists and other scholars report as the 'cultural advantage' of Mexican immigrant women during pregnancy and childbirth are inseparable from a legacy of poverty and what they view as

'backward,' home-based health care. . . . Here, we have a different kind of paradox, in which 'health care' can lead to ill health, and healthful practices are willfully, even happily, left behind" (2011, 12).

3. It is certainly possible that the peer-professional staff at WIC, for example, engaged in racialized professionalism with co-ethnic recipients.

4. Children frequently did not feel entitled to ask questions; in instances when they or their families were treated poorly by an institution's staff, they were more likely to justify those behaviors than to feel that they could assert or defend themselves.

5. García-Sánchez (2014) details how child brokers made similarly complex cultural negotiations for their Moroccan-origin parents in a Spanish clinic.

6. These feelings sometimes led to parents selecting a different child to help them when interactions were potentially face-threatening. For example, although Alejandro relied heavily on Milagro's brokering assistance, he felt more comfortable taking his eldest daughter to consultations related to his reproductive health, as he felt Milagro was "still too young for these kinds of experiences."

7. Small's "unexpected gains" concept (2010) parallels Alba and Nee's (2005) argument about immigrant assimilation processes; that is, that few immigrants calculatedly pursue connections that assure their integration into American life. Rather, these changes are "unintended consequences" of simply doing what they need to do to achieve everyday goals related to settlement (Alba and Nee 2005, 35).

CHAPTER 6 — SHORTCHANGING THE IMMIGRANT BARGAIN?

1. Education is one of the most common pathways for children to honor the immigrant bargain, but certainly not the only one. For some children, forgoing college or dropping out of high school to work is a viable way to honor the immigrant bargain, having already exceeded their parents' educational attainment (though not having achieved parity with the native born; see FitzGerald 2012). Only two child brokers had dropped out, but due to pregnancy rather than plans to work. Since I was most concerned with children's contributions to families' institutional connections, my focus in this chapter is limited to how brokering relates to the immigrant bargain and educational attainment.

2. See chapter 2 for detailed descriptions of both schools.

3. Even demonstrating aesthetic caring was a challenge in these schools, given the low levels of academic performance school-wide (see table 2.3). In these environments, student achievement and grades earned were relative assessments. Ms. Lynworth, a Teach for America seventh-grade teacher at Tyler, said, "What we end up giving an A for here would earn a C in one of the schools on the Westside [a wealthier neighborhood in Los Angeles]. I mean, it's all relative, but I know that a kid with all A's here would be struggling to even make it at a better school."

4. Vivian Louie (2012) noted the same neutral feelings toward teachers among her respondents.

5. These patterns contrasted with the experiences of African American parents I interviewed whose children were in the same classes at Tyler and Bellum; their children were more likely to find math and science a struggle and language-based subjects easier.

6. Math and science are often linked, but mastery of both was only evident among high-achieving child brokers. Most struggled in science, even though math came easily to them. This pattern likely reflects how limited funds were for demonstrative science

learning, like conducting experiments and other lab work. Without it, science was reduced to "just sentences" in a textbook, which is how Rolando (age seventeen) had described learning history.

7. Teach for America is an American nonprofit organization that hires recent college graduates to teach in low-income communities for two years or more, in furtherance of their mission to eliminate inequalities in public education.

8. There were fewer Latino teachers and administrators at Bellum than Tyler. Ms. Hernandez, the ESL coordinator at Bellum, was Latina but was a fourth-generation American who spoke very little Spanish. Since she had a Spanish last name, immigrant parents came in to see her expecting that she spoke the language. As a result, she was defensive about her ethnic identity and downplayed it in her professional interactions.

9. Bellum Middle School was not actually predominantly African American since children of African and Caribbean immigrants were included in this racial designation. See chapter 2 for more details.

10. See chapter 3 for a discussion of California's bilingual education policy.

11. Marjorie Orellana also noted that Mexican immigrant parents taught their children different methods for long division (2009, 78).

12. Although one of Graciela's brothers was sixteen, he was struggling in school and came to her for assistance, rather than the reverse.

13. Compare with Dorner, Orellana, and Li-Grining (2007, 458).

14. Juliana benefited from her high school teachers and administrators being effective resource brokers. They held numerous informational meetings about financial aid and the college application process, and individual staff members provided her with support as she completed these documents.

15. See chapter 4 for more details on children's media brokering.

16. Vivian Louie argued that even if parents experience a downturn in social status after migration, professional status in their country of origin enabled them to help their children negotiate the US education system better than parents with no prior or current professional status (2012, 81).

17. Marjorie Orellana and her associates had found this same pattern; see Orellana (2009); García-Sánchez and Orellana (2006).

18. See chapter 5 for more details.

19. For example, see Buriel et al. (1998); and Dorner, Orellana, and Li-Grining (2007).

20. For example, see Kam (2011), Tse (1995), and Weisskirch and Alva (2002).

CHAPTER 7 — BROKERING AND ITS CONSEQUENCES

1. Massey and Sánchez (2010) extend Alba and Nee's (2005) formulation of assimilation theory; see more discussion of the former in chapter 1.

2. Delvecchio-Good and colleagues (2011) describe the struggles of providing healthcare in an age of "hyperdiversity" in rich detail.

3. Orellana found that children did not correct teachers' misperceptions in parent-teacher meetings (2009, 93).

4. Buriel and de Ment note, "For some children, the role of cultural broker is a lifelong responsibility that continues even after parents have lived in the United States for many years and have learned English. . . . [Child brokers are] still required to make doctor appointments, translate documents, and negotiate business transactions for parents" (1998, 190).

5. Guilamo-Ramos and his colleagues (2006) report the same mother-daughter communication pattern; even when Latina mothers talk openly about sex-related topics, daughters fear their mothers' reactions if they actually seek help or advice from them.

6. See Feliciano and Rumbaut (2005) and Lopez (2003) for discussion of differential college matriculation rates among boys and girls from Latino immigrant families.

7. See Vivian Louie (2012) for extended discussion of the loneliness that children of immigrants viewed as the price paid for pursuing higher education.

8. For example, see Sampson, Morenoff, and Gannon-Rowley (2002).

APPENDIX

1. The Metamorphosis Project is led by Dr. Sandra Ball-Rokeach and housed at the USC Annenberg School for Communication and Journalism.

2. Erzinger (1999) noted a similar dynamic between Spanish-speaking patients and English-speaking doctors who asked for patience with their elementary Spanish capabilities.

3. Orellana followed a similar strategy in these instances (2009, 59).

4. In 2008 and 2009, I interviewed service providers and conducted observations in the four institutions described in chapter 2.

5. Valdés describes these difficulties poignantly in her work as well (1996, 9–13).

REFERENCES

Abrégo, Leisy, and Roberto G. Gonzales. 2010. "Blocked Paths, Uncertain Futures: The Postsecondary Education and Labor Market Prospects of Undocumented Youth." *Journal of Education for Students Placed at Risk* 15 (1): 144–157.

Alba, Richard, and Victor Nee. 2005. *Remaking the American Mainstream: Assimilation and Contemporary Immigration.* Cambridge, MA: Harvard University Press.

Aldridge, Jo, and Saul Becker. 1999. "Children as Carers: The Impact of Parental Illness and Disability on Children's Caring Roles." *Journal of Family Therapy* 21: 303–320.

Ariès, Phillipe.1962. *Centuries of Childhood.* Translated by Robert Baldick. New York: Vintage Books.

Barry, Christine A. 2002. "Multiple Realities in a Study of Medical Consultations." *Qualitative Health Research* 12: 1093–1111.

Benítez, José. 2006. "Transnational Dimensions of the Digital Divide among Salvadoran Immigrants in the Washington, DC, Metropolitan Area." *Global Networks* 6 (2): 181–199.

Berroll, Selma C. 1995. *Growing Up American: Immigrant Children in America Then and Now.* New York: Twayne Books.

Bloemraad, Irene, and Christine Trost. 2008. "It's a Family Affair: Inter-generational Mobilization in the Spring 2006 Protests." *American Behavioral Scientist* 52: 507–532.

Bourdillon, Michael, Deborah Levison, William Myers, and Ben White. 2010. *Rights and Wrongs of Children's Work.* New Brunswick, NJ: Rutgers University Press.

Brittain, Carmina. 2003. *Crossing Borders in the Schoolyard: The Formation of Transnational Social Spaces among Chinese and Mexican Immigrant Students.* San Diego: University of California, Center for Comparative Immigration Studies. http://www.ccis-ucsd.org/PUBLICATIONS/wrkg76.pdf.

Buriel, Raymond. 1993. "Childrearing Orientations in Mexican American Families: The Influence of Generation and Sociocultural Factors." *Journal of Marriage and the Family* 55: 987–1000.

Buriel, Raymond, and Terri de Ment. 1998. "Immigration and Sociocultural Change in Mexican, Chinese, and Vietnamese American Families." In *Immigration and the Family*, edited by Alan Booth, Ann Crouter, and Nancy Landale, 165–200. Mahwah, NJ: Lawrence Erlbaum Associates.

Buriel, Raymond, William Perez, Terri de Ment, David V. Chavez, and Virginia R. Moran. 1998. "The Relationship of Language Brokering to Academic Performance, Biculturalism, and Self-Efficacy among Latino Adolescents." *Hispanic Journal of Behavioral Sciences* 20: 283–297.

Burt, Ronald. 2001. "Structural Holes versus Network Closure as Social Capital." In *Social Capital: Theory and Research*, edited by N. Lin, K. Cook, and R. S. Burt, 31–56. New York: Aldine de Gruyter.

California Department of Education. 2007. "Data and Statistics." http://dq.cde.ca.gov/dataquest/.

California Women, Infants and Children Program (WIC). 2011. "WIC Fact Sheet." http://www.cdph.ca.gov/PROGRAMS/CENTERFORFAMILYHEALTH/Pages/WICFactSheet.aspx.

Cannon, Lou. 1999. *Official Negligence: How Rodney King and the Riots Changed Los Angeles and the LAPD*. New York: Basic Books.

Chao, Ruth. 2006. "The Prevalence and Consequences of Adolescents' Language Brokering for Their Immigrant Parents." In *Acculturation and Parent-Child Relationships: Measurement and Development*, edited by Marc Bornstein and Lisa R. Cote, 271–296. Mahwah, NJ: Lawrence Erlbaum Associates.

Chàvez, Christopher, and Sandra J. Ball-Rokeach. 2006. "Exploring the Role of Religious Affiliation on Civic Engagement amongst New Immigrant Latinos in Los Angeles." Paper presented to the Annual Meeting of the International Communication Association, Dresden, Germany, June.

Child Trends. 2010. "Immigrant Children." Accessed February 12, 2012. http://www.childtrendsdatabank.org/?q=node/333.

Chinn, Sarah E. 2009. *Inventing Modern Adolescence: The Children of Immigrants in Turn-of-the-Century America*. New Brunswick, NJ: Rutgers University Press.

Clark, Lynn S. 2005. "The Constant Contact Generation: Exploring Teen Friendship Networks Online." In *Girl Wide Web: Girls, the Internet, and the Negotiation of Identity*, edited by Sharon Mazzarella. New York: Peter Lang.

———. 2011. "Parental Mediation Theory for the Digital Age." *Communication Theory* 21 (4): 323–343.

———. 2013. *The Parent App: Understanding Families in the Digital Age*. Oxford: Oxford University Press.

Coe, Cati, Rachel Reynolds, Deborah Boehm, Julia Hess, and Heather Rae-Espinoza, eds. 2011. *Everyday Ruptures: Children, Youth, and Migration in Global Perspective*. Nashville: Vanderbilt University Press.

Cohen, Jerry, and William Murphy. 1966. *Burn, Baby, Burn! The Los Angeles Race Riot, August 1965*. New York: Dutton.

Cohen, Suzanne, Jo Moran-Ellis, and Chris Smaje. 1999. "Children as Informal Interpreters in GP Consultations: Pragmatics and Ideology." *Sociology of Health & Illness* 21: 163–186.

Cordasco, Francesco. 1976. *Immigrants in American Schools*. New York: Kelley Books.

Covello, Leonard. 1958. *The Heart Is the Teacher*. New York: McGraw-Hill.

Dailey, Dharma, Amelia Bryne, Alison Powell, Joe Karaganis, and Jaewon Chung. 2010. "Broadband Adoption in Low-Income Communities." Washington, DC: Social Science Research Council. http://webarchive.ssrc.org/pdfs/Broadband_Adoption_v1.1.pdf.

de Block, Liesbeth, and David Buckingham. 2008. *Global Media, Global Children: Migration, Media, and Childhood*. London: Palgrave Macmillan.

Delvecchio-Good, Mary-Jo, Sarah Willen, Seth Hannah, Ken Vickery, and Lawrence Park, eds. 2011. *Shattering Culture: American Medicine Responds to Cultural Diversity*. New York: Russell Sage Foundation.

de Souza, Rebecca. 2009. "Creating 'Communicative Spaces': A Case of NGO Community Organizing for HIV/AIDS Prevention." *Health Communication* 24 (8): 692–702.

de Souza Briggs, Xavier. 2003. "Bridging Networks, Social Capital, and Racial Segregation in America." Harvard University School of Government Faculty Research Working Papers Series, RWP02–011.

Dodson, Lisa, and Jillian Dickert. 2004. "Girls' Family Labor in Low-Income Households: A Decade of Qualitative Research." *Journal of Marriage and Family* 66: 318–332.

Domínguez, Silvia. 2011. *Getting Ahead: Social Mobility, Public Housing, and Immigrant Networks*. New York: NYU Press.

Domínguez, Silvia, and Celeste Watkins. 2003. "Creating Networks for Survival and Mobility: Social Capital among African-American and Latin-American Low Income Mothers." *Social Problems* 50: 111–135.

Dorner, Lisa, Marjorie Faulstich Orellana, and Christine Li-Grining. 2007. "'I Helped My Mom' and It Helped Me: Translating the Skills of Language Brokers into Improved Standardized Test Scores." *American Journal of Education* 113: 451–478.

Doty, Melissa M., and Alyssa L. Holmgren. 2006. "Health Care Disconnect: Gaps in Coverage and Care for Minority Adults." The Commonwealth Fund. http://www .commonwealthfund.org/Publications/Issue-Briefs/2006/Aug/Health-Care-Disconnect --Gaps-in-Coverage-and-Care-for-Minority-Adults--Findings-from-the-Commonwealt .aspx.

Dreby, Joanna. 2010. *Divided by Borders: Mexican Migrants and Their Children*. Berkeley: University of California Press.

Duffy, Mignon. 2011. *Making Care Count: A Century of Gender, Race, and Paid Care Work*. New Brunswick, NJ: Rutgers University Press.

Dumas, Firoozeh. 2004. *Funny in Farsi: A Memoir of Growing Up Iranian in America*. New York: Random House.

Duranti, Alessandro. 1997. *Linguistic Anthropology: A Reader*. Cambridge: Cambridge University Press.

Durham, Meenakshi. 2004. "Constructing the 'New Ethnicities': Media, Sexuality, and Diaspora Identity in the Lives of South Asian Immigrant Girls." *Critical Studies in Media Communication* 21: 140–161.

Ebaugh, Helen, and Janet Saltzman Chafetz. 2000. "Structural Adaptation in Immigrant Congregations." *Sociology of Religion* 61 (2): 135–153.

Elias, Nelly, and Dan Caspi. 2007. "From *Pravda* to *Vesty*: The Russian Media Renaissance in Israel." In *Every Seventh Israeli: Patterns of Social and Cultural Integration of the Russian-Speaking Immigrants*, edited by Alek D. Epstein and Vladamir Khanin, 175–198. Jerusalem-Ramat-Gan: Bar-Ilan University Press.

Elias, Nelly, and Dafna Lemish. 2008. "Media Uses in Immigrant Families: Torn Between 'Inward' and 'Outward' Paths of Integration." *International Communication Gazette* 70: 21–40.

———. 2011. "Between Three Worlds: Host, Homeland, and Global Media in the Lives of Russian Immigrant Families in Israel and Germany." *Journal of Family Issues* 32: 1245–1274.

Elman, Richard. 1967. *Ill at Ease in Compton*. New York: Pantheon Books.

Epstein, Helen. 1979. *Children of the Holocaust: Conversations with the Sons and Daughters of Survivors*. New York: Bantam Books.

Erzinger, Sherry. 1999. "Communication between Spanish-Speaking Patients and Their Doctors in Medical Encounters." In *Rethinking Ethnicity and Health Care: A Sociocultural Perspective*, edited by Grace Ma and George Henderson, 122–140. Springfield, IL: Charles C. Thomas.

Fabiano, Laurie. 2011. *Elizabeth Street*. New York: Mariner Books.

Fass, Paula S. 2007. *Inheriting the Holocaust: A Second-Generation Memoir*. New Brunswick, NJ: Rutgers University Press.

Federal Communications Commission. 2010. "National Broadband Plan: Connecting America." http://www.broadband.gov/plan/.

Feliciano, Cynthia, and Rubén Rumbaut. 2005. "Gendered Paths: Educational and Occupational Expectations and Outcomes among Adult Children of Immigrants." *Ethnic and Racial Studies* 28 (6): 1087–1118.

Félix, Adrián, Carmen Gonzalez, and Ricardo Ramírez. 2008. "Political Protest, Ethnic Media, and Latino Naturalization." *American Behavioral Scientist* 52: 618–634.

Fiscella, Kevin, and Ronald M. Epstein. 2008. "So Much to Do, So Little Time: Care for the Socially Disadvantaged and the 15-Minute Visit." *Archives of Internal Medicine* 168: 1843–1852.

FitzGerald, David. 2012. "A Comparativist Manifesto for International Migration Studies." *Ethnic and Racial Studies* 35: 1725–1740.

Fulton, William. 1997. *The Reluctant Metropolis: The Politics of Urban Growth in Los Angeles*. Baltimore: Johns Hopkins University Press.

Gálvez, Alyshia. 2011. *Patient Citizens, Immigrant Mothers: Mexican Women, Public Prenatal Care, and the Birth-Weight Paradox*. New Brunswick, NJ: Rutgers University Press.

Galvin, Kathleen, Fran C. Dickson, and Sherilyn R. Marrow. 2005. "Systems Theory: Patterns and W(holes) in Family Communication." In *Engaging Theories in Family Communication: Multiple Perspectives*, edited by D. O. Braithwaite and L. A. Baxter, 309–324. Thousand Oaks, CA: Sage Publications.

García-Sánchez, Inmaculada M. 2010. "(Re)shaping Practices in Translation: How Moroccan Immigrant Children and Families Navigate Continuity and Change." *mediAzioni* 10. http://mediazioni.sitlec.unibo.it.

———. 2014. *Language and Muslim Immigrant Childhoods: The Politics of Belonging*. Hoboken, NJ: Wiley-Blackwell.

García-Sánchez, Inmaculada, and Marjorie Faulstich Orellana. 2006. "The Construction of Moral and Social Identities in Immigrant Children's Narratives-in-Translation." *Linguistics and Education* 17: 209–239.

Gavazzi, Stephen. 2011. *Families with Adolescents: Bridging the Gaps between Theory, Research, and Practice*. New York: Springer.

Georgiou, Myria. 2001. "Crossing the Boundaries of the Ethnic Home: Media Consumption and Ethnic Identity Construction in the Public Sphere: The Case of the Cypriot Community Centre in North London." *Gazette* 63 (4): 311–329.

Goffman, Erving. 1959. *The Presentation of Self in Everyday Life*. New York: Anchor Books.

Gonzales, Roberto. 2011. "Learning to Be Illegal: Undocumented Youth and Shifting Legal Contexts in the Transition to Adulthood." *American Sociological Review* 76 (4): 603–604.

Gordan, Milton. 1964. *Assimilation in American Life: The Role of Race, Religion, and National Origins*. Oxford: Oxford University Press.

Granovetter, Mark. 1973. "The Strength of Weak Ties." *American Journal of Sociology* 78 (6): 1360–1380.

Guilamo-Ramos, Vincent, Patricia Dittus, James Jaccard, Vincent Goldberg, Eileen Casillas, and Alida Bouris. 2006. "The Content and Process of Mother-Adolescent Communication about Sex in Latino Families." *Social Work Research* 30 (3): 169–181.

Hakuta, Kenji. 1986. *Mirror of Language: The Debate on Bilingualism.* New York: Basic Books.

Hargreaves, Alec, and Delila Mahdjoub. 1997. "Satellite Television Viewing among Ethnic Minorities in France." *European Journal of Communication* 12 (4): 459–477.

Havighurst, Robert. 1953. *Human Development and Education.* London: Longmans, Green & Co.

Heath, Shirley Brice. 1983. *Ways with Words: Language, Life, and Work in Communities and Classrooms.* Cambridge: Cambridge University Press.

Heritage, John, and Douglas W. Maynard. 2006. "Problems and Prospects in the Study of Physician-Patient Interaction: 30 Years of Research." *Annual Review of Sociology* 32: 351–374.

Hirsch, Jennifer. 1999. *A Courtship after Marriage: Sexuality and Love in Mexican Transnational Families.* Berkeley: University of California Press.

Holmes, Seth. 2007. "'Oaxacans Like to Work Bent Over': The Naturalization of Social Suffering among Berry Farm Workers." *International Migration* 45: 39–68.

Hondagneu-Sotelo, Pierrette. 1994. *Gendered Transitions: Mexican Experiences of Immigration.* Berkeley: University of California Press.

———. 2001. *Doméstica: Immigrant Workers Cleaning and Caring in the Shadows of Affluence.* Berkeley: University of California Press.

Hoover, Stewart, Lynn Schofield Clark, and Diane Alters. 2004. *Media, Home, and Family.* New York: Routledge.

Hseih, Elaine. 2007. "Interpreters as Co-diagnosticians: Overlapping Roles and Services between Providers and Interpreters." *Social Science and Medicine* 64: 924–937.

Hunt, Darnell. 1996. *Screening the Los Angeles "Riots": Race, Seeing, and Resistance.* Cambridge: Cambridge University Press.

Hunt, Darnell, and Ana-Christina Ramon. 2010. "Killing 'Killer King': The *Los Angeles Times* and a 'Troubled' Hospital in the 'Hood." In *Black Los Angeles: American Dreams and Racial Realities*, edited by Darnell Hunt and Ana-Christina Ramon, 283–322. New York: NYU Press.

Ito, Mimi, Sonja Baumer, Matteo Bittanti, Danah Boyd, Rachel Cody, Becky Herr, Heather A. Horst, Patricia G. Lange, Dilan Mahendran, Katynka Martinez, C. J. Pascoe, Dan Perkel, Laura Robinson, Christo Sims, and Lisa Tripp. 2009. *Hanging Out, Messing Around, and Geeking Out: Kids Living and Learning with New Media.* Cambridge, MA: MIT Press.

Janowitz, Morris. 1967. *The Community Press in an Urban Setting: The Social Elements of Urbanism.* Chicago: University of Chicago Press.

Johnson, Julia Overturf, Robert Kominski, Kristin Smith, and Paul Tillman. 2005. *Changes in the Lives of U.S. Children: 1990–2000.* Working Paper No. 78, Population Division. Washington, DC: US Census Bureau.

Jones-Correa, Michael. 1998. "Different Paths: Gender, Immigration, and Political Participation." *International Migration Review* 32 (2): 326–349.

Kam, Jennifer A. 2011. "The Effects of Language-Brokering Frequency and Feelings on Mexican-Heritage Youth's Mental Health and Risky Behaviors." *Journal of Communication* 61: 455–475.

Katz, Vikki S. 2010. "How Children Use Media to Connect Their Families to the Community: The Case of Latinos in Los Angeles." *Journal of Children and Media* 4: 298–315.

————. 2014. "Children as Brokers of Their Immigrant Families' Healthcare Connections." *Social Problems* 61 (2).

Kibria, Nazli. 1993. *Family Tightrope: The Changing Lives of Vietnamese Americans*. Princeton, NJ: Princeton University Press.

Kim, Yong-Chan, and Sandra J. Ball-Rokeach. 2006. "Community Storytelling Network, Neighborhood Context, and Civic Engagement: A Multi-level Approach." *Human Communication Research* 32: 411–439.

Kim, Yong-Chan, Joo-Young Jung, and Sandra J. Ball-Rokeach. 2006. "'Geo-Ethnicity' and Neighborhood Engagement: A Communication Infrastructure Perspective." *Political Communication* 23: 421–441.

Kishon, Ephraim. 1967. *So Sorry We Won*. Jerusalem: Maariv Library.

Lareau, Annette. 2003. *Unequal Childhoods: Class, Race, and Family Life*. Berkeley: University of California Press.

LeCompte, Margaret. 2008. "Negotiating Exit." In *Sage Encyclopedia of Qualitative Research*, vol. 2, edited by L. Given, 553–556. Thousand Oaks, CA: Sage Publications.

Le Espiritu, Yen. 2001. "'We Don't Sleep Around like White Girls Do': Family, Culture, and Gender in Filipina American Lives." *Signs* 26: 415–440.

Leidner, Joel D. 1965. "Major Factors in Industrial Location." In *Hard-Core Unemployment and Poverty in Los Angeles*, prepared by University of California, Institute of Industrial Relations. Washington, DC: US Dept. of Commerce.

Lenhart, Amanda. 2005. "Protecting Teens Online." Washington, DC: Pew Internet and American Life Project. http://www.pewinternet.org/PPF/r/152/report_display.asp.

Lenhart, Amanda, Sousan Arafeh, Aaron Smith, and Alexandra Macgill. 2008. "Writing, Technology, and Teens." Washington DC: Pew Internet and American Life Project. http://www.pewinternet.org/PPF/r/247/report_display.asp.

Lievrouw, Leah, and Sonia Livingstone. 2005. "Introduction to the Student Edition." In *The Handbook of New Media: Social Shaping and Consequences of ICTs*, edited by L. Lievrouw and S. Livingstone, 1–24. London: Sage Publications.

Light, Ivan. 2008. *Deflecting Immigration: Networks, Markets, and Regulation in Los Angeles*. New York: Russell Sage Foundation.

Lin, Wan-Ying, and Hayeon Song. 2006. "Geo-ethnic Storytelling: An Examination of Ethnic Media Content in Contemporary Immigrant Communities." *Journalism, Theory, Practice* 7: 362–388.

Lippi-Green, Rosina. 1997. *English with an Accent: Language, Ideology, and Discrimination in the United States*. London: Routledge.

Lipsky, Michael. 2010. *Street-Level Bureaucracy: Dilemmas of the Individual in Public Service*. Thirtieth Anniversary Expanded Edition. New York: Russell Sage Foundation.

Livingstone, Sonia. 2002. *Young People and New Media: Childhood and the Changing Media Environment*. London: Sage Publications.

Livingstone, Sonia, and Leslie Haddon, eds. 2009. *Kids Online: Opportunities and Risks for Children*. Bristol, UK: Policy Press.

Livingstone, Sonia, and Ellen J. Helsper. 2007. "Gradations in Digital Inclusion: Children, Young People, and the Digital Divide." *New Media and Society* 9 (4): 671–696.

Lopez, Nancy. 2003. *Hopeful Girls, Troubled Boys: Race and Gender Disparity in Urban Education*. New York: Routledge.

Louie, Josephine. 2003. "Media in the Lives of Immigrant Youth." *New Directions for Youth Development* 100: 111–130.

Louie, Vivian. 2004. *Compelled to Excel: Immigration, Education, and Opportunity among Chinese Americans*. Palo Alto, CA: Stanford University Press.

——. 2012. *Keeping the Immigrant Bargain: The Costs and Rewards of Success in America*. New York: Russell Sage Foundation.

Madden, Mary, Amanda Lenhart, Maeve Duggan, Sandra Cortesi, and Urs Gasser. 2013. "Teens and Technology 2013." Pew Internet Project. http://www.pewinternet.org/Reports/2013/Teens-and-Tech.aspx.

Mangual Figueroa, Ariana. 2013. "*La Carta de la Responsibilidad*: The Problem of Departure." In *Humanizing Research: Decolonizing Qualitative Inquiry with Youth and Communities*, edited by D. Paris and M. T. Winn, 129–146. Thousand Oaks, CA: Sage Publications.

Massey, Douglas S., Jorge Durand, and Nolan J. Malone. 2002. *Beyond Smoke and Mirrors: Mexican Immigration in an Era of Economic Integration*. New York: Russell Sage Foundation.

Massey, Douglas S., and Magaly Sánchez R. 2010. *Brokered Boundaries: Creating Immigrant Identity in Anti-immigrant Times*. New York: Russell Sage Foundation.

Matei, Sorin A., and Sandra J. Ball-Rokeach. 2005. "Watts, the 1965 Los Angeles Riots, and the Communicative Construction of the Fear Epicenter of Los Angeles," *Communication Monographs* 72: 301–323.

Matsaganis, Matthew D., Vikki Katz, and Sandra Ball-Rokeach. 2011. *Understanding Ethnic Media: Producers, Consumers, and Societies*. Thousand Oaks, CA: Sage Publications.

Mayer, Vicki. 2003. "Living Telenovelas/Telenovelizing Life: Mexican-American Girls' Identities and Transnational Telenovelas." *Journal of Communication* 53 (3): 479–495.

McCone, John. 1965. *Violence in the City: An End or a Beginning? A Report*. Los Angeles: California Commission Report. http://www.usc.edu/libraries/archives/cityinstress/mccone/contents.html.

McDevitt, Michael, and Steven Chaffee. 2002. "From 'Top Down' to 'Trickle Up' Influence: Revisiting Assumptions about the Family in Political Socialization." *Political Communication* 19: 281–301.

McKenzie, Kwame, Rob Whitley, and Scott Weich. 2002. "Social Capital and Mental Health." *British Journal of Psychiatry* 181: 280–283.

Medina, Jennifer. 2012. "In Years Since the Riots, a Changed Complexion in South Central." *New York Times*, April 24. http://www.nytimes.com/2012/04/25/us/in-south-los-angeles-a-changed-complexion-since-the-riots.html?_r=1.

Menjívar, Cecilia. 2000. *Fragmented Ties: Salvadoran Immigrant Networks in America*. Berkeley: University of California Press.

Menjívar, Cecilia, and Leisy Abrégo. 2009. "Parents and Children across Borders: Legal Instability and Intergenerational Relations in Guatemalan and Salvadoran Families." In *Across Generations: Immigrant Families in America*, edited by N. Foner, 160–189. New York: New York University Press.

Miller-Day, Michelle, and Carla Fisher. 2006. "Communication over the Life Span: The Mother–Adult Daughter Relationship." In *Widening the Family Circle: New Research in Family Communication*, edited by K. Floyd and M.T. Morman, 3–19. Thousand Oaks, CA: Sage Publications.

National Assessment of Educational Progress. 2005. "The Nation's Report Card." http://nationsreportcard.gov/reading_math_2005/s0006.asp.

Office of Minority Health. 2010. "Obesity Data/Statistics." http://minorityhealth.hhs.gov.

Olsen, David. 2000. "Circumplex Model of Marital and Family Systems." *Journal of Family Therapy* 22: 144–167.

Ong, Aihwa. 2003. *Buddha Is Hiding: Refugees, Citizenship, and the New America*. Berkeley: University of California Press.

Orellana, Marjorie Faulstich. 2009. *Translating Childhoods: Immigrant Youth, Language, and Culture*. New Brunswick, NJ: Rutgers University Press.

Orellana, Marjorie Faulstich, Lisa Dorner, and Lucila Pulido. 2003. "Accessing Assets: Immigrant Youth's Work as Family Translators or 'Para-Phrasers.'" *Social Problems* 50: 505–524.

Orfield, Gary, and John Yun. 1999. "Resegregation in American Schools." UCLA Civil Rights Project/Proyecto Derechos Civiles. http://civilrightsproject.ucla.edu/research/k-12 -education/integration-and-diversity/resegregation-in-american-schools/?searchterm =Resegregation.

Oznobishin, Olga, and Jenny Kurman. 2009. "Parent-Child Role Reversal and Psychological Adjustment among Immigrant Youth in Israel." *Journal of Family Psychology* 23: 405–415.

Park, Lisa Sun-Hee. 2001. "Between Adulthood and Childhood: The Boundary Work of Immigrant Entrepreneurial Children." *Berkeley Journal of Sociology* 45: 114–135.

———. 2005. *Consuming Citizenship: Children of Asian Immigrant Entrepreneurs*. Palo Alto, CA: Stanford University Press.

Perrow, Charles. 1984. *Normal Accidents: Living with High-Risk Technologies*. New York: Basic Books.

Pessar, Patricia. 2003. "Engendering Migration Studies: The Case of New Immigrants in the United States." In *Gender and U.S. Immigration*, edited by P. Hondagneu-Sotelo, 20–42. Berkeley: University of California Press.

Pew Research Center. 2011. *Demographics of Internet Users*. Washington, DC: Pew Research Center Internet and American Life Project. http://www.pewinternet.org/Static-Pages/ Trend-Data/Whos-Online.aspx.

Portes, Alejandro, and Lingxin Hao. 2002. "The Price of Uniformity: Language, Family, and Personality Adjustment in the Immigrant Second Generation." *Ethnic and Racial Studies* 25: 890.

Portes, Alejandro, and Ruben Rumbaut. 2000. *Legacies: The Story of the Immigrant Second Generation*. Berkeley: University of California Press.

Portes, Alejandro, and Min Zhou. 1993. "The New Second Generation: Segmented Assimilation and Its Variants." *Annals of the American Academy of Political and Social Science* 530: 74–96.

Putnam, Robert. 2000. *Bowling Alone: The Collapse and Revival of American Community*. New York: Simon & Schuster.

Pyke, Karen. 2000. "'The Normal American Family' as an Interpretive Structure of Family Life among Grown Children of Korean and Vietnamese Immigrants." *Journal of Marriage and Family* 62: 240–255.

———. 2005. "'Generational Deserters' and 'Black Sheep': Acculturative Differences among Siblings in Asian Immigrant Families." *Journal of Family Issues* 26: 491–517.

Reese, Leslie. 2001. "Morality and Identity in Mexican Immigrant Parents' Visions of the Future." *Journal of Ethnic and Migration Studies* 27: 455–472.

Reynolds, Jennifer, and Marjorie Faulstich Orellana. 2009. "New Immigrant Youth Interpreting in White Public Space." *American Anthropologist* 111: 211–223.

Rideout, Victoria, Ulla Foehr, and Donald Roberts. 2010. "Generation M2: Media in the Lives of 8- to 18-Year-Olds." Menlo Park, CA: Kaiser Family Foundation. http://kff.org/other/event/generation-m2-media-in-the-lives-of/.

Rideout, Victoria, Ulla Foehr, Donald Roberts, and Mollyann Brodie. 1999. "Kids and Media @ the New Millennium." Menlo Park, CA: Henry J. Kaiser Foundation. http://kff.org/hivaids/report/kids-media-the-new-millennium/.

Romich, Jennifer L. 2007. "Sharing the Work: Mother-Child Relationships and Household Management." *Journal of Early Adolescence* 27: 192–222.

Rueda, Robert, Lilia D. Monzó, and Angela Arzubiaga. 2003. "Academic Instrumental Knowledge: Deconstructing Cultural Capital Theory for Strategic Intervention Approaches." *Current Issues in Education* 6. http://cie.asu.edu/volume6/number14/index.

Rumbaut, Ruben, and Alejandro Portes. 2001. *Ethnicities: Children of Immigrants in America.* Berkeley: University of California Press.

Sampson, Robert J. 2011. "Neighborhood Effects, Causal Mechanisms, and the Social Structure of the City." In *Analytical Sociology and Social Mechanisms*, edited by Pierre Demeulenaere, 227–250. Cambridge: Cambridge University Press.

———. 2012. *Great American City: Chicago and the Enduring Neighborhood Effect.* Chicago: University of Chicago Press.

Sampson, Robert J., Jeffrey D. Morenoff, and Thomas Gannon-Rowley. 2002. "Assessing 'Neighborhood Effects': Social Processes and New Directions in Research." *Annual Review of Sociology* 28: 443–478.

Shakur, Sanyika. 2004. *Monster: The Autobiography of an L.A. Gang Member.* New York: Grove Press.

Sharf, Barbara. 1993. "Reading the Vital Signs: Research in Health Care Communication." *Communication Monographs* 60: 35–41.

Shin, Hyon, and Robert Kominski. 2010. *Language Use in the United States.* Washington, DC: US Census Bureau. http://www.census.gov/hhes/socdemo/language/data/acs/ACS-12.pdf.

Sides, Josh. 2004a. *L.A. City Limits: African American Los Angeles from the Great Depression to the Present.* Berkeley: University of California Press.

———. 2004b. "Straight into Compton: American Dreams, Urban Nightmares, and the Metamorphosis of a Black Suburb." *American Quarterly* 56: 585.

Sitton, Tom, and William Deverell, eds. 2001. *Metropolis in the Making: Los Angeles in the 1920s.* Berkeley: University of California Press.

Small, Mario L. 2006. "Neighborhood Institutions as Resource Brokers: Childcare Centers, Interorganizational Ties, and Resource Access among the Poor." *Social Problems* 53 (2): 274–292.

———. 2010. *Unanticipated Gains: Origins of Network Inequality in Everyday Life.* Oxford: Oxford University Press.

Smith, Robert Courtney. 2002. "Life Course, Generation, and Social Location as Factors Shaping Second-Generation Transnational Life." In *The Changing Face of Home*, edited by P. Levitt and M. Waters. New York: Russell Sage Foundation.

Song, Miri. 1999. *Helping Out: Children's Labor in Ethnic Businesses.* Philadelphia: Temple University Press.

Stack, Carol, and Linda Burton. 1993. "Kinscripts." *Journal of Comparative Family Studies* 24: 157–170.

Stanton-Salazar, Ricardo D. 2001. *Manufacturing Hope and Despair: The School and Kin Support Networks of U.S.-Mexican Youth.* New York: Teachers College Press.

Stanton-Salazar, Ricardo D., and Stephanie Urso Spina. 2003. "Informal Mentors and Role Models in the Lives of Urban Mexican-Origin Adolescents." *Anthropology & Education Quarterly* 34: 231–254.

Stevens, Gillian, and Hiromi Ishizawa. 2007. "Variation among Siblings in the Use of a Non-English Language." *Journal of Family Issues* 28: 1008–1025.

Strasburger, Victor, Barbara Wilson, and Amy Jordan. 2009. *Children, Adolescents, and the Media.* 2nd edition. Thousand Oaks, CA: Sage Publications.

Street, Richard. 1991. "Accommodation in Medical Consultations." In *Contexts of Accommodation: Developments in Applied Sociolinguistics*, edited by Howard Giles, Justine Coupland, and Nikolaus Coupland, 131–156. Cambridge: Cambridge University Press.

Suárez-Orozco, Carola, Marcelo Suárez-Orozco, and Irina Todorova. 2008. *Learning a New Land: Immigrant Students in American Society.* Cambridge, MA: Harvard University Press.

Takeuchi, Lori, and Reed Stevens. 2011. *The New Coviewing: Designing for Learning Through Joint Media Engagement.* New York: Joan Ganz Cooney Center at Sesame Workshop.

Taylor, Steven J., and Robert Bogdan. 1998. *Introduction to Qualitative Research Methods.* 3rd edition. New York: John Wiley.

Telles, Edward, Mark Q. Sawyer, and Gaspar Rivera-Salgado, eds. 2011. *Just Neighbors? Research on African American and Latino Relations in the United States.* New York: Russell Sage Foundation.

Thoman, Elizabeth, and Tessa Jolls. 2004. "Media Literacy: A National Priority for a Changing World." *American Behavioral Scientist* 48 (1): 18–29.

Thorne, Barrie. 1993. *Gender Play: Boys and Girls in School.* New Brunswick, NJ: Rutgers University Press.

Thorne, Barrie, Marjorie Faulstich Orellana, Wan Shun Eva Lam, and Anna Chee. 2003. "Raising Children, and Growing Up, across National Borders." In *Gender and U.S. Immigration*, edited by P. Hondagneu-Sotelo, 241–262. Berkeley: University of California Press.

Tripp, Lisa M. 2011. "'The Computer Is Not for You to Be Looking Around, It Is for Schoolwork': Challenges for Digital Inclusion as Latino Immigrant Families Negotiate Children's Access to the Internet." *New Media & Society* 13: 552–567.

Tse, Lucy. 1995. "Language Brokering among Latino Adolescents: Prevalence, Attitudes, and School Performance." *Hispanic Journal of Behavioral Sciences* 17: 180–193.

———. 1996. "Who Decides? The Effect of Language Brokering on Home-School Communication." *Journal of Educational Issues of Language Minority Students* 16: 225–233.

Urban Institute. 2009. *Children of Immigrants.* Accessed January 5, 2012. http://datatool .urban.org/charts/datatool/pages.cfm.

US Bureau of the Census. 2000. "American Factfinder." www.census.us.gov.

———. 2010. "American Factfinder." www.census.us.gov.

US Commission on Civil Rights. 1960. *Hearings Held in Los Angeles and San Francisco, January 25–28, 1960,* 158–159. Washington, DC: Government Printing Office.

US Department of Agriculture Food and Nutrition Service. 2013. "How to Apply: WIC Eligibility Guidelines." http://www.fns.usda.gov/wic/howtoapply/incomeguidelines.htm.

US Department of Defense. 2010. "Recruiting and the All-Volunteer Force (AVF)." Washington, DC: US Dept. of Defense. http://www.defense.gov/news/d20101012handout.pdf.

US Department of Health and Human Services. 2009. "Office of Minority Health." http://www.omhrc.gov/templates/browse.aspx?lvl=1&lvlID=2.

Valdés, Guadalupe. 1996. *Con Respeto: Bridging the Distances between Culturally Diverse Families and Schools.* New York: Teachers College Press.

———. 2003. *Expanding Definitions of Giftedness: The Case of Young Interpreters from Immigrant Communities.* New York: Routledge.

Valenzuela, Abel. 1999. "Gender Roles and Settlement Activities among Children and Their Immigrant Families." *American Behavioral Scientist* 42: 720–742.

Valenzuela, Angela. 1999. *Subtractive Schooling: U.S.-Mexican Youth and the Politics of Caring.* New York: State University of New York Press.

Varghese, Anita, and Sharon Rae Jenkins. 2009. "Parental Overprotection, Cultural Value Conflict, and Psychological Adaptation among Asian Indian Women in America." *Sex Roles* 61: 235–251.

Vygotsky, Lev. 1978. *Mind in Society: The Development of Higher Psychological Processes.* Cambridge, MA: Harvard University Press.

Waldinger, Roger, and Claudia Der-Martirosian. 2001. "The Immigrant Niche: Pervasive, Persistent, Diverse." In *Strangers at the Gates: New Immigrants in Urban America*, edited by Roger Waldinger, 228–271. Berkeley: University of California Press.

Waters, Mary C., Van C. Tran, Philip Kasinitz, and John H. Mollenkopf. 2010. "Segmented Assimilation Revisited: Types of Acculturation and Socioeconomic Mobility in Young Adulthood." *Ethnic and Racial Studies* 33: 1168–1193.

Watkins-Hayes, Celeste. 2009. *The New Welfare Bureaucrats: Entanglements of Race, Class, and Policy Reform.* Chicago: University of Chicago Press.

Watson, Bernadette, and Cindy Gallois. 2004. "Emotional Expression as a Sociolinguistic Strategy: Its Importance in Medical Interactions." In *Language Matters: Communication, Culture, and Identity*, edited by Sik Hung Ng, Christopher Candlin, and Chi Yue Chiu, 63–84. Hong Kong: City University of Hong Kong Press.

Weisner, Thomas, Gery Ryan, Leslie Reese, Kendall Kroesen, Lucinda Bernheimer, and Ronald Gallimore. 2001. "Behavior Sampling and Ethnography: Complementary Methods for Understanding Home-School Connections among Immigrant Latino Families." *Field Methods* 13 (1): 20–46.

Weiss, Bernard J. 1984. *American Education and the European Immigrant, 1840–1940.* Champaign: University of Illinois Press.

Weisskirch, Robert, and Sylvia Alva. 2002. "Language Brokering and the Acculturation of Latino Children." *Hispanic Journal of Behavioral Sciences* 24: 369–378.

Wellman, Barry, and Milena Gulia. 1999. "The Network Basis of Social Support: A Network Is More Than the Sum of Its Ties." In *Networks in the Global Village: Life in Contemporary Communities*, edited by Barry Wellman, 83–118. Boulder, CO: Westview Press.

Weston, Kath. 1997. *Families We Choose: Lesbians, Gays, Kinship.* New York: Columbia University Press.

Whaley, Shannon E., Lu Jiang, Judy Gomez, and Eloise Jenks. 2011. "Literacy Promotion for Families Participating in the Women, Infants, and Children Program." *Pediatrics* 127 (3): 454–461.

Wilkin, Holley A., Sandra J. Ball-Rokeach, Matthew D. Matsaganis, and Pauline H. Cheong. 2007. "Comparing the Communication Ecologies of Geo-ethnic Communities: How People Stay on Top of Their Community." *Electronic Journal of Communication* 17 (1–2). http://www.cios.org/EJCPUBLIC/017/1/01711.HTML.

Wilkin, Holley, Vikki Katz, and Sandra Ball-Rokeach. 2009. "The Role of Family Interaction in New Immigrant Latinos' Civic Engagement." *Journal of Communication* 59 (2): 387–406.

Willen, Sarah. 2011. "Pas de Trois: Medical Interpreters, Clinical Dilemmas, and the Patient-Provider-Interpreter Triad." In *Shattering Culture: American Medicine Responds to Cultural Diversity*, edited by M. J. Delvecchio-Good, S. S. Willen, S. D. Hannah, K. Vickery, and L. T. Park, 70–94. New York: Russell Sage Foundation.

Wilson, William J. 1987. *The Truly Disadvantaged: The Inner City, the Underclass, and Public Policy*. Chicago: University of Chicago Press.

———. 1996. *When Work Disappears: The World of the New Urban Poor*. New York: Knopf.

Wong, Janelle, and Vivian Tseng. 2008. "Political Socialization in Immigrant Families: Challenging the Top-Down Parental Socialization Models." *Journal of Ethnic and Migration Studies* 34: 151–168.

Yerby, Janet. 1995. "Family Systems Theory Reconsidered: Integrating Social Construction Theory and Dialectical Processes." *Communication Theory* 5: 339–365.

Yoshikawa, Hirokazu. 2011. *Immigrants Raising Citizens: Undocumented Parents and Their Young Children*. New York: Russell Sage Foundation.

Zarate, Maria. 2007. "Understanding Latino Parental Involvement in Education: Perceptions, Expectations, and Recommendations." Los Angeles: Tomas Rivera Policy Institute. http://eric.ed.gov/?id=ED502065.

Zelizer, Viviana. 1985. *Pricing the Priceless Child: The Changing Social Value of Children* Princeton, NJ: Princeton University Press.

Zentella, Ana Celia. 1997. *Growing Up Bilingual: Puerto Rican Children in New York*. Oxford: Blackwell Publishing.

Zhou, Min, and Carl Bankston III. 1998. *Growing Up American: How Vietnamese Children Adapt to Life in the United States*. New York: Russell Sage Foundation.

Zuñiga, Victor, and Edmund Hamann. 2006. "Going Home? Schooling in Mexico of Transnational Children." *Confines* 2 (4): 41–57.

INDEX

Page references followed by T denote tables.

ABOUT THE AUTHOR

Vikki S. Katz (PhD, Communication, University of Southern California, 2007) is an assistant professor of communication in the School of Communication and Information at Rutgers University.

CPSIA information can be obtained at www.ICGtesting.com
Printed in the USA
BVOW05s1736090514

352674BV00001B/1/P